The Intelligence Advantage
Organizing for Complexity

The Intelligence Advantage
Organizing for Complexity

By Michael D. McMaster

Butterworth–Heinemann
Boston Oxford Johannesburg Melbourne New Delhi Singapore

Recognizing the importance of preserving what has been written, Butterworth–Heinemann prints its books on acid-free paper whenever possible.

Library of Congress Cataloging-in-Publication Data

McMaster, Michael D., 1943-
   The intelligence advantage : organizing for complexity / by
Michael D. McMaster
     p. cm.
   Includes index.
   ISBN 0-7506-9792-X (pbk.)
   1. Organization. 2. Management. I. Title.
HD31.M38561996
  656—dc20   95-48258
                                              CIP

British Library Cataloguing-in-Publication Data
A catalogue record for this book is available from the British Library.

The publisher offers discounts on bulk orders of this book.
For information, please write:
Manager of Special Sales
Butterworth–Heinemann
313 Washington Street
Newton, MA 02158-1626
Tel: 617-928-2500
Fax: 617-928-2620

For information on all Business Books available, contact our World Wide Web home page at: http://www.bh.com/bh/

If you would like to explore the themes of this book please contact http://vision-nest.com/BTBookCafe on the Internet's World Wide Web for a lively dialogue.

10 9 8 7 6 5 4 3 2 1

Printed in the United States of America

To Marion, who has unwaveringly supported my expression, believed in my contribution and been a companion and partner who has maintained balance and joy in my life.

To my family, who have taken me the way that I am and given back only love.

To Howard Sherman, my friend and mentor whose contribution to my development made this particular work possible.

This book is written as a fulfillment of these and all the contributions that have been made to me, and as my contribution to life on this planet.

Table of Contents

Preface

My intention in writing this book is to explore the possibility of human organization. Throughout the book, I will explore ideas recently made available through advances in philosophy, science and technology (especially communication). These advances, and the way in which I intend to present them, will foster insight into ways of organizing productive activity that are consistent with the nature of human beings and society. This book will provide access to a way of thinking and questioning that is capable of transforming our current corporations into organizations that will meet the demands of the Information Era.

The phrase "iron cage of capitalism" refers to a way physical production is organized that dehumanizes those working for money. The organizations of the Industrial Era were compatible with machines but not with human beings who wanted to have full, rich lives. The way we organized during the Industrial Era perfectly suited times in which information costs were very high. As we reorganize for the Information Era, we begin the process of freeing ourselves from the confines of the iron cage, without having to reject the marketplace or hinder the human spirit or intelligence.

The ideas presented in this book evolved over a long period of time. My father was a lawyer who spent most of his time working for people who were persecuted. He argued for and defended the Dukhobors, who were always in trouble in British Columbia, the families of those in Japanese internment camps, and the members of the labor unions. His practice involved work with the credit unions in Canada and legislation that kept Canadian cooperatives "member owned with one vote per member." My father was Calvinist in his belief in the value and integrity of work. There was no such thing as "good enough" with any job. Some of my earliest memories are of going to his office to play with the machines. From an early age, I worked in his law firm taking care of small support tasks. The world of work has fascinated me as far back as I can remember.

This book is the result of a lifelong inquiry. My inquiry was fueled by hopes that it might reveal something that would contribute to the possibility of human productive activity. I have always been puzzled by people who don't love their work. And I have always wondered why they continued on such a path, rather than undertaking the journey of discovering what it would take to love their work. From my early teens, I said that I wanted to be a philosopher of business when I grew up. My father always laughed at me when I told him this and responded "There is no such thing." Well, there is now.

During my school years, I was taught that an atom was the smallest particle in existence. At that time, such information was about 50 years out of date. The degree of outdatedness of such facts is nothing compared to the degree of change in the thinking models that have been influencing philosophy, science and technology for the past century. The way of thinking used by the general population is about 100 years behind the times. I can say this with confidence, because the commonly accepted thinking in philosophy, physics, evolution and economics, to name just a few fields, altered dramatically decades ago and yet the thinking of the general educated population would be familiar to the people of 100 years ago.

My countless conversations with boards of directors and senior managers have revealed that these people are completely unfamiliar with current thinking. In fact, many executives and managers become hostile when they hear that there is fundamental thinking with which they are not familiar. Many are skeptical about the usefulness or potential application of any new way of thinking. It never fails to amaze me when this kind of response is aimed at thinking that has been accepted by scientists and philosophers for decades. These very same breakthroughs in thinking are responsible for generating the technologies that are reshaping life for everyone in the world and are being applied in every science and by virtually every master practitioner in all fields of human endeavor. Politics, business and education have managed to remain far behind in their integration of new thinking.

This book is an inquiry into the nature of a new way of thinking about the world we live in and its significance in organizational design and management practices. I have been told by early readers of my manuscript that the chapters read like separate inquiries or meditations. You will not find simple packaged answers here. Nor will you find neatly outlined models for analysis. Rather, you will find this new thinking being integrated with the challenges facing executives and managers responsible for the success and survival of their organizations, for which they have the privilege of responsibility. This book will raise useful questions and provide principles for initiating the transformation of an organization.

If you are struggling to make a profit, or struggling to provide a future and livelihood for the community of people around you, you will find what is presented here invaluable. If you are finding that more and more energy is producing less and less return, there are parts of this book you will find very useful. It is intended for people who are dissatisfied with the way things are and have a sense of how they might be, but cannot get their organizations to behave in a way that is appropriate to the current circumstances. It is for all those who are engaged in efforts to change, or know they should be, but are not confident of success.

The book is divided into sections. The first section provides the foundations of the new thinking and outlines the approaches generated by viewing a corporation as an independent entity with its own intelligence. In the next section, the new thinking is translated into fundamental principles, and in the final section, we will explore the processes of transformation and the nature of the journey from a design based in the principles of the Industrial Age to those based in the Information Age.

The courage and commitment of the people I have worked with—from the board room to the factory floor—has allowed this body of knowledge to unfold in the way that it has. In each of the companies I consulted, we worked in partnership—a partnership of ideas and practical concerns—to develop approaches and practices capable of turning around the performance of corporations. Each endeavor brought its surprises, learning and rewards. And the process continues.

There are, as yet, no definitive answers regarding how best to accomplish a transformation. And there likely will never be because the processes of change are more developmental and evolutionary than ever before. We are in the early stages of the transformation from machine-based to information-based organization. It is likely that in the next couple of decades our understanding of the process of transformation will become more refined, and models and formulae will be created to assist that change.

It became clear to me, during my years working with corporations in the area of organizational transformation, that the executives and managers who suffered the dangers and frustrations of being leaders—*showing by going first*—also realized enormous benefits. People involved in corporations that are being redesigned to match the principles of the Information Era report that their work is a more satisfying experience than ever before in their careers. This is occurring at the same time that sales and profits are increasing for their companies.

I would like to thank Howard Sherman, my intellectual mentor for many years, for his contributions to the emerging process of my thinking and my work. Combining experience gained from a professorship in philosophy and a successful business career, Howard has shown me the power of ideas throughout history. He has stirred in me an appreciation of both the depth and limits of thinking that can be called upon from history. In particular, Howard opened doors that gave me access to interpretive philosophies as a pragmatic and powerful approach to the challenges of our times. Howard has enabled me to work with new challenges and confront the larger questions of organizational design and management practices.

I would also like to extend my gratitude to members of the faculty of the Santa Fe Institute, who shared their thinking, models and understanding of the sciences of complexity. The faculty has been remarkably willing to engage in dialogue with me, even though I'm not a member of the scientific community. The Institute has contributed language, principles and metaphors with which to think about organizations. The work of the faculty includes investigating ways of taking questions beyond metaphor and analogy. Their research is opening up enormous possibilities for application in business fields such as risk analysis, scheduling, strategic analysis, computer programming, new product invention and learning approaches.

Complexity is becoming a common word in business literature. It is being used in many different ways, and each use of the word has a slightly different meaning and produces significantly different results. I will use the word *complexity* frequently in this book. But before I distinguish the word "complexity" in the way in which I intend to use it, let's consider other uses of the word and their consequences.

The earliest popular use of the word came out of chaos theory in physics. Popular references use "chaos" and "complexity" as a pair, often interchangeable. When the word complexity is used in this way, it refers to applications in physical sciences that describe events using mathematical formulae. These applications of the word describe physical entities, the forces that affect them, and any patterns that occur (or do not occur). This field of science provides a way to break down our embedded view of the world, but it has limited direct application to the understanding of human systems.

The other approach to complexity is Systems Dynamics: this approach appears to be more relevant to corporations. It provides new insight into complex living systems and assists us in considering their properties when the systems are seen holistically. This field of complexity has created breakthroughs in our understanding of communication and information, and the systems dependent on them, and provides models and metaphors for considering systems beyond the understanding of linear mathematics. The tools the developers of Systems Dynamics had available were the computers of their day, which provided some very interesting work on scenarios and modeling. The terminology and computer systems used were inert systems which reduced the systems to parts and studied the interrelationships which were not alive. Again, this approach to complexity is of limited use for living organizations and human systems.

The approach to complexity developed by the Santa Fe Institute is rooted in living systems such as ecology, biology, evolution and economics. The term *complex adaptive systems* is used to distinguish the field currently being worked on at the Institute. Features such as adaptation, learning and self-organization, mark the interests and research endeavors of the Institute. Terms such as *emergent, threshold points* and *co-evolution* suggest a field of independent agents operating with local rules that create increasingly complex patterns of activity and results. These ideas are amenable to use in the marketplace and organizations where the agents are independently intelligent and independently intentional.

The basis of this book is a combination of complexity, as it is being developed at the Santa Fe Institute, and interpretive philosophical approaches to dialogue, inquiry and the nature of human existence. This combination provides a way of speaking about and viewing organization that is acceptable to business and compatible with the way that we actually experience organizations. Blending complexity and interpretive philosophical thought provides useful metaphors and analogies, as well as practical design principles and effective management and work practices.

Two other people deserve special mention. Katrina Schnieder provided an editing service beyond my fondest hopes. She has made my work accessible. Most of the difficulty that remains is due to my insistence that a difficult expression is sometimes necessary to convey a sufficient depth of understanding. Paula Alter, who has been a close associate in consulting over the years and an integral part of the development of this work, has provided invaluable insight and simplicity. She has been able to understand whatever I write, whatever I am attempting to communicate, and translate it into an expression that was far easier to comprehend, yet always maintained perfect integrity with my intentions. Her contribution went far beyond editing.

Love, family, creativity and contribution are very special aspects of our life. These elements can bring a tremendous sense of fulfillment if they are given the attention and care they deserve. I consider *work* another aspect of life that can be equally fulfilling. Without fulfillment in our work, we cannot live the full possibility inherent in our lives, nor can we understand what it means to be fully human.

The joy, beauty and satisfaction that result from the cooperative endeavors of human beings toward a common end are seldom matched by anything else. Community emerges out of such work endeavors. Full expression of our humanity requires such endeavors. And a sense of making a difference in life is impossible without them.

Mike McMaster

Introduction:
Thinking in a New Way

"Every few hundred years throughout Western history, a sharp transformation has occurred. In a matter of decades, society altogether rearranges itself, its world views, its basic values, its social and political structure, its arts, its key institutions. Fifty years later a new world exists. And the people born into that world cannot even imagine the world in which their grandparents lived and into which their own parents were born."
PETER DRUCKER

The next time you are sitting in an executive or management meeting, or anywhere that people accountable for the performance of a corporation are engaged in a discussion, listen very carefully to what is said. Listen to the ideas, and notice if they resonate with a new way of thinking—a way of thinking that is capable of achieving a marketplace advantage in today's rapidly changing environment. As you listen, set aside the current buzzwords and notice what remains. Do you hear theory that is different from what you might have heard decades ago? More importantly, listen for signs of a kind of speaking that has the power to generate the pursuit of new action, the intelligence to revitalize our ailing corporations, and an openness towards learning that is sufficient to make effective use of ever-improving technologies.

For most of us, our ideas about the world, our models and our structures of interpretation arise from a few fundamental assumptions. We use these assumptions to design and operate our corporations and relate to the people in those corporations. The thinking, logic and language that surround these assumptions are based on a view that the world works like a machine and that it is predictable and understandable in considerable detail. This way of thinking was a perfect match for the Industrial Era and it allowed us to function with ease and effectiveness throughout that era. In fact, this way of thinking "created" the Industrial Era. Only under rare circumstances do we approach anything in a way that is not linear, mechanistic, reductionist or analytic. For most of us, this is the only way we know of approaching action, organization and events. Our "Industrial Era" thinking is the only acceptable way of approaching organizational issues.

The Industrial Era and its approaches are rapidly being displaced and a new way of thinking about the world is emerging—one that is far too different from that of the past for mere adaptation. This new way of thinking, and the theories and approaches that accompany it, are emerging out of our awakening to new levels of understanding in the areas of complex systems, intelligence, information and language. Our new understanding of these areas is spawning new technologies that are now sweeping the commercial world. These new technologies are demanding changes in every aspect of our organizational structures and management practices. Innovative ways of working together, utilizing information and spreading knowledge are being employed by our associates and competitors in ways that are taking market territory.

THE EMERGENCE OF A NEW ERA

To be worthy of the label "new era," the changes that take place must be so pervasive that the very structures of society are affected. When an era changes, everything that we used to count on becomes shaky. Old "truths" are no longer reliable. The world that we are familiar with and competent in seems to be more and more mysterious. Yet an era change is not really very mysterious. In fact, it is filled with countless opportunities for those who take the trouble to learn the new ways of thinking from which the era change arises.

A glance through history reveals countless examples of one era being transformed into another and the ramifications of not making the necessary shifts in the thinking and approaches that accompany that era change. To name only a few examples: a dramatic shift in thinking occurred everywhere when human beings began to redefine their relationship to one another, thus abolishing slavery. Countless landowners, dependent on slave labor, failed to alter their way of thinking—and therefore their estates—to the new way of thinking that was abolishing slavery. These landowners sent their estates into terminal decline. Owners of lucrative cottage industries, who failed to learn new ways of organizing around large central systems of energy and machinery, were unable to compete with businesses that reorganized. The emergence of literacy created a fear in those who were illiterate or those who used literacy as an advantage. People failing to adjust to the reorganization that occurred as the literacy rate began to rise found themselves in the midst of enormous struggles. Today, we are watching similar setbacks involving people and companies that are failing to learn the ways of thinking and organizing that accompany computers.

The beginning of a new era always has its roots in new theories and new ways of seeing the world. When these new theories and new ways of thinking are applied in diverse ways, a compelling and all-inclusive change begins to ignite. Take for example the idea of freedom. The idea has been in the world for centuries. It was not until it was applied by people fleeing non-democratic systems, and used to establish a place in which the ideas of freedom could be put into practice, that freedom was expressed as never before. America's founding ideas and their subsequent applications have fueled changes in every part of the globe.

In a similar way, the ideas that made possible the design and production of machinery were around for centuries before they were specifically applied. The ancient Greeks had a working steam engine, but it was not until steam power was introduced in England that the methods of organizing work changed dramatically. The changes caused by steam power made the production line, as we know it, virtually inevitable. In a similar way when electric motors were invented, other major changes in the organization of work were inevitable. The anticipated economic benefits of using electric motors went unrealized for decades. It was not until the organization of machinery, work flow and productive activity were radically changed that the benefits became available. Economic benefits were not made available by merely changing the source of power, because it was a long time before line management saw the need for change.

Once ideas are applied to create technology, a society changes forever. The transformation of ideas—in physics, communication and information theory, systems thinking and methodologies of inquiry—that fueled the recent explosion of information has been occurring for over 100 years. But the countless applications of these ideas—television, computers, integrated circuit chips, lasers, and distributed accountabilities—have been developing for about half that time. Our way of organizing work has altered very little during that time and yet the speed of change in our thinking and our technologies is accelerating. We are not going to have the time to adjust that was available in previous era changes.

The shift we are making is made possible by computers and includes increasingly extensive (and effective) use of information technology, but the shift is not really about computers. It is about information itself and includes communication technology, display and public access, graphics, algorithms, organizing our work practices, organizing information, accessing information and generating information.

The Age of Information might better be called the Age of Knowledge. But irrespective of what we call it, it is unfolding rapidly and we are a part of it, whether we want to be or not. Unfortunately, most of us are not aware of how fundamental the shift is. Most of us do not know how to generate the kind of organization and action that is a match for the new era. Instead, we think in a way that is suitable for an Industrial Era. To make the shift in thinking, we need the willingness to unlearn the old and the courage to grapple with the new and unfamiliar.

The times ahead will demand new theories, new thinking capabilities, new capacities for transforming chaotic data into useful information, and new levels of innovation capable of designing practical applications for that information. We must be ready to innovate, adapt and invent as never before. To meet the onslaught of new and unfamiliar circumstances in the future, we must learn new cooperative behaviors at every level. It will become increasingly common to join hands with former competitors, former "adversaries" or customers who were previously considered to have different interests. Efforts accomplished in dialogue between individuals, teams and organizations will far surpass efforts made by individuals. The coordination of information and action occurring across boundaries will be the order of the day for those who are to succeed in an information-based economy.

CONVERGENCE OF THINKING INTO COMPLEXITY THEORY

As we break the grip that the Newtonian-Cartesian paradigm has had on Western minds for centuries, we become able to create a new relationship with what occurs within and around us. We are beginning to reinterpret every aspect of ourselves, our ways of being and the universe in which we live. Every science and discipline is going through a process of breaking free of its old interpretations. The transformations that have taken place in Western physics and philosophy have converged until each sounds like the other, only expressed in different terms. Furthermore, the thinking of Western physics and Eastern meditative disciplines is beginning to converge. Fritjof Capra was ahead of his time when he saw this underlying unity in the 60s. David Bohm explored the East/West convergence and went on to create useful developmental material that can be used to facilitate dialogue and group processes.

The explosion of new approaches and new theories is a blend of a multiplicity of fields, including language, philosophy, physics and even computer sciences. Science's reinterpretations of reality are producing profound insights in the areas of learning, development and corporations. One resulting expression in the world of biology speaks of the alphabet and grammar of DNA which interact to produce understandable evolution, immense creativity and rich variety. Grammar and syntax can be seen in the organization of cells, immune systems, languages, companies, economies and ecologies. Our new perspectives on learning, adaptation and survival are contributing to our understanding and design of corporations.

Scientists are discovering that they can integrate the insights of physics and philosophy (especially linguistic theories) and open doors to new levels of understanding by exploring biological entities as creators of information and influencers of the ecology in which they live. As computer technologies are applied to these approaches, we are recognizing new aspects of learning, adaptation and production-line scheduling that do not fit our old pictures of how things should occur. These applications are resolving problems in the areas of production, scheduling and computer programming in ways far superior to those using the best engineering methods available.

For example, drugs are being invented by computer models that use evolution to create potential structural matches for the offending virus. These new approaches produce a variety of possible solutions that are unimaginable using analytic techniques. Genetic algorithms are solving scheduling challenges that are beyond the capabilities of some of the most advanced mathematics. Ideas using genetic algorithms are being developed for diverse companies and uses: Citicorp for risk management, Canadian Pacific for railway scheduling and John Deere for productivity challenges.

Some of the most interesting work in the area of interdisciplinary science is being conducted by a colorful group of Nobel Laureates, scientists, economists and computer wizards at the Santa Fe Institute in Santa Fe, New Mexico. The Institute's work is referred to as the "science of complexity." Their approach to complexity deals with the emergent phenomena of life and living systems in ways appropriate to those types of phenomena, rather than those suited to the strictly physical and material universe. Much of what we are interested in cannot be mechanically generated or understood in a linear fashion and complexity addresses these areas. These areas include evolution, adaptation in living systems, learning and the development of languages, societies and communities.

Phenomena such as life, learning, relationship, team and organization emerge from a complex interplay of forces and elements. These phenomena unfold, influenced by a network of a few simple principles that allow rich and varied patterns to develop. These are unpredictable, unspecifiable and unrepeatable in detail. Although the network of principles shapes what emerges, it does not control in detail what is unfolding. The network of principles does, however, ensure that a pattern is maintained while keeping creativity at a maximum. Some level of prediction and control can be exercised regarding the shape of the patterns, but we cannot control the rich detail from which the patterns emerge. The exercise of specific control at a detailed level kills the patterns that would otherwise emerge.

Breakthroughs in the various sciences are opening doors in the areas of communication and computational ability. These breakthroughs are shedding light on the fact that there are some organizational structures that are more supportive of communication, computation and creativity than others. Our learning about an organism's capacity for communication, computation and flexibility in service of its growth and survival (i.e. its intelligence), can potentially be applied in many other areas, such as our companies and other productive organizations. Corporations are facing the same challenges that all living beings face in their attempt to survive in an ecosystem.

When the theories and principles resulting from the new developments of the scientific world are pursued, these theories and principles may revitalize or totally transform many of business's recent trends (TQM, re-engineering, etc.) and bring them to new levels of power and effectiveness. W. Edwards Deming provided us with one very important clue: "What is missing is a theory of management." I'm going to go one step further and suggest that what is needed first is *a theory of organization*. Until this is created, whatever strategy we apply (whether TQM, re-engineering or the "learning organization") will continue to flounder because of the gap between our current thinking, language and approaches and what is actually needed. This gap must be bridged if we are to lead our corporations into the next century without unnecessary struggle and suffering.

THE PATHWAY TO MARKETPLACE ADVANTAGE

Between 1970 and 2000 there will be approximately a 500 million-fold increase in our ability to access, move, create and process information. A great deal of technology has already been created. Yet, compared to the increase in our capacity to move, process and store information, our way of organizing and working together has not been transformed to meet that increase. The source of marketplace advantage may be seen as the organizational capacity to develop and apply knowledge in ways consistent with the power of available technology. Developing this capacity will enable the corporation to deliver on the promise of both the knowledge and the technology.

The superficial activities that the various management fads provide will not accomplish the depth of transformation that is required. What is required is more profound and more at the heart of how we think than what is proposed by popular programs, such as TQM and re-engineering. What is required is a level of organizational intelligence and learning that goes far beyond that which any mechanistic or engineered approach can provide. This level will not be approached until we begin to think of a corporation as having an intelligent existence of its own. This new level of organizational intelligence and learning must totally transform the way in which we organize for work and organize work itself.

Most companies have not even begun to grasp the implications of the Knowledge Era, much less take on relevant issues and think about them in powerful ways. Certainly, most of us are concerned with information technology, investment and the effectiveness of what we have or what is readily available. But how are we going to access what is not available to us through our normal pathways? To begin to master this way of thinking, we must understand the possibilities of the technology and the ideas behind it, and be willing and able to question our approaches to many things. Namely, we must question the way that we think about work, the way that we organize our cooperative productive activities and the relationships with those with whom we will work.

Development and learning are natural processes for human beings, but pain and struggle are not inherent in these processes. Changing the past or changing habits and familiar structures do not have to be painful processes. In order to learn and develop, in a way that is not filled with difficulty, we will have to be willing to let go of some of the things we learned in the past, as well as some of the habits we have acquired, such as being right and knowing everything. Although our current way of thinking and designing our organizational structures may have had some very beneficial effects in the past, the world is changing dramatically and these structures are inhibiting the natural flow of learning and the natural emergence of intelligence. A recognition of this condition is the first leap forward in removing the sense of desperation from the process of development and learning and transforming the process into one of joy, excitement and great reward.

Corporations exhibit many of the same characteristics as individuals. It is as though corporations have personalities and make decisions and take actions that are independent of the individuals in them. Corporations also appear to resist learning. A corporation is a phenomenon that emerges from the interaction of individuals within various social environments, but the corporation itself is independent of the individuals involved in the corporation at any given time. Organizations have an intelligence of their own. Corporations have the ability to learn and they have the ability to embody knowledge that cannot be found in any one individual, a few individuals, or even everyone in the corporation at any given time.

The reductionist ways of thinking that we have inherited and continue to cultivate are incapable of grasping the notion that our corporations have an intelligence of their own. But this seemingly strange notion of corporations having intelligence begins to appear possible if you look at the fact that you can't locate a mind by looking at what is in each of the cells of a brain or the nervous system. If this is so—that corporations have intelligence— then it might also be possible that our corporations are more intelligent than the combined intelligence of all of the individual members in that corporation. And if this is so, then we are open to the possibility that organizational learning can take place at a much greater rate than if many individuals were learning independently.

THE CRITICAL ROLE OF STRUCTURE

Until recently, management has been able to inherit gracefully and effortlessly the organizational structures that suited the contemporary landscape. These organizational structures consist of machinery, processes, legal agreements, habits, language patterns, accountabilities, and the like which proved successful in our past productive efforts. We have learned how to use them in our work almost unconsciously and we have only had to make occasional minor adjustments in the structures. But the organizational and economic landscape is changing dramatically and management's great legacy of structures is not going to work much longer.

Executives and managers argue that they know a great deal about structure. But what they actually know is how to use the structures that exist. Few executives and managers are competent in design, in formulating new structures and bringing them into existence. Most of the failures related to TQM initiatives are attributed to a lack of commitment. This is inaccurate. The failed efforts are testimony to a lack of understanding and facility in the area of structure—both physical and linguistic. I, for one, am reticent about accusing executives of a lack of commitment. If they lack commitment, how did they get into a position of responsibility?

To begin something new, to keep it in existence, and to alter the course of what is occurring, we must be able to bring into being the physical structures, practices, and language patterns appropriate to the new theories upon which the alteration is based. If we don't succeed in bringing the essential elements into existence and interrelating them, the new structures will not remain in existence and the old structures will reassert themselves. Such is the power of structure. Without structure, we would be living in a chaotic world.

We must design structures that allow energy and/or information to be converted into something intended and not into something else. These structures will guide us and allow us to do many things effectively without demanding that attention be placed on the influencing structure. We are then free to create, innovate and access what is otherwise not possible. This is one of the areas in which complexity theory offers us a wealth of information. Structures that are a match for our intentions and understanding allow us to expend our energy and attention where it will have the most effect. The difference, between a productive and a nonproductive culture, can be found in the culture's ability to use structure without having to place awareness on it and the ability to keep structure in existence without great energy. When we are ignoring structure, or it is inhibiting or continually disintegrating, then the situation is "remedial" rather than productive.

Perhaps the most powerful area of organizational and managerial development in the future will be the creation of operational definitions with which we can redesign every aspect of our approach to work. "Operational definitions" is one of the areas in which W. Edwards Deming said that management needed to be educated. Operational definitions turn ideas and theories into the "linguistic tools" with which we can work and produce results; they have been effective working tools for scientists, mathematicians and engineers for a long time. It is time for management to access the power available through use of operational definitions.

A NEW ERA EMERGES INTO A TRADITION

The sweeping nature of the changes that are occurring in the world can be seen to extend far beyond the world of corporate concerns. Governments and social systems are being transformed or toppling—sometimes both. The Soviet Union could endure being uncompetitive or economically unsuccessful, but it could not endure the bright light of information and communication as its citizens broke free of the grip of suppression. In country after country, governments and leaders are being turned out of office. For everyone everywhere, security is becoming elusive and old beliefs are coming under attack. Every level of every current social structure, whether it is corporate or government, is falling in the light of new thinking and new practices.

Our new Era of Information, with all its speculation, creation and uncertainty, is actually the flowering of a tradition. Although the tradition is young, there are many who have gone before us and there are many who have expressed their ideas in theories and proven them in application. The journey of organizational transformation is being undertaken by many who have dared to lead and dared to create the space of possibility for the rest of us. Join the game early. Embrace the fact that profoundly new ideas are always possible. Thoroughly enjoy the satisfaction of every aspect of your own development and that of your organization. To do so provides a possibility for the entire world—the possibility that the transformation of our organizations will provide the environment and conditions for a realization of a new level of human existence.

Complexity Theory

This section of the book presents an introduction to complexity theory and explores how complexity provides a new way of looking at corporations. The first chapter looks at the nature of intelligence and how it applies to corporations. Chapter 2 provides a context for a new theory of organization and illuminates the importance of a new theory for operational success. The final chapter of this section reveals the importance of language for the development and application of new ideas within a culture.

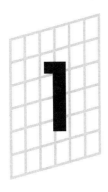

Organizational Intelligence

"But to commonplaces of sound common sense, what is unthought in any thinking always remains merely the incomprehensible. And to the common comprehension, the incomprehensible is never an occasion to stop and look at its own powers of comprehension, still less to notice their limitations. To the common comprehension, what is incomprehensible remains forever merely offensive proof enough to such comprehension, which is convinced it was born comprehending everything."
MARTIN HEIDEGGER

"No question is so difficult to answer as that to which the answer is obvious."
GEORGE BERNARD SHAW

Prelude

Organizational intelligence refers to the capacity of a corporation as a whole to gather information, to innovate, to generate knowledge, and to act effectively based on the knowledge it has generated. This capacity is the basis of success in a rapidly changing or highly competitive environment.

Organizational intelligence refers to a capacity which is inherent in a system of organization. It is greater than the sum of the intelligence, information, and knowledge of each individual in that organization. Organizational intelligence includes the historical knowledge that has been "wired in" to the design. It also includes the generative possibility of dialogue between individual intelligent agents—this includes each and every human being.

Organizational intelligence refers to the source of marketplace advantage which can be developed intentionally but cannot be copied successfully by others. It is the source of contact with the world as well as the source of the contribution of value made to the world. It is the source of being unique in the marketplace, evolving with the marketplace, and having something to say about the shape of the marketplace.

LEARNING AND INTELLIGENCE

The rate at which a corporation learns determines its ability to adapt, innovate and ultimately survive in a changing competitive environment. The challenges of organizational learning are timeless. The name and focus of such challenges may change but the issue of organizational learning is likely to be of more interest in the future than our concern for individual human learning. The ability to learn and its application to practical concerns are central to the continued healthy functioning of our corporations and institutions.

Exploration of the theory and methodology of learning has produced powerful processes for the corporations that have inquired into the area. However, most of the research and development has focused on the individual and group behavioral aspects that create the conditions for learning. Little effective work has been done to understand organizational learning or the conditions for its occurrence. As the exploration of organizational learning continues, it leads to the discovery that something is missing in our approach. It is becoming obvious that we are not organized for learning and that the conditions necessary for learning are missing in most corporations.

A deeper inquiry reveals that the learning that is typically explored is incremental, based on experience, and mainly a matter of sharing existing knowledge. When learning is discussed, most of the conversations are about individual learning and how to share what has been learned with the larger corporation. What is not being discussed is that learning has a much broader scope than merely what is derived from experience. What management is not exploring is the potential for learning as a generative process.

In order to have real insight and understanding that will allow us to capture the value of this generative organizational learning, it is essential that we develop a theory of organization compatible with that challenge. We need a theory of the nature of an entity that can learn. What is missing is a theory of organization which includes the ability to learn.

Intelligence is a matter of design. What is required for learning to occur? At a fundamental level, the answer is intelligence. The nature of intelligence, particularly organizational intelligence, is important to understand. When we see that a corporation's ability to learn and its rate of learning are a function of organizational intelligence, then we become interested in the designs and practices that increase intelligence. Understanding organizational intelligence will create the possibility for breakthroughs in organizational learning. As groundwork for understanding organizational intelligence, let us first look carefully at our current theory of organization.

UNDERSTANDING ORGANIZATION

What we are distinguishing here is not something "new" that has never existed before. What we are looking for is much more difficult to get at than that. We are looking for a new and deeper understanding of a phenomenon that already exists. What makes the inquiry especially difficult is that we are already too familiar with the phenomenon. In fact, we are so familiar with it that we are completely confident of our understanding of it and our operational relationship to it.

What we are attempting to do is to call into question our traditional definition and understanding of organization and to create new distinctions regarding organization which give us new power. When looked at from the perspective of complex adaptive systems, we see that theory, the sciences of biology, evolution, and economics can provide us with new distinctions regarding organization that are useful for our purposes. Management's inherited understanding of organization leaves it unable to design its corporations for developing intelligence and incapable of managing in ways consistent with such a design. Our task is to develop new theories of organization that lead to operational definitions that provide useful tools for organizational design and management practices.

Business news is filled with two very different kinds of reports that are symptoms of a single phenomenon. The first type includes the unpleasant surprises of major corporations losing large sums of money, household names disappearing, sudden or massive layoffs, and a mood of fear and uncertainty in corporate boardrooms. The second type of report includes the proliferation of management fads that are relatively ineffective and short-lived. They are being replaced by even more current approaches—the next fads—such as "quality circles," "just in time," "one minute" everything, "cycle time," "culture change," "visioning," "continuous improvement," "kaizen," "re-engineering," "reinvention," and the list goes on.

The ideas contained in these fads are not necessarily wrong-headed. In practice, many of them have produced significant gains and, in some cases, even transformations. The problem is that producing results from the application of these fads is far from reliable. Even when some of the sound initiatives, such as TQM, are approached in the same manner as the more current fads, the results are equally uncertain. TQM publications report that

5

80% of all quality initiatives fail, even though everyone "knows what it takes" to have them succeed.

What do the losses, failures, uncertainty, and surprises have to do with the proliferation of fads? While they all may be blamed on "short-termism," incompetent management, or your favorite scapegoat, the chosen reason is likely to have its source in the same theories and understanding that created the problem. The common factor, the single element that explains the existence and ineffectiveness of fads as well as the unpleasant surprises, is the lack of a theory of organization that accounts for intelligence.

W. Edwards Deming, one of the creators of the quality movement and someone who thought deeply about organization and management, said, "There is no management theory; therefore the problems of our enterprises are predictable." How can there be a management theory when there is no theory of organization, and vice versa? How can a new management approach be expected to succeed unless there is a theory to support it? How can executives be confident without a theory that both makes sense and withstands the test of the competitive marketplace?

Our theories of organization are hierarchical and mechanistic. Instead of saying, as W. Edwards Deming did, that there is no theory, let us say that there is a theory. However it is out of date and is based on design principles that are not appropriate for the current state of thinking and technology. This inherited theory is based on the view of an organization as a production machine, people as the major parts of the machine, and systems as engineered linear structures. The management theories that accompany this thinking treat people as tools to serve the goals of the systems. As a result of this thinking, management considers systems as controls on people, communication as directional (certain kinds "upwards" and certain kinds "downwards"), authority as hierarchical, and reward systems as a means for motivation. In this theory, the job is to engineer a production machine where the parts, including people, will act in reliable and predictable ways. There is no allowance for creativity or intelligent reaction to unpredictable changes in the environment.

The foundation of the theory of management that currently exists is commonly thought to have its origins in the church or the military. It is more accurate to locate the roots in the fundamental theory, cosmology, and language that was dominant when the church and the military were developing their own structures. We can find that its origins are woven through at least 2,500 years of Western thinking. The tapestry includes Aristotle as well as the more recent and obviously relevant work of Newton and Descartes, who gave us their own applications of this materialistic, mechanistic kind of thinking for science, technology, and an almost all-pervasive world view. It is this type of thinking that has been replaced in the fields of the sciences, philosophy and technology during the last century. It is now time for it to be replaced by appropriate theories in the human sciences—including those of organization and management.

A NEW THEORY OF ORGANIZATION

If we are to leave behind the outdated theories which emerge out of a view that the universe is a machine that can be analyzed, broken into small parts, and engineered for reliable production, then what sort of a view might provide a new foundation from which new theories will emerge? The view of the universe as a dynamic self-organizing system will provide such a foundation. This view will see the marketplace as an ecology in which each entity is ever-changing and continually adapting to its environment, while simultaneously influencing its environment. It sees corporations as adaptive, learning, innovative entities. This view implies that each entity will influence the environment in both predictable and unpredictable ways through its own actions. This also means that it will affect its own future in unpredictable ways.

We organize around historical accidents.

When using this new way of thinking and its corresponding theory of organization, we begin by recognizing that corporations arise in an environment that existed before the corporation was formed and that the pre-existing environment was instrumental in shaping the corporation. Similarly, how we organize work today is largely determined by how it is organized by the other corporations also in existence. The operating environment was created by the successes and failures of similar corporations in the past. This same principle holds true for legislation that is created, schools that develop, and what managers learn about managing.

Corporations now emerge from the social environment with great frequency. While individuals can be said to create corporations, when a corporation is successful, it occurs almost independently of the founder. It is important to see corporations as phenomena in their own right that have emerged from a certain complexity of interaction between society at large and the people and resources that have been brought together for productive pursuits. It is equally important to see corporations as emerging from an historical environment and being shaped only to a limited extent by the individuals who start them, and influenced even less by later executives.

If intention, design, and intelligence had been the operational factors at IBM, then John Akers would have succeeded in the attempt to turn the company around. If what happened is that the "frozen historical accidents" determined the structure, and the structure continued while the environment changed, then the source of the failure becomes clear. For example, "close to the customer" remained a significant IBM slogan long after the operational meaning had gone out of it. This demonstrates that the system had become rigid and disconnected from any theory. It had lost its intelligence and thereby become ineffective. The source of this cannot be traced to any single part of the design; nor can the blame be laid at the feet of any single person or even a small group of people.

Let's assume IBM demonstrates this emergent nature of organization. Initially it manufactured and sold weighing equipment in traditional markets, using traditional methods of organizing work. It had employee relations that were good but not particularly noteworthy for the times. It was considered successful in its field.

Someone in the company suggested the idea of producing a "computing machine" for commercial use. Tom Watson, the company's leader, saw possibility in the idea and invested in research and development until a marketable machine was created.

After a few initial sales the market began to expand and sales far exceeded the initial estimate of a world-wide market of 15 machines.

In response to a depression occurring in the U.S. at this time, most manufacturers began to curtail hiring and investment. Tom Watson, however, decided to continue hiring and investing.

Through the historical accidents of a depression, a growing market, new technology and the personal beliefs of the owner, a new company began to emerge that captured the attention of the world.

The ideas of the founder became well known as well as becoming enshrined in the organization's credo. These ideas included significant items such as a commitment to ongoing employment and valuing the individual. They also included peculiarities such as prohibiting facial hair and colorful dress in the workplace.

A dynasty emerged when a combination of historical accidents became frozen into an organization, complete with a personality and culture.

Many skillful decisions were made and, continually, the results far surpassed the expectations of the company. Other major events occurred, such as an anti-trust suit, to which the company adjusted and as a result of which the company created new policies and procedures. (Dramatic changes were introduced because of the *bringing* of the suit—probably more so than were caused by the final judgment.)

Although various influences can be pinpointed and events in the history of the company can be said to have been intentional, the specifics of the resulting company were unpredictable and largely unintended. It would be more accurate to say that the company unfolded or emerged.

This point of view and the company's later rigidity also give us some insight into the manner of its spectacular failure.

Companies emerge rather than being designed.

I have not yet spoken to the founder of a company who does not admit in private that it "just sort of happened" in the particular way that it did. They have plenty of explanations of what they were attempting to do. There were theories or personal values from which they operated. But the actual result was not what they had intended or predicted, except in the most general terms. They are happy and often relieved to see their companies as an emergent phenomenon that unfolded from the interplay between numerous accidents and their own approaches. Also, they freely admit that their organizations have passed the threshold point of control and although they have something to say about how their organizations will develop in the future, they have little direct control over these matters.

The new theory of organization that we are exploring relates to a corporation as though it has characteristics of its own, such as intelligence, ability to learn, and a culture (or personality)—its own *being*. This theory implies that these qualities exist independently of the founder, management, and people currently in that corporation. Even though some of the specifics that were intended and planned by individuals can be traced to individual personalities or to the results of specific historical accidents, what now exists has a life of its own.

In this new approach to organizational development, the responsibilities of executives and managers are altered. They become much more like horticulturists in a rain forest in which they are responsible for the health and survival of a particular plant species in that forest. By doing their job well, the species will flourish. If they fail at their task, the species will not survive and the forest will be occupied by other plants. To meet the challenges of survival in an ecology we must come to understand the nature of the entire rain forest and the plant species themselves, so that we do as little damage as possible and provide as much assistance as possible toward a successful result.

CORPORATION AS A COMPLEX INTELLIGENT SYSTEM

Management has less to say about organization than it likes to think.

A corporation is a complex adaptive system. That is, it is capable of learning and adapting to its environment. Its environment is simply a greater self-organizing complex system. An entity's survival depends on its own self-organization and self-renewal. Because it is created by and composed of human beings, we refer to corporations as complex *intelligent* systems. It is only through intelligence that a corporation can grow, adapt, and survive. An enterprise is not considered a corporation until it is operating on its own intelligence (similar to adulthood in the animal kingdom). Another way of saying this is that an enterprise becomes an (adult) corporation when its intelligence exists independently of its founder's intelligence. That is, it is able to operate without the founder and is beyond the direct control of the founder.

Intelligence needs to be defined operationally to be useful.

To operate effectively using this way of thinking, we must develop an operational definition for intelligence that is appropriate to our current understanding of corporations. From this definition will emerge the design principles of the corporation and the responsibilities of management. Without this distinction we are left with the mechanistic model in which we only have available to us already existing approaches broadly termed as "engineering."

Transf. structures

Our operational definition of intelligence is *"that capacity for computation which can be applied to information that is externally gained or internally generated to meet survival challenges."* Computational capacity refers to the system of capacities that can obtain input from the environment, generate information, interpret information, and translate the resulting interpretations into action. In the case of corporations, this ability is extended to include creativity, multiple interpretations, choice, and imaginative intention.

The elements of intelligence, for our purposes, include:

- the capacity to receive signals from the external world
- the capacity to interpret these signals according to a variety of internal structures and intentions
- the capacity to generate variations from the input received
- the capacity to treat internally generated signals in the same manner as externally generated signals (and to combine both)
- the capacity to create an infinite variety of combinations (to construct worlds and imagine their interactions)
- the capacity to generate a variety of output (communication and action) from interpretations, however they are generated

The elements of intelligence include the full range of possibilities, such as receiving input from the environment, creating information internally, generating meaning from external and internal information, and maintaining that information in such a way that it is available as knowledge and for action. These elements describe the conditions for creating information that is available for action as and when needed, as well as supporting self-generated action independent of circumstances.

The elements of intelligence suggest criteria for measuring intelligence. The expected results of intelligence can also suggest measures. Some measures of intelligence include:

- the variety of responses possible to externally generated input
- the variety of models that can be created
- the amount of input (information) and the number of sources of input that can be integrated
- the degree to which past interpretations are open to question and that past input is available for reinterpretation
- the speed with which input can be processed and interpretations can be changed and/or generated (flexibility)
- the ability to receive feedback and adjust accordingly
- the number of relationships that can be maintained at any one time
- relative success in altered circumstances
- the percentage of products and processes that are new or that others do not have
- various measures of relative survival success (i.e., market share direction)

A corporation is a computational entity—its design and function emerge from that state.

Organizational intelligence and computational ability may perhaps be the same thing. In the way in which it is used here, computation is not a mathematical term, but instead a broader term which includes the ability within the organization to make sense of input and internally generated output. "Make sense of" means the ability to create abstractions that need not have a referent in reality but can be worked with internally to create more input and output. What is created can be tested against other data or models, is capable of generating potential behaviors or actions, and is capable of choosing between alternatives. Said another way, this computational ability can make symbols and operate with those symbols, whether or not they are directly connected to an external reality. In corporations the symbols will be almost exclusively linguistic.

Intelligence, as distinguished here, is what gives a corporation the ability to adapt, learn, innovate, increase its knowledge, select from among alternatives, and do these as responses to the environment through creative combining or purely generative acts. This goes well beyond what adaptation implies and also beyond what is commonly understood as "learning from experience." It includes the creativity of art, poetry, and scientific breakthrough.

Our operational definition for Organizational Intelligence is *"that intelligence which resides in the organization itself; which is beyond and outside the individual intelligence of the people in that organization."* It is the intelligence present within the systems, habits, procedures, processes, practices and physical layouts. It includes the intelligence of individuals to the extent that it is available to the system. It also includes phenomena that extend beyond the individuals who possess that intelligence.

Marketplace advantage and survival depend on intelligence.

Organizational intelligence has an obvious relationship to marketplace advantage and continuous survival. Nearly every current challenge that is laid at the doorstep of management requires organizational intelligence to be accomplished successfully. The need for strategy, information, market knowledge, quality, strategic alliances and more, requires organizational intelligence for both their initial development and their execution in real life.

It can also be seen that the results obtained by TQM, re-engineering, and all the other management approaches are in direct relation to the organizational intelligence that exists in any given company. They not only *require* intelligence for their execution but, when they succeed, they also *increase* intelligence. Evidence of this is that while the majority of these initiatives are failing, there are those that are using the same methods and systems and that employ individuals who are no smarter or more committed and yet are succeeding in dramatic ways. Furthermore, these same organizations continue to get better and increase the distance between themselves and their competitors and imitators.

The "learning organization" is suffering a similar fate almost before it begins. Yet, we have not even scratched the surface of its possibility. How can "the learning organization" mean anything until we understand that organizations have intelligence? Surely there can't be learning without intelligence.

It is still commonly thought that the capacity of intelligence is limited and cannot be increased. It is also thought that the only increase possible is in the ability to use that capacity. While this is a questionable assumption for human beings, it is definitely not the case for organizations. The distinctive nature of organizations is that we can *design them* for intelligence and we can increase or decrease that capacity by design. We can also increase or decrease the capacity by action without benefit of design—by accident. Your organization already has intelligence. At some level, you are already trusting that intelligence. For instance, although to a certain degree you trust your people individually to be intelligent, that confidence increases to the extent that you trust the systems that provide guidance and restraint to the exercise of that individual intelligence.

Because the existing design for intelligence is something beyond the boundaries of our awareness, it is continually opposed and hindered by the application of new management fads and theories. Instead of allowing the intelligence that is available in our old systems to emerge and develop, we have applied theories based on command-and-control, hierarchies and mechanistic approaches; this creates blocks and inhibitors for the already existing intelligence.

These mechanistic organizational and management theories interact in a way contrary to new technological developments that are attempting to increase intelligence.

Intelligence, creativity, and energy are waiting only for a design to release them.

By not interfering with the existing design for intelligence and with only minimal effort and design, we can release the intelligence, creativity, and energy of our organizations for immediate and substantial returns. The difficulty in a transformation to such an approach is that we have been restraining and opposing the natural occurrence of these elements for so long, and in such an all-inclusive way, that the release may go far beyond what feels controllable. We may find ourselves reverting back to familiar patterns that would kill an initiative. Witness the People's Republic of China. It is experiencing tremendous growth but is continually re-establishing old authoritarian controls whenever fear of loss of control arises in its leadership.

COMPLEXITY AND INTELLIGENCE

Complexity is a way of seeing things that transforms the chaotic and complicated into something simple and amenable to understanding.

By exploring some of the major principles of "design for intelligence," we can reveal the nature of the immediate changes we can make in our corporations. Such changes will release new intelligence capacity. Understanding these principles will also provide an indication of our direction for future designing. This will result in an ever-increasing capacity to design for intelligence. Before exploring these principles, it will be helpful to understand a little about complexity theory.

Complexity is a burgeoning new field of study in the world of science. It is concerned with the phenomena that occur when systems are beyond linear understanding, beyond simple cause/effect, and beyond particular analysis, but have not yet "spilled over" into the area of chaos.

Complexity has been described as "at the edge of chaos." In this state, patterns can be seen and even understood, but the rich interplay of individual elements cannot be reduced to individual elements. This area has great significance because it is the area of most information. It is also robust and

Seeing phenomena through the lens of complexity continuously brings more of the unknown and unmanageable into the realm of adaptation and innovation.

viable while not being a place that can be located by formula. Nobody knows exactly where "the edge of chaos" is.

If developed, this approach continually claims space from chaos and uncertainty and increases the amount of information that a system is able to handle effectively. We can think of complexity as extending further and further into the unknown in developmental stages. As mastery is attained "at the edge," the "edge" moves further out from the center; just as your ability to master new concepts or skills expands, so too the already-mastered base expands. Similarly, when you discover something about yourself, new possibilities open for another level of discovery.

For the purpose of understanding organizational intelligence, there is another term from complexity theory that will be very useful to understand. It is the concept of "emergence." Our operational definition of emergence is *"a phenomenon that occurs out of the interplay of forces, information or en-*

The lack of organizational intelligence is stunning in its pervasiveness and its cost. Most of the cost is hidden because we are not considering what is happening from the point of view of intelligence.

An example of how application of organizational intelligence can resolve problems can be found in the shareholder service operation of a giant telecommunications company.

The company was using a large computer for its record-keeping. Initially, the various shifts had no system for communicating with each other, which resulted in continual breakdowns.

The enormous breakdowns were resolved through the simple design principles of intelligence. That is, by designing the communication links between shifts directly into the processes of the shifts themselves, the communications were not left to chance.

Another example of how applying the design principles of intelligence can quickly resolve organizational problems lies within a production process that was industry standard in cost and quality.

The process was costing the company millions a year in wasted effort and physical stockholding problems. This occurred because a simple process for off-site construction and delivery wasn't being followed.

No one was discussing it in ways that resolved the situation. The problem wasn't a poor system design, but rather a lack of communication among the various entities: connections that were essential for the existence of intelligent coordination of action. This was simply a problem of lack of intelligence in organization.

Examples such as these are usually considered to be merely individuals being unintelligent because of idiosyncrasies in personality or ability. However, when viewed from the perspective of organizational intelligence, they are design matters that are amenable to rapid resolution and immediate profit gains.

ergy being channeled through a system composed of a few basic principles (or 'attractors') and beyond a threshold point of containment. This interplay results in an identifiable phenomenon of rich variety and expression."

Intelligence is such a phenomenon. It arises from a particular form of energy interacting with a structure of particular design; however, it cannot be located in any one part of the process and cannot be sufficiently explained by causality or by examination of its particular "parts." Life itself is also such a phenomenon. The varied and rich array of biological forms of life all come from a simple four-letter code and relatively few principles similar to the grammar and syntax of language.

INFORMATION THEORY AND INTELLIGENCE

Our everyday understanding of information is that it is the part of communication that is most specific, has no ambiguity, and is clear. Information theory and communication theory tell us something different. Our operational definition of information is *"that part of communication that resolves uncertainty."* There is the highest information value when the ambiguity is the greatest, and the communication (eventually) resolves that ambiguity in the most surprising way. To the degree that a communication is predictable, it carries the least information value.

This introduction to organizational intelligence has given us sufficient concepts, tools, and vocabulary to begin to consider the issues of organizational "design for intelligence." By starting with a new theory of organization and a new set of operational definitions with which to work, we can begin to reinvent or design our organizations instead of merely tinkering with their existing designs. In the process of designing our organizations, we can transform many of the management fads into useful and reliable tools. We can replace our insatiable hunger for new fads with an ability to create for ourselves the organizations for which we are responsible and of which we are a part.

QUESTIONS FOR THIS CHAPTER:

- Where is intelligence already manifesting itself in your corporation?
- Where is it least present?
- What is occurring in the corporation that indicates a lack of intelligence and a lack of understanding of intelligence?
- What factors most inhibit intelligence?

- What is the cost in the areas of creativity, aliveness, and satisfaction that lack of intelligent design and related practices cause?
- What would be the biggest payoff in developing organizational intelligence? Where are the biggest apparent risks?
- Where do we not want more intelligence in the system?
- Where do we want "hardwired intelligence" rather than human intelligence?

The World of Theory

"Along with the saying, 'I found out I'd always been writing prose' we might now say, I found out I'd always been using theory."
M. MCMASTER

"Unaware, we are ruled by theories of a defunct economist."
JOHN MAYNARD KEYNES

Prelude

It is time that we claim theory for ordinary people—people like you and me. Scientists and philosophers are a special case; they have more or less rigorous operational definitions of theory. These definitions and the mystique that goes with them keep theory out of our reach and prevent us from using theory as a tool in our productive conversations. We can claim the use of theory by creating operational definitions for ordinary life, organizational life, and social understanding.

We operate from *theory* whether we are aware of it or not. So, it looks as though our only choice is between being unconscious or aware; and that choice determines whether or not we have something to say about what we do.

We are all scientific in our approach. We have theories about everything because we live in an age of science. We have a "because" for everything, even if we aren't aware of it. Even though these theories continue to go unnoticed and unquestioned, they are still determining our approach to everything and our general effectiveness.

What becomes possible as we learn to reshape the theories determining our actions is generative learning, profound exploration, and exciting new approaches. We are freed to explore the world of possibility itself. This is as true in the arenas of welding, sewing, and paperwork as it is for strategy and management.

THE PERVASIVENESS OF THEORY

What do Disney, IBM, Sony, McDonald's, Mercedes-Benz, Coca-Cola and all other great (or once great) companies have in common? Not many specifics. They're all organized differently and they're all in very different businesses. What they do have in common (aside from far exceeding their competition for significant but differing periods of time) is that each had a unique approach or a unique way of doing things; they had a *theory*. Each of these winners had its own unique approach based on theories of how people work together, the nature of the company's business and a way to organize. Their theories were both unique and operational. What made these companies extraordinary was that their theories were explicit, effective and drove literally every aspect of the business.

All success is based on theory. This is also true of smaller companies, divisions and even brand names: Connor Peripherals, GM's NUMMI plant, Midas Muffler, Frito-Lay, Southwest Air, Super Cuts, Unipart, Visa and Gillette, to name only a few. More significant perhaps are the many, many examples of small businesses right in your own backyard that have continually operated well beyond the norm. All these companies have unique approaches developed from simple theories. While businesses often attempt to copy successful approaches, they seldom concern themselves with the theories that spawned those approaches. The attempts to copy seldom succeed. Why is it that we are so blind to the source of success for these and countless other companies? Why

In one of our recent programs, the executive team of the company we were working with was asked to examine the way work is currently done in the company, the way people communicate, and other issues of concern for the company. Following that, the team members were asked to state the theories from which those actions arose.

Initially, they saw this exercise as trivial. As it progressed it revealed that they no longer subscribed to many of the theories and that there were many conflicting theories in existence. As the process continued they began to see that

they were going to have to develop and share new theories if they expected a behavioral change in the company.

When they were asked to create new theories around which the business would be organized, the already apparent conflicts increased and the actual theories proposed were weak.

Finally, a breakthrough occurred when the Chief Executive Officer stood and announced, "I don't know what a theory is." From that point on, the team was able to begin to work powerfully when dealing with questions of strategy, organization and the development of employees.

are we satisfied with shallow and automatic explanations about size, luck, commitment, or surface structures?

Theory is forever getting a cold shoulder at management meetings. The focus is always directed toward action, immediate application and, above all, what will produce the needed results for the next quarter. Even though executive and management development programs touch on a bit of theory, it is not expected to be talked about back at work. I have seldom seen people return from one of these programs and be asked to share with others in their corporation what they learned about theory from the program. Nor have I ever heard a lively dialogue about the relevance of any of these theories to their organizational structures.

" Story "   Fact vs. Story

A GENERAL VIEW OF THEORY

To explore theory in any depth, we'll have to create an operational definition that will make it relevant and return it to the field of everyday life in our corporations. In order to pursue organizational intelligence, our operational definition of theory is *"a group of statements, taken as a related whole, that is used as our basis for design, judgment, and guidance of action."* These are the statements that provide patterns, meaning and order as we approach the world. They identify the standards that are constantly being tested against the results they can produce. They are the clearest expression of our approaches and act as a source of information, creativity and integration within a group of people. For maximum usefulness and accessibility over time, we must be able to express these statements explicitly (verbally, visually or by demonstration), so they remain available to be challenged, tested and changed.

Theory creates the identity of corporations.

A theory is tentative in the sense that it is always on trial, always being tested, and always being challenged. Its function is to be operational, rather than to be an ideal. A theory emerges and continues to evolve and transform through the process of life itself. It acts as a reference point; not one that is permanent but one that is dynamic and up-to-date. Theory provides flexibility and information. Absence of theory leaves us with either chaos or being limited by experience. In corporations, people are unconscious of theory because it is obscured by explicit systems, by control mechanisms and by accepted management platitudes. Theory is what creates the identity of a corporation. It is the way we approach the world and something with which the world can interact. A corporation's identity will tend to remain the same, even though countless circumstances have changed. But when theory is altered, identity is also altered. The significance of this, which we'll explore later, is that theory determines the kinds of interaction that are possible with the environment and the quality of the information gained. These may be the most significant factors influencing the quality of a corporation's existence and its ultimate survival.

To gain access to theory, we must begin to see that it is everywhere.

The problem with our usual understanding of theory is that we see it as somehow separate from our day-to-day actions. To understand and utilize theory fully, we must place whatever we currently understand about theory into a much broader and richer context. This extends beyond specifics and includes many loosely and tentatively formulated statements, as well as any assumptions that underlie the theory—often beyond awareness. A powerful exploration of theory revives something old, as well as invents something new. A more complete understanding of theory recognizes that there is always more to understand or say.

By expanding our understanding of theory, we are able to reclaim it and bring it back to the level of our day-to-day lives. We all use theory (or are used by it) and engage in theoretical thinking and conversation every day of our lives. It is very common to hear management insist, "You can't discuss theory with the direct workforce." My own experience is that you can talk about theory more easily there than at management level. People in the workforce already have a sense that they are using theory. Welders know intuitively that they have a theory of welding and recognize immediately the potential power of a new theory.

THEORY AS AN EMERGENT PHENOMENON

Let's consider the theory that theory is emergent. We will then be doing in practice what we are talking about.

Let's consider theory as an emergent phenomenon and see what power that gives us. To consider theory as emergent, we will have to discover the elements and interactions from which it arises, discover the conditions in which it occurs, and reveal how it functions. Emergent phenomena cannot be traced to specific "root causes." They cannot come into existence until the necessary conditions are present and they do not exist independently prior to the emergence of the phenomenon. The conditions and the phenomenon arise together in a sort of dance. An example of this would be that language cannot arise without a certain level of intelligence and that same intelligence cannot arise without language. While certain things must pre-exist for language to occur (such as some kind of sound-production system), this alone is not sufficient. When something emerges it can be explained by *emergence from complex interaction* and cannot be understood by reduction into parts, specific actions, or preceding causes.

THE NATURE OF THEORY IN EVERYDAY LIFE

To understand theory at a new level, it will be helpful to leave our operational definition of theory behind temporarily. Let's observe theory "as it occurs," without the constriction of an operational definition. By "working backwards" and retracing the way theory occurs, the emergent nature of theory will reveal itself. With this new understanding we can then work with theory in a way that may prove to be quite valuable.

Theories are guiding the activities of our life long before we understand the nature of theories.

We all make sense of the world using the theories we have inherited from the culture around us. We are socialized into the fundamental theories and the prevailing cosmology, before we can become aware of such things as theories. We do not discover them as theories until we discover theory itself. And by then it is too late. We already have in place most of the important theories for living before we discover that such a thing as theory even exists. Because theories are invisible to us, if we are not looking for them, they remain transparent and unavailable for examination and adjustment. They just *are*. They exist as the basic fabric of our lives and determine the way in which we see the world.

If we intend to meet the demands of the rapidly changing markets of today, we must create more powerful approaches and theories for our businesses. The process for doing so is best accomplished by first waking up to where we are, rather than trying to figure out what those theories should be.

Once the existing theories are revealed, work "backwards" and explore the connections and relationships that were the source of their emergence and understand the relevant theories at that level. Only then will powerful new theories begin to present themselves.

For years Midas Muffler dominated muffler manufacturing in the USA. When it began losing market shares, the company analyzed its business and confirmed that its existing theories were sufficient for manufacturing mufflers and maintaining its manufacturing position. But that didn't explain the losses. When a consultant who appreciated language and theory was brought in, Midas generated a new theory for its business. That was that the company had become something else and would be more effective seeing itself as a marketing organization.

This first level of theory gave way to the specific theories of effective marketing organization and the company began to design a franchise system. Midas has maintained its competitive edge to this day.

Using similar thinking—that is, looking at the theories of the business—McDonald's (the hamburger chain) changed its approach to be in the real estate business.

Sears decided, decades ago, it was in the business of being "a buyer for middle-class America" rather than in the business of retail sales, and dominated many markets for a long time.

We might say that the existence of theory at this very fundamental level is what creates the possibility of understanding. If we have become aware of the fact that there is such a thing as theory and that theories can be examined, challenged, invented and reiterated, we have typically learned this through specific circumstances and know the specific applications for these theories. Even though it is common knowledge that theories play an instrumental role in the various sciences, few people are aware of the fact that these theories are based on layers of other theories. Few people see the value to be gained from examining some of the more fundamental theories. Even professionals who are dealing with theories on a daily basis are seldom familiar with this level of thinking and conversation. So whether we are working at an abstract level or at a pragmatic level, we are constantly acting and making choices guided by the theories that are part of our personal or social culture—with no awareness of what those theories are. And for the most part, we are unaware of the source of those theories.

The phrase "what we don't know that we don't know" expresses the phenomenon in which something is in the background and completely unavailable for examination and effective use. What we 'know' is contained within the context of our generally accepted understanding. What we don't know is also within that same context. We know that we don't know it but

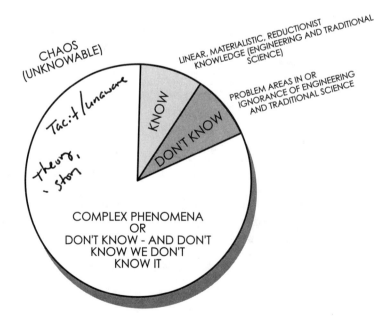

Theory / story
↓
perception / judgment
↓
Conversation / Lang.
↓
Behavior

we could learn it, find out about it, or gain access to it if necessary; i.e. physics, technical subjects, or motherhood.

However, "what we don't know that we don't know" is a vast realm of possibility. Concealed within this realm is all the useful knowledge that we don't even think to consider. If it was offered to us for consideration, we would probably dismiss the opportunity because we fail to see any relevance in it. For example, we are unaware of the nature or power of the phenomenon of listening—but we think we are aware.

When we join an organization, the theories are transparent rather than explicit.

When a new employee strides through the front door of a new company, there are already countless theories operating. Some were inherited from a larger social culture, some emerged through the process of education, some were borrowed from other institutions, and others were acquired from very fundamental levels of human understanding. A company's theories have taken on a particular expression because they were shaped by the unique history of that company. The theories that determine how we organize productive activity, do business, coordinate how people work together, and manage products or markets were already in operation and determining the interpretation of every action or accident that happened within that company. In any company of significant size and duration, the theories that are actually fueling the day-to-day operations will be mainly out of sight and out of mind. The explicit theories expressed in a company's "banner," slogan, or vision statement may be totally unrelated to the theories actually in operation.

When our consulting group is working with executives who are having difficulty engaging others within their organization in a new initiative, we continually stress that the key element missing may be listening. In the beginning, they're not sold on the idea.

But after months of work, with progress still lagging far behind projections, these same executives begin to understand that there actually is something about the capacity of listening that they have failed to consider. They begin to realize that it has always been important but has always been taken for granted.

Many times during the writing of this book, I discussed listening with various people. And do you know what? Most of them demonstrated this same lack of interest and understanding. They didn't get it. They could only understand listening in the ordinary way and could not see its power.

The way that we are listened to is directly related to the way we approach listening. Most people consider the capacity trivial and fail to demonstrate any interest in learning to listen.

Good therapists, top sales people, effective executives and managers realize that listening encompasses far more understanding and far more power than is generally realized.

It is probably becoming obvious that theories are something much more extensive than a logical set of clearly understood principles that guide us. While some theories may be understood and some may be logical or specific, a clear set is very unusual and never complete. There are always more theories than we can articulate, more connections between them than we can begin to imagine, and more contexts surrounding them than we can hope to comprehend. There are ongoing conflicts at varying levels at different times, and when these are worked out, the result is that more theories are produced. This process changes the entire original configuration. So in understanding this and using it to look at theories, we can begin to get a sense of the complexity of it all.

The accumulation of theories tends to become complicated, uncoordinated and unfathomable.

When theories become too numerous and begin to create conflict between themselves and earlier ones, either complicated systems and confusion will occur, or higher levels of theory will be sought. At times the edifice of theory may become so unwieldy that all our old theories will be displaced by a new generation of redesigned theories—and the whole cycle starts again. It is at this point that "meta-theory" emerges. It offers the theories that provide integration and continuing complexity. New and simpler principles or theories are generated. Or, if we fail to do the required thinking and redesigning, the whole structure will begin to get so complicated that it will collapse or break apart.

Our operational definition of theory is intended to create a much broader view of theory than the more commonly accepted view, which often refers to a specific theory or logic and rigorous standards of explanation and testing. Our approach sees theory as a vast network of statements

> *Organization as a Series of Complex Conversations*

IBM may be a practical example of the failure to develop new theory resulting in all four wheels flying off at once.

Now, the question remains, what will follow? Will everything flying apart result in a crash-and-burn grand finale? Or will the flying parts settle into patterns and create independent units, each with its own unique set of theories and approaches?

Don't you wonder how long such a monster can remain on its life-support system of yesterday's theories and a multitude of old habits?

IBM's theories of the business of computers and the way to organize for production have both remained largely unchanged.

IBM's rigid theories prevented it from capturing the PC market. Failure to capture the PC market significantly affected the company's mainframe business, even though that division of the company was very successful in its field.

that form the basis for our actions. By approaching theory in this way, we do not attempt to locate *the* theory that applies to all; instead, we are referring more to a *gestalt* of all the statements, assumptions and perceptions with which we make sense of things. Remember: most of us live right in the midst of theory without being aware of how it arose, what it is specifically, or even that there are theories in operation. The IBM example does not imply that any one specific theory is the source of the company's breakup. It merely illustrates that the apparent lack of attention to theory is currently destroying the company and the possible breakup would be merely the result of the same lack of concern for theory. In the event of a breakup, if the individual units are unable to address issues at the level of theory, then they are unlikely to succeed any more than the original dinosaur from which they came.

When using this approach to theory, we can see that the specific and clear theories that we developed and attempted to use came about in one of the following ways:

1. They arose from a background of unexamined theories.
2. They were designed using insufficient information and were then imposed over the top of, and often in spite of, other operating theories.

However they came to be, we will defend rationally (and often with great emotion) theories that cannot stand on their own or would be contradictory if we examined them in any depth. One situation will demand that the theories be interpreted one way and another situation will demand that they be interpreted another. People will often argue adamantly in favor of a theory they are attempting to implement, and completely ignore the realities preventing the theory from being implemented. Hence the insistence that a theory be of a very precise nature (frequently heard in relation to TQM), and when it fails to operate as intended, the failure is blamed on others' lack of commitment, others' lack of caring, or just plain "human nature."

So, as we "work backwards" and retrace the emergence of a theory, we can see that there are already countless theories operating and that they are loosely integrated with one another. This network of theories was in existence long before we arrived and will continue to be "doing its thing" long after we leave. For the most part, all these theories remain unexamined, and it doesn't even occur to most people that there are theories in operation. No one is very interested in theories because we don't seem to need them—especially since the whole thing is automatic. But once we realize that we are awash in a sea of theories and that they are impacting upon the way that we think, speak and act, we will quickly become very interested in discovering which ones are playing a critical role in our lives, how to invent new ones, and how to master the task of *integrating new theories into the web or ecology of existing theories.*

GETTING TO WORK WITH THEORY

Let's return to our operational definition of theory and bring to it everything we have just explored. Again, theory is ***the body of statements, taken as a related whole, that is used as the basis for design, judgment and guidance of action.*** We make this body of statements explicit by inquiring into the source of our actions. Or we intentionally create another set of statements that we use to generate our actions.

Now that we understand theory as having emerged out of a process of simple everyday occurrences, we open up the field to each and every person. Theory should concern every one of us. Every person at every level of any organization is affected by theory. With only a little investigation, it starts to look as if theory has a lot to do with success and failure. It just might be that the greatest source of failure is a lack of awareness of theory, rather than the possession of a wrong theory. Underlying corporate failure is the seemingly complicated nature of a business. This is not a result of wrong theory but, rather, a lack of thinking at the level of theory.

When a company evolves without sufficient thinking and awareness at the level of theory, then the "fixes" and adaptations to circumstances create an increasingly complicated system in which rule books look like your only salvation. And we wonder why things go downhill rapidly from here. Given the emergencies that knock on our doors every day of business, each one demanding action with little time for reflection, is it surprising that our actions end up being conflicting, confusing and a poor match for the larger whole?

Developing theory results in coordinated and reliable operations, as well as allowing management to work on continuous improvement (by developing more theories).

With theory as the source, management is accomplished with minimal effort or intervention. There's no need for tight control on those doing the work when theory is what guides the work. Incompetence gets turned around through education and training by using theory to guide the process. Continuous improvement in performance can be expected to occur naturally when theory is guiding our actions. Without theory, management is reduced to a life of making rules, overseeing in detail, interfering, and basically "getting in the way" of productivity. And you can forget continuous improvement without theory. Without theory, you are left only with the hope of "automatic" learning or the fatiguing job of motivation. Management's long-standing fascination with motivation is the result of not being able to make its theories explicit so that the theories can be learned or by its unwillingness to put them to the test.

Combining our new accomplishment of understanding theory (*a testable network of statements from which our actions emerge*) with our realization that we are the heirs to a world of endless unexamined theory, we can now anticipate some power and effectiveness in the domain of theory. Theory need no longer be remote but, instead, a practical tool for everyday use. Everyday assumptions and statements are just as much a part of theory as highly-developed and specialized theory. A simple statement can become a statement of theory. Deadbeat slogans like "Putting the customer first" or "Zero defects" transform into dynamic statements of theory put to the test of action, moment by moment, in our daily work. Statements such as these transform into theory when we take them seriously and continually match what's being said with our actions. When the interplay between theory and action stops, a theory returns to the world of slogans.

If your organization is still alive, then obviously the network of existing theory has been adequate for survival so far. Your current network of theory is what provides the existing level of productivity and creates your success in the marketplace. So if what you're looking for in your corporation is a leap, a turnaround, or any other unprecedented result, it is only going to happen as a result of dramatic unpredicted changes in circumstances, or new theory.

John Seely Brown of Xerox recently wrote a paper about how our basic theories in business conflict with what works in human organization, if learning is to occur. He pointed out that the hierarchical way of organizing leads to manuals, which lead to rigid practices—that manage everything in detail using command-and-control procedures—which leads to a structure that doesn't work.

You don't have to look far to see that the actual working practices of effective people do not involve picking up a manual and working from a set of rules.

When people are trying to get their jobs done, they may very well avoid communication with management or refuse to cooperate, seeing it as their only means of being able to do what they need to get done. As disdain amasses toward management and the system, the classic "us" and "them" syndrome makes its way into the mind of every person at every level of the organization.

As part of his paper, Seely Brown offers some alternative theories about human beings and organizations that provide a basis for different ways of working. He then points out our general lack of understanding of theory and our gross inability to use theory rather than be used by it.

Since the first is beyond our knowledge and control, I suggest concentrating on the second, if you're after significant results.

THEORY AND INFORMATION

At this point in the game it should be easy to see that theory is the source of information. We interpret data "through the lens" of our theories. Said another way, data becomes information (patterned data, meaningful data) via theory. Without a theory, we cannot interpret data, so we either become lost in chaos or look for aid by helplessly grasping old structures no longer adequate for the task.

Information is a result of context, of meaning, and of making a particular message from the many possible messages that could be made. It is our theories that provide structures through which data are processed. Without such structures, we are left with meaningless data or "noise." The best approach is not to search out and then start with the *right* theories (we cannot even expect to end up with *right* theories). Instead, we can consider ourselves on track if we know what our theories are and use them to generate information that will continually challenge and upgrade our existing theo-

A specialty chemical company, having recently spun off from a larger company, realized that its future depended on creating new processes.

The hurdle it needed to leap was not one of science or manufacturing processes; it needed to build production facilities for a cost that would meet the capital return requirements. The market was wide open for the company's products—the price just needed to be in the right area.

When the engineering division realized how important it was in the success of the process, it declared its commitment to reducing the costs of designing and building by 50%.

After an heroic attempt and a failure to deliver, the engineering department sent up the white flag and agreed that it needed to do a thorough review of its theories of engineering, contracting and construction.

Throughout the process of a couple of workshops, it transformed one of its slogans, "minimalist engineering," to the level of theory. The department began to put it into use everywhere.

Although the phrase had been around for some time, the department discovered that it had been using it as an excuse to set aside the ideas of others and to justify everything that it already had in place.

Aided by the rigor of a new theory, the chemical company reviewed all the procedures that affected the final cost of the process. The company reduced the cost of capital projects by 50% in four months.

ries. This self-referential loop is difficult for our rational, linear Western minds to grasp. But it is this self-referential aspect of theory that keeps the theories we already have alive and fresh.

Theory and information used to come pre-packaged; now we need direct access to them.

One of the reasons we are still uncomfortable and unfamiliar with theories in the world of business is that the theories of the past were embedded in the systems and the machinery. You didn't have to understand any of the theories to use them; they came prepackaged in all the physical stuff with a set of instructions to boot (along with a few experts to make them work). Any necessary information was built into the package. The Age of Information, however, demands flexibility and the ability to manage ever-expanding qualities and quantities of information. Those who wait for packaged answers will find themselves at the end of the line in the areas of learning and innovation. Those who embrace theory will have access to information, understanding and the ability to innovate far beyond those who do not.

Since the existing theory is producing the current results, new levels of results will require new theory. Obviously, not all new theory will become integrated with the existing theories, so the first steps of development and introduction should be approached with an attitude of experimentation. The point of an experiment is to gather information. This information allows for the evolution of the theory itself as well as its integration into the existing systems of thinking and practice.

Theory needs a safe space for its development and a protected space for its integration.

A new theory is not to be believed; it is to be explored and tested. A theory is valid if it produces results in the desired direction. Initial testing is best done in a limited environment because the kind of information needed will not be produced if the theory is subjected immediately to the world of production, with all its complexity and immediate demands. As information is gained, as the initial theory is modified, and as theory reshapes practices, additional conditions of reality can be included until enough information has been gathered, and the theory has been developed sufficiently for production to proceed.

Remember: theory doesn't belong to the world of specialists and geniuses. Theory is an everyday sort of thing always present, always operating, and doing so at many levels in an integrated way. There are times to examine theories of a higher order and times to examine those of a lower order; there are times to re-examine very obvious theories. More important than where you start is *that* you start. Once familiar with the various levels of theory, move freely from one level to another. If you're stuck, check to see if perhaps you're unwilling to dig around in your past. Or you may be working with the wrong level; if so, merely change levels until you crack the impasse. Here are some good questions with which to check your theory: "Does it reduce effort in producing a specific result? Does it increase the net payback from the energy expended?"

QUESTIONS FOR THIS CHAPTER:

- What theories are the basis of your corporation's design?
- What theories regarding people and production organize your work flow?
- What theories are indicated by your approaches to research, production, new methods and technological innovation?
- What few simple theories form the basis of your approach to your particular business or industry?
- What theories are active in your corporation regarding competition, cooperation and relationships?
- What theories guide your corporation in regard to the marketplace?
- What theories organize your strategic thinking?
- What theories do you have about motivation and why people work?
- Look at your practices, structures and actual operations to test your answers against the current structures and results.

3 Language

"People always rely on certain 'language,' which, like the languages we speak, allows them to articulate and communicate an infinite variety of designs within a formal system which gives them coherence.

"It is not just the shape of towns and buildings which comes to them from pattern languages, it is their quality as well. Even the life and beauty of the most awe-inspiring great religious buildings came from the languages their builders used.

"Now we shall begin to see in detail how the rich and complex order of a town can grow from thousands of creative acts. For once we have a common pattern language in our town, we shall all have the power to make our streets and buildings live, through our most ordinary acts . . . The language, like a seed, is the genetic system which gives our millions of small acts the power to form a whole."

CHRISTOPHER ALEXANDER
A PATTERN LANGUAGE

Prelude

It is said that "there are three mysteries in the universe: air to a bird, water to a fish, and language to a human being." Things that are transparent to us, or remain in the background of our lives, remain mysteries to us. They do so not because of *their* nature, but because of *our* nature; we usually fail to explore and question something that is always present.

To become an engineer, a mathematician, or a doctor you must learn a different language. To become a master in any of these or other fields, you must develop further distinctions. Masters speak differently from anyone else in their field. When people reach a level of mastery, it is not merely their words that are different, but also the meaning of their words, and their understanding of the world. To begin to change anything, we must change the way we speak about it. And as we begin to alter the way in which we speak about something, we begin to change our experience of it. The process is an interactive loop.

A language rooted in a linear, mechanistic view of the universe creates different actions and opportunities from a language that emerges from a complex intelligent view of the universe. A linear perspective compels us to use language in a rigid and dehumanizing way; the purpose of language in this approach is to *describe* reality. But when a complex open-ended perspective is seen as the source of our language, there is room for expression, creativity and freedom; the role of language in this approach is to *bring forth* reality.

ORGANIZATION FIRST APPEARS IN LANGUAGE

Language is at the center of society, cooperation and the coordination of action. All social organization occurs in language. Community is a function of language. How we distinguish those who "belong" from those who do not is by the way they speak. Even when the distinction is based on common practices, these practices emerged from a society where language was the fundamental organizing medium.

A corporation, like a community, is held together by its language, given meaning by its language, and is distinguished from other corporations by its language. IBM, Apple, and NEC all have unique languages, unique stories, and unique ways of speaking. Equally important, they have unique ways of understanding things and listening. These ways of speaking, listening and understanding not only constitute the culture of a company, but they also constitute a company's unique way of organizing, managing and relating to the marketplace. Xerox is unique because of the conversations that take place in the corporation. Motorola changed its language and parlayed itself into a position of world leader in quality. When you are inside a McDonald's, it doesn't sound like Burger King or any other fast-food outlet.

Language constructs worlds.

For human beings, the world becomes manifest in language. Language includes actions and the interpretation of those actions; these actions range from reactions to body language to habits, and include the meaning we add to those. Our personal understanding of something is what we say something is. And what we say is first given by our culture and only later becomes colored by personal integration. A particular corporation is created by what people say while in it and understood through what others say about it. Perhaps one of an executive's most important tasks is to provide a "pattern language" (to borrow a term from the world of architecture) that will ensure that a corporation maintains a design consistent with its self-organizing nature and produces a language of interpretation for those who are part of the corporation.

It is rare to find executives or managers who understand the relevance and power of language. Mechanistic approaches put language in the back seat; but as the world shifts toward approaches organized around information and knowledge, language assumes a role of primary importance. What indicates whether or not a major shift or turnaround is about to happen? I suggest that the most reliable place to look (listen) is in the language. If there is no change in the way that problems are described, the way challenges are spoken about, or the way values are stated, then it is very unlikely that any major change is occurring in that corporation.

The world occurs for us *as something* when it occurs in language. There are occurrences outside language, but until they are brought into the domain of language, they cannot be shared, nor can anything complex be retained or recalled about them. We are born and socialized into a linguistic world. The nature of the physical and experiential world is forever obscured by language. What we can share with others, what we can coordinate our action around and what produces organization is created in language.

Corporations are a linguistic phenomenon. A corporation exists for us in the same way that anything exists for us and that is in language, in our speaking and in our (linguistic) understanding. In addition, a corporation is composed mainly of conversations, communications, and interactions with linguistic interpretations as a main component of each. So, a corporation can be said to exist, as a phenomenon, in language. Although this idea may seem somehow distant to someone working at a desk or a machine, it is not such a strange idea to a manager or an employee whose main activity is talking, listening and conversation. It becomes more obvious when organization is explored distinct from the immediate activity of work. It is nearly impossible to be a part of a corporation and not be involved in the integration of activities, which requires extensive use of linguistic interpretation and direct communication. Even the physical aspect, such as production machinery layout, contracts and procedure manuals of a corporation, find their meaning through the linguistic act of interpretation.

Work is organized in relation to machinery, buildings and offices, which themselves have been organized by the human design of the corporation itself. This design occurs in language, and the patterns of language allow for the phenomenon of design and all the possibilities of design.

MOVING FROM LINEAR TO COMPLEX

A complex system such as a corporation can only occur in a linguistic culture. And it can only occur in a system of language that allows for complex systems. The linear language, which we have inherited both socially and for business affairs, does not allow for emergent phenomena or complex systems; it therefore leaves us powerless when dealing with such things. Those who have developed the understanding and vocabulary of complex systems can see certain things that are invisible to others. Thus, they have a greater range of action, possibility and power available to them.

As we broaden our ability to speak and think about complexity, the more things appear as complex systems. Each new appearance of this phenomenon allows for more insightful views of whatever we are dealing with. During the early stages of developing an understanding of the language and phenomena of complex adaptive systems, insights are gained that could yield great rewards, but we are poorly equipped in knowing how to work with them. As we gain familiarity with the application of the ideas of complexity, the variety of results that can be produced expands rapidly.

Our greatest obstacle in exploring ideas of complexity and complex systems is that we do not experience our world as occurring in language. For us, the world just "is." And the way it "just is" is the way in which our lan-

When you walk through the doors of BMW in Munich, you are immediately impressed by every element of the architecture and layout. By the time you arrive at the executive suites, you already have a pretty clear idea of how the company works. Its hierarchical and functional ways of organizing are obvious everywhere. Each level of the building is a perfect match for the various levels of the company.

And if you have been noticing all these features about the physical structures, you will also be aware of the fact that the ways in which people speak mirror the physical layout exactly: the kinds of problems, the ways that problems are expressed, and the way day-to-day tasks are spoken about. It is not difficult to imagine that any attempt at change, dramatic cost reduction, or any other new initiative will founder on the rocks of traditional ways.

It is also easy to predict the kinds of problems that will be encountered as the required changes demand the crossing of departmental or functional lines—such as who can talk to whom or who should influence whom.

The precision and form of BMW's enterprise are reflected in its products—and both are a perfect match for a particular era, the era that is rapidly being displaced. The current trends sweeping the globe will demand many changes everywhere, including at BMW. Either the language changes to match the current era or the needed changes are not going to happen.

guage of linear, materialistic systems represents it to us. We don't have a recollection of the world manifesting itself for us in any other way. We are competent with any language that we have inherited and been educated with; this competence obscures what we might otherwise easily see. Competence with an inherited language prevents discovery, innovation, and breakthroughs in our ability to produce remarkable results.

Competence is the ability to use things (our bodies, tools, systems, etc.) without having to bring conscious attention to them. The ease of performance of a professional athlete or craftsman is an example of this. Executives and managers must also operate with competence. They cannot operate effectively without an unconscious shared understanding of an organization and the unconscious competence to operate within it.

LANGUAGE AND AUDITING

If corporations are complex systems of language, then we must begin to design, manage and audit them for ever-increasing intelligence. Let's take a look at how corporations are assessed. Those engaged in TQM are always assessing potential supplier organizations. This assessment activity is mostly composed of audits in which systems, procedures and processes are evaluated for their effectiveness and completeness. However, looking at the systems will not provide the information that is crucial. Instead, where we must look is people's relationship to those systems. Obviously, the systems, as they exist on paper, do not produce results. Just as obvious: the systems that are operating correctly in a technical way are not in the same category as those systems operated by intelligence.

For corporations, intelligence exists in language.

"Going by the rules" never really happens; if we get close, it is only when a system has become rigid. We understand that when unions say "work to rule," the intelligence of a system and the individuals doing the work are lost. How do we test for intelligence? How do we test people's relationship to a system? How do we test attitude? These are crucial questions and until now we have ignored their relevance. Our first step is to realize that the answers are embedded in language and that language is available for study and analysis. Language patterns and language structures offer information as well as insight into relationship. We don't need only correct formal systems, we need intelligent ones. Intelligence is in the design of a system as well as in people's relationship to a system.

To see if the principles of TQM are sufficiently integrated into a system (i.e. the system is both intelligent and dependable) is impossible using a simple linear cause-effect approach. The systems that can be analyzed by most audits are linear and have no intelligence potential. To the extent that systems have intelligence, they appear contrary to most audits. The British BS5750 (and similar standards in other countries) are almost totally unintelligent; hence their bad reputation and their inability to be anything other than a marketing survival tool. For a system to be counted on, it must not only be intelligent (because it is operating within a complex system), it must also be an intrinsic part of the system in a way that is integrated with the automatic behavior and thinking of the whole corporation.

The standard tests for integration include the observation of practices of a system that have been independently judged to be effective in theory. Because an observation cannot be made without the observation itself being part of the event, the value of such an observation is limited. (This does not mean that observation changes all events; just that it changes events in which the agents are intelligent and aware of being observed.) In the following example of the computer manufacturer and the ISO 9000 procedures, the problems occurred only when the system was being installed or when it was being audited. The rest of the time, the useful information cards stayed in operation. The same lack of sense and integrity can be observed in almost every installation of similar standards. What this lack highlights is the mismatch between formal systems designed to be audited and processes designed to match the productive work of complex beings at work in complex systems.

There is another test that becomes obvious when we recognize the linguistic nature of corporations and systems such as TQM. We can listen to whether or not there is an integration of language into the everyday conver-

One of the leading computer manufacturers is now in strong pursuit of its ISO 9000 certification. The company continually demands that its customer service representatives follow procedures as laid out in a standards manual designed specifically for this purpose.

The performance of the service reps is hindered because it has become more important *to management* to have the manual followed than provide service. For example, information cards that speed service are continually re-

moved from the representatives' desks because the cards aren't listed in the ISO 9000 procedures.

The cost of viewing systems as physical things rather than information, or viewing the organization of work as something other than a complex system, becomes apparent in real costs. Using these perspectives devolves a system into something that can be audited in old ways but prevents it from evolving into something that works.

When the world is approached and man-

sations about operations. This does not mean listening to responses to questions about the subject of interest (i.e. TQM), but instead, listening to what's being said about everything else related to the corporation, its operation and its productive activities. In fact, you might even learn all that you need to know by simply listening to the language used in personal relationships, social assessments and the approach taken in the face of challenges. Of course, to be able to do this will require that you develop a new appreciation for language and a new ability to listen.

Language includes practices of speaking and action.

Practices, disciplines, and routines are all part of the language of an organization. The practices of individuals in an organization are also language. When the CEO of Jaguar/GKN (a joint venture for making auto bodies) escorted me from the car park to his office and stopped to pick up a piece of scrap paper that was lying near our path, I was immediately confident about the level of integration that the principles of TQM had reached in his company. His action was automatic and unconscious; it said as much to me as his one hour talk on quality that followed. The power of the talk was not in what he said about quality; rather, his grammar, language, thinking and actions reflected those principles—no matter what he was talking about. The grammar of his actions was consistent with what he said. This nonordinary relationship to an ordinary subject carries with it the ability to influence the thinking and behavior of others. This was a man who was leading—*showing the way by going first.*

That the world occurs for us in language becomes particularly important when our concerns are directed toward the organization of human productive activity. Everything that emerges from the complex interplay of factors,

aged in a material and mechanistic way, an audit is conducted by looking at material things. But if we shift our perspective and see everything as information and grammar, how is an audit then conducted?

The principles for conducting an audit in the information world are just as real and just as rigorous as they are in the material world, but they are different. In the material world, auditing what exists in material form is sufficient. However, in the world of information, we must audit what exists there. That world includes language, grammar, design, inherent structures, relationships, the resulting interplay of information and the things which create order as a result of their functioning.

What will those audits contain? And how will we design them? How will we test them?

Initially, computer accounting systems were audited in the same way as manual systems—by checking outputs against inputs. Later, it was done statistically. Finally, we progressed to auditing the program itself, a level consistent with the (non-material) technology.

whether material or energetic, can only be understood in linguistic terms. More abstract "things" are also available only in language; they are creatures of language and emerge, as themselves, only when language is created to distinguish them. Phenomena such as organization, life, energy, leadership, relationship, intelligence, learning, quality and courage emerge from a rich and varied interplay of factors. A more refined understanding of the language and concepts of complexity provides access to these phenomena in ways previously understood only by those who took the time to understand the relationship between language and the world we live in—or other such marvelous adventures.

LANGUAGE, REALITY AND WHAT WE "TAKE FOR GRANTED"

Our current way of speaking and thinking has things occurring one-dimensionally in the world as "objects" disconnected from both the world around them and the language structures through which they are presenced. That is why, for instance, we have so many books on leadership, the reading of which does not produce leadership. The phenomenon of "leadership" is not one of character, personality, style, or anything nearly as personal as we have made it out to be. The phenomenon has at least as much to do with the complex systems in which leadership occurs as a natural phenomenon, the systems in which leadership is a wanted occurrence and those in which leadership is a missing element when not present. The com-

The Liberal Democrats in Great Britain have been the third party for a long time—a very distant third party. They speak a language that is different from the other two parties. When their language becomes the language of the majority, they will become a majority party.

They think that their job is to fight for ideas. In doing so, they fail to realize that their real job is to change the language of the country. As they begin to develop a language that alters the language of the country, they can expect a breakthrough at the polls.

It is beginning to dawn on some of the older institutions attempting social change—for example, the various libertarian organizations or many of the newer movements, such as women's rights and environmental groups—that language is the crucial factor in their work. Emotional diatribe is giving way to education; out of it is emerging a new language with which to conduct dialogue with regard to our social concerns.

plex systems we are talking about may be corporations, or they may be the circumstances of larger systems, such as political affairs. In some systems, leadership is always present. In others, it is present only under certain conditions. But in all cases, it has relatively little to do with an individual's desire or ability to be a leader.

For all of us, meaning is created in language. For most of us, fundamental meaning is already given by the structure and accepted patterns of our language. The job of an executive has more to do with the use of language to create meaning for communities of people than with personality traits inherent in a person.

Similarly, when a CEO wants to transform an organization, he or she must change the language of that company. Gerstner, now at the helm of IBM, is off to a bad start by using the same language as his predecessor. John Neill, of Unipart, turned a dismal manufacturing capacity into a world leader by changing the language of the company. Not only is the speaking and listening of everyone at Unipart consistent with the company's concern for quality of an extraordinary level, but the company has continual learning built into every element of its language, whether it is practices or investments.

Language is a structure of interpretation first, and a descriptive medium after that.

It will take new ways of speaking and thinking—a special language—to move away from our obsolete mechanistic approaches and move toward operating as a complex intelligent system that learns. Providing a new language of interpretation for a corporation may be an executive's most important undertaking. The role of language in a corporation is paramount; it contains the design of the organization, determines the intelligence of the corporation, and limits the possibility of the corporation. Language may be considered the ultimate structure within a corporation in that it allows for infinite variety within an existing identity and maintains the structure's integrity at the same time as it is developing or evolving. For a corporation to transform, its language and grammar must change. Language will be the source of change. Organizational transformation is the linguistic change that allows for the transformation of thinking, activity and even possibility. When the language of interpretation is altered, new information may be generated and put into practice.

Pattern languages, or grammar, are not only found in corporations and their designs; they are also a part of anything in which design is an element. Engineers and architects have pattern languages. Scientists and artists have pattern languages. DNA can be seen as a pattern language—four letters and rules of combination depending on the species. Physics and chemistry are

Part of the power of language is that we learn it unconsciously and it uses us.

starting to illuminate the grammar of the elements of the universe. A pattern language can be found everywhere we find order or design.

The basics of a language provide a grammar, which in turn provides a structure of interpretation for those who use it. When we are socialized into a language, it becomes part of us at an automatic "beyond awareness" level. Language structures our society by providing a means to understand or create meaning. As we learn a language, we are acquiring a structure for interpreting the world (a cosmology). Without even knowing that it is happening, we learn both a language and a cosmology, and use them without awareness. This illustrates the power of such a system.

Corporate language is much the same. Even though it is composed of a broader social language, it has particular patterns that are unique to each corporation. These patterns are already in existence when we show up in a corporation, and we are socialized into the particulars in the same way as we are socialized into the broader language; that is, we learn them automatically from subtle interactions with a complex environment.

The introduction of a new grammar—not just new words—is the key to organizational transformation. The distinction is crucial. Changing the words alone, which frequently is attempted in introducing vision or TQM or some other program, will not produce results. Fitting new words into familiar phrases, sentences and conversations will not produce results. No new grammar, no new possibility of change. For an initiative to be successful, a whole new language is required, one that allows for and demands powerful new thinking, speaking and grammar.

We structure reality with language: reality doesn't structure language.

As the power of language is revealed to us, the role of thinking must be addressed. Language provides the tools with which we think, interpret and generate meaning. Language is the means by which we structure reality, construct our world and interrelate in our relationships. Speaking is often thought to be the primary use of language: but our speaking is a result of what we have thought. And what we have thought is a function of what we've been able to listen to, understand and integrate. When we say that the language of an organization must change if a transformation is to take place, we mean that the thinking must change: our new way of thinking will then automatically be reflected in our speaking. When we say that the language must change, we are not saying that the words people speak must change. We are saying that the words, grammar, and sentences that they think with must change. The words that are spoken will change. This is an interactive and self-reflexive process. Different speaking will change the thinking and different thinking will change the speaking in a spiral of accelerating impact.

We must dwell in a language to make it operational.

The extraordinary complexity and diversity of language allows us to learn a new language and not forget the old. To the extent that interactions with the outside world (or the internal operations) still require the old language to be used, it is completely available. The challenge is very much like learning any new language: until we can think in the new language, we think in the old and translate. We learn the nuances of a new language by engaging in the translation and communication processes until finally we are dwelling in that language. When beginning a process of organizational transformation, the principles may seem clear and the pathway obvious; but until the corporation is dwelling in their new language, we can be certain that it is not fully integrated into the daily operations of the corporation.

When we see that language is at the heart of the matter for major transformational undertakings, it provides us with a freedom to act. We have access to language. It is a public phenomenon. If we had to approach the

Do you remember the saying, "Don't call them problems, call them opportunities"? At the time of its debut, the saying was effective for people for brief periods of time. A few people, who heard it correctly, were actually able to benefit from it on a long-term basis.

But for most, the remedy wore off quickly. The source of the failure was not the idea but the shallowness of people's interpretation of the idea.

For those who did nothing more than swap words in a few places, the remainder of their language patterns stayed intact and particular situations were still perceived as problems, no matter what they were called. But for those who brought a little insight to the saying, they saw that the entire structure of interpretation needed to be altered in relationship to certain situations.

The standard interpretation of the word "problem" was loaded with detrimental meaning. For a shift to occur in relationship to problems, it must occur at the level of interpretation—and that alters the grammar.

On a broader scale, the investments of time and money into vision statements and the various elements related to them are, for the most part, wasted. The losses are not a result of having the "wrong" vision statement. Instead, the language and grammar of an organization are never influenced by the vision work; thus, there is no way to maintain a new approach or idea, and it quickly goes out of all practical existence.

An example of an incomplete fulfillment of vision can be found at Hilton. If you walk into one of its many hotels throughout the world, you'll notice that the speaking and action of the staff, in the ordinary course of their working conversations, is frequently not a match for the vision statement of Hilton. So why the gap between what the company says it is and how the world sees it? Hilton is inconsistent with that vision in the language that its staff uses when they are dealing with each other. The language of Disney World matches their vision, inside and out— at least in the USA.

changes we wanted to make by first changing the physical existence of things, we'd be hopelessly bound by "reality."

If we had to change the ideas, beliefs, values, or personal attributes of every person taking part in an initiative, we would be faced with an impossible task. But all we need to do is change the language, grammar and structure of interpretation that is used and we have provided everyone with an accessible, malleable and effective tool for any transformation effort. The real challenge is to find ways to say what is in our hearts and minds—a way that reflects the world as it occurs today.

QUESTIONS FOR THIS CHAPTER:

- How do you currently talk about your business?
- Will this way of speaking lead to the future you want or will it merely continue to extend what is already in existence?
- What language patterns exist in your corporation that inhibit the expansion of its values, goals, and possibilities?
- Do the functions, specialties and levels of authority in your corporation have a grammar that maintains exclusion?
- What specific words and grammars keep them in place?
- How would you like the people of your corporation to think about the company?
- Does your way of speaking encourage that way of thinking in others, or not? Examine your everyday way of speaking, not just the special occasions when you are attempting to get a message across.
- Is the language that you use forming and strengthening a sense of community, or is it undermining it?

II Organizational Theory

In this section the basis for a new theory of organization based on complexity is developed. Chapter 4, *Breaking Free,* deals with the obstacles to new theory and the challenge of breaking with the past. The next chapter explores the nature of design as it applies to corporations. The following chapters take into consideration the fundamental issues of design and management of human organization. These include leadership, learning and freedom.

4 Breaking Free

"The culture that admires truth and effectiveness, at least at work, will produce more than the culture that prefers observance of traditional forms and cares little about truth and effectiveness."
MAX SINGER
PASSAGE TO A HUMAN WORLD

"Two monks who had taken a vow to never touch women came across such a creature standing in front of a small stream which she was afraid to cross. One monk swept her up in his arms, carried her across and put her down on the other side. Many miles later, the other turned to his companion and said, 'We've taken a vow not to touch women. How could you pick her up and carry her across the stream?' The monk responded, 'My friend, I put her down many miles back. Why are you still carrying her?'"
A TIBETAN STORY

Prelude

The past is always with us. There is no escape from it. The challenge is to achieve the freedom to invent a future that is not merely an extension of the past. We have the ability to choose to go beyond that past—but only when we are fully aware of its nature.

The future is open to choice and to design. This openness is a dangerous thing when viewed from the perspective of continuation and survival. The existing patterns seem to be the source of our survival. Any change may lead to destruction. To go beyond the past, we cannot forget or reject it; we must use it instead of being used by it. We must keep the past firmly in the past without attempting to lose it or deny it. Any such attempts will fail. The past will reassert itself if denied.

For human beings and their institutions, the past is kept alive in language and by physical structure. Physical structure makes concrete the thinking and action of the past. Language provides meaning for those physical structures and keeps them protected. It is the ability to give new meaning through new language (words, meanings, uses, combinations and patterns) that gives us our power to create a future. When we realize this power in language, we become free to use the past for its information value without being trapped by that past. We can expect to be free and to use this freedom intelligently and profitably when we are aware of its nature.

WHAT DOES IT TAKE TO TRANSFORM SOMETHING WITH A PAST?

Imagine you are John Akers and you have the job of transforming IBM. IBM is a perfect example of the worst possible situation for such an effort. Aside from having a large number of employees, the company has a long history—and success has been the name of the game for most of it. IBM had a reputation as the best managed company in America, if not the world. As a leader promoted from within, you have many well-established relationships and a long history within that organizational culture. You simply had the bad fortune of "being on watch" when the damned thing began to come apart.

Now what are the chances of you being able to turn the company around? None! So the directors bring in a new man and for the most part ignore the fact that they also were on watch when the wheels came off. Next, imagine yourself to be the new leader, Lou Gerstner, and you've been given the job of transforming IBM. What's different except that you were not there when things started falling apart? Can you imagine your chances of turning the company around to be much better?

To transform anything with a past requires: 1. understanding of the historical nature of things and 2. new theory.

What it takes to transform anything with a past (that is, literally *anything*) is an understanding of the phenomenon that you're dealing with and a new theory generating your actions—one that is different from the one which created the past that failed you. Given the current state of affairs it doesn't appear that Gerstner has either a new theory or an understanding. This shouldn't be surprising, because the board that hired him is also operating without either of these.

In the same way that "everyone" knew IBM to be one of the best-managed companies, "everyone" now knows what is wrong. Sure. But nobody knows how to fix it—not even those who say they do. Listen carefully to any of the suggestions and you won't hear anything other than conventional, everyday "wisdom" spoken in a way that clearly will not make a difference, even if you are CEO. Witness Gerstner. During his first year in the executive suites, did he say anything that was profoundly different? Was there anything in his approach that suggested he possessed a profound new understanding of the nature of the organization, or that he was in the midst of creating a remarkable new theory? Then how can we possibly expect him to do any better than Akers did, except for the simple fact that he is not bound by old relationships and attachments?

If we want to move into a new level of understanding corporations and the transformation of organizations, then we must begin to explore the historical and conservative nature of being. *Being* refers to anything that has an existence of its own. It refers to anything that has survived long enough to be considered to have an identity. Another feature of being is *becoming*. Everything that exists in its own right has an historical basis, embodies a design that continues or maintains that historical being and has available a limited range of possible futures. Even when *becoming* has a very large range of possibilities, what an entity can become is inherent in the current design and circumstances. Any action intending to generate a transformation must take into account these elements because they are fundamental to the identity or being of a corporation. A caterpillar has in its design the possibility of becoming a butterfly—but not a bird.

What a corporation can become, given that we can alter the design itself, has much greater possibility for transformation than the caterpillar. Unfortunately this possibility is seldom able to develop. We tend to lose sight of the design principles and get attached to a particular form of design that is not much more than an historical accident. Through the ideas presented in this book we intend to engage in the development of the capacity to design and implement principles that will continually and effectively balance the need to adapt to the environment with the need to impact the environment to suit our intentions. This capability will allow us to realize the possibility that is inherent in the existing identity of our organizations and the evolving social and commercial environment.

Corporations are complex intelligent systems and can therefore transform. The difference in the size of corporations will not proportionately affect the length of time it takes to transform an enterprise or the difficulty involved. Obviously, it is likely to take longer to transform a corporation of 100,000 people than one of 1,000 people, but the difference in time will not be proportional. If it took more "per pound" to transform a large corporation, that would imply that large corporations were less intelligent than small ones and that they are the dinosaurs of our times. The reason that large corporations are relatively easier to transform than small ones is expressed in the theory of complex adaptive systems.

It may turn out that the most significant thing Gerstner did in his second year was to abolish the dress code that was a mainstay of the IBM mythology. A small change in a complex system affects all parts of the system. So significant changes can be accomplished through minimal effort and small disturbances to the system. If this were not the case, then transformation would not be possible at all. If a system were large and linear, then a small change would have a small impact and a large change (larger than is possible in most cases) would be required to have any sizable impact. If a system were beyond a certain size, a change of the required scope would not be possible. However, large linear systems are not our concern here. It is interesting to note that as linear systems increase in size, they become subject to the principles of complexity and the laws of their operation change accordingly. A complex intelligent system, such as a corporation, is subject to the principles of complexity from the moment it passes the threshold point of size and becomes a corporation.

A small set of principles or attractors provides a simple and effective basis for breaking free of the past.

The theory of complex adaptive systems allows us to access the grammar and syntax of transformation so that we can be effective with relatively little effort. Understanding this theory allows us to see that a relatively small set of principles, or *attractors,* will be sufficient to create the elements by which a system self-organizes. If the *attractors* are robust and certain boundary conditions are maintained, we can rely on the system to continually renew itself in an effective manner.

Structures that are put into place, consistent with the design principles, continue to inform all participants within the system and draw them to appropriate behavior while releasing creativity and energy. The remaining challenges of education and development occur over an extended period of time and require varying amounts of resources. The size of the corporation influences the time and resources required, but not proportionately. In fact, a larger corporation has the advantage of minimizing spending and increasing internal competence by educating its own educators. Ideally managers, a powerful in-house resource, become competent at the continuing education and development process in the course of their day-to-day activities. Transformation occurs in the complex interactions and practices of everyday work.

KEEPING THE PAST FIRMLY IN THE PAST

"We are victims of the past and it calls us towards it."
HEIDEGGER

Another reason why the size and age of a corporation has little to do with the amount of time it takes for transformation to occur is that the past has an equally strong grip on every individual and every corporation without respect to their differences in size or content. To transform a corporation (or a human being), the tenacious grip of the past must be broken. This is accomplished by clearly distinguishing the past as the past, thereby giving us complete accessibility to it without being controlled by it. Relating to the past in this way gives us an enormous amount of freedom with respect to that past. We can access its information and knowledge when needed, as well as unlearn and set aside that information in order to create a future.

We seldom learn from the past. More often, we use a more distant past to make sense of the present which merely reinforces a still earlier past in a continuing "vicious circle." When this is occurring, learning takes place only marginally. Even when we *do* learn from the past, we tend to put what is learned in place as a permanent rule and it becomes the new standard of interpretation that prevents new learning.

The past is valuable for its information not its conclusions or "learnings."

When the past is clearly defined as the past, we have the freedom to access the wide range of *information* which can be used creatively for new learning and innovation. We can reinterpret the past as many times and in as many ways as may be productive for our current purposes. We can revisit the past with the same flexibility at any time in the future. While it is sometimes useful to revisit the past to recover the conclusions that we made, it is generally more useful for acquiring additional data for our current creative processes. When this information is combined with new ideas, new technology and new circumstances, it enables us to produce otherwise unforeseen insights and possibilities.

It is not merely useful information from the past that we are concerned with here; looking at the "dark side" is also of interest. It's the past that we don't want to question or consider in a new way that prevents us from breaking free. It is the "dark side" that we protect from challenge by keeping

---

For almost a century Avon wore the crown of success. Since the company's policies and practices had been successful in the past, it kept them in place through changing times.

In the '80s the company began a decline and margins dropped, but it was unable to access critical information contained in its history in a way that would be useful for producing new insights and possibilities.

The company's only option was to repeat the past. Executives kept pointing to their profitable growth that spanned 100 years and used it to justify not listening to new ideas.

Finally it changed: it got worse. The changes made were inconsistent with the information the past could have provided. Relationship, convenience and personal reward were still key operating principles, but the nature of what would satisfy those principles had changed in the last few decades.

Avon's recovery in the '90s occurred when it broke free of the way it had been relating to the past. The company discovered new ways of learning from the information of the past and integrated it skillfully into current information. This is the renewal that breaking free of the past allows.

it hidden even from ourselves. The information value of the past is not available to us until we are aware of our relationship to it and we are free to recall, reassess and reconceptualize any part of it. By developing a new awareness we become able to do this when necessary.

It is important to remember that we are not talking about an individual being able to do this, but rather a corporation as a whole. (This process can be useful for individuals but that is not our concern here.) Even though we may have free access to the past and are able to transform our interpretation of that past on an individual basis, groups of people are generally not very skillful at this. Corporations (identities to which our personal identities have become attached in many different ways) find this process almost impossible. There are many cases, however, where a group or corporation can look at its past while certain key individuals cannot. We can begin to see in this that a corporation or team can be more intelligent than the individuals on their own, when a certain competence in dialogue is present.

It is not the past itself but the interpretations which create our identities that make it difficult to break free.

When an individual challenges the accepted interpretations of the past that have become part of the culture, values, or cherished beliefs of a corporation, there will always be a significant percentage of any group or meeting who will kill that challenge. This is particularly noticeable when an outsider, such as an educator or consultant, does the challenging. It is particularly noticeable only because those inside the system have learned either not to challenge, or to ignore or ridicule anyone doing the challenging.

The limits of a corporation arise from a particular interpretation of past events that shapes the interpretations of current events.

The past is not the problem. The problem is a *particular* past. We didn't learn not to touch a hot stove when others burned their hands. We learned not to touch a hot stove when we burned our own hands. The structure of interpretation which we carry forward from our learning is unique to us. Said another way, the problem is our own particular past. The same is true for corporations. The past that limits the future possibilities of a corporation is not just any past; it's not a general past; it's not even a "real" past. The past

At one point, I did consulting work in a hospital in which I frequently heard the phrase, "Sister Mary doesn't allow that here." or "Sister Mary said . . . "

I wondered why we were doing such important organizational work without such an influential person as Sister Mary at the meetings.

When I asked why she wasn't there, the response I received was, "She died ten years ago."

that limits a corporation is a very specific past that is part of the organizational memory. It is this past that is brought to every conversation, action, interaction and structure of a corporation.

There are two features to notice about the past. One is that the past is an interpretation unique to the corporation and not necessarily based on what actually occurred. The other is that this particular past determines the context for current actions. I've been in many companies in which people say, "You can't do that because if you do you'll be fired." Yet, if you search through those same companies, you can't find anyone who knows of anyone else having been fired for the behavior mentioned. What's interesting is that frequently you'll find past occasions of that same "forbidden" action in the leaders of the company.

THE NATURE OF ORGANIZATIONAL MEMORY

We are examining the past in such detail because we cannot break free of it until we are aware of both the nature of its existence and its contents. It is essential to understand the mechanisms and structures by which the past keeps itself alive and continues to influence a corporation in limiting ways. If we are to become competent at keeping it firmly in its place (that is to say, firmly in the past) we need to understand the nature of organizational past and organizational memory.

The past has a particularly powerful grip in corporations because it is inherited as reality. An inherited past is different from a past which you

When I joined IBM, its identity, culture, and particular inherited way of doing things were as real as anything else.

If you had been there since the company started, you would know its history as a series of accidents, differing interpretations of those accidents, and direct personal experiences more or less accessible to questioning. If you showed up later, as in my case, the history was implied, expressed in the culture, and conveyed in various ways during one's indoctrination.

Nothing was subject to recall, re-evaluation, or questioning with regard to the past. Historical accident had become intentional design. Another example of this same phenomenon, except on a more personal level, is our marital relationships.

As one of the partners in the relationship we have access to all the incidents that form our past with our spouse. As a child born into that relationship, none of that history is available to us and the relationship is just the way that it is.

helped to create. This is why experienced managers and professionals often have an ability to see the whole and break with the past, whereas it is lacking in some of the younger ones from whom we expect more intelligent challenges.

To understand fully the phenomenon of the past, we must notice that when most of us deal with the past, it does not exist *as* the past. It exists undistinguished from the present as the present. Within our corporations there are contexts, structures, rules, beliefs, habits, customs, unspoken constraints, physical structures (buildings, etc.), and an endless variety of things inaccessible in their totality. These occurred in response to interpretations in the past. The structures, systems and particularly the language patterns form the organizational memory. We have little access to the past that was the source of all of this, even though we live inside the stories, context, and *interpretative* mechanisms that it gives us.

One of the most subtle and yet most powerful aspects of the past's grip on us is the influence of structure on our daily lives. We become competent managers and employees when we are able to operate within the structures of our corporations without much thought or effort. In the same way, our competence as adults and citizens is determined by the extent to which we are able to operate effectively within the already existing structures of society and its institutions. What then defines competence is the ability to function without conscious attention or serious interruption when there is a variation in the circumstances. We are born into a world of organized struc-

DEC fired its founder after decreasing market share and increasing losses. The new CEO brought in as a replacement created a new vision and strategy, and announced that there would be a major reorganization of the company.

Within the year, the reorganization was declared a success. However, in the next year, losses continued to mount and the new structures were abandoned.

The new structures were nothing more than a reshuffle of the old structures and they exhibited a profound lack of anything original.

The new CEO and the board displayed no understanding of structure. Like many before and after them, they thought that a change in executive positions or a shift within departments would make a difference.

What they actually did was destroy some organizational memory and overlook the fact that new structure would have to increase intelligence to make up for the loss. *They didn't know that they didn't know anything about structure.*

The reorganization only occurred at a superficial level and not at a level of reassessing the past or exploring organizational memory.

tures and become competent at using those structures for our ends. We become so competent that the structures fade completely into the background and we are no more aware of them than we are of the existence of the ground as it supports our competence in walking. It is not until we find ourselves running in soft sand or navigating on an icy pavement that the idea of the supportive nature of the ground even enters our awareness.

Most of the structures of organization are like that. We are bound by the history embedded in the structures because we are unaware of its nature, its importance, or its daily relevance to the future.

The insight provided by this view has recently enabled me to understand what has been a puzzling phenomenon during my career as an educator/consultant. I had always assumed that executives and managers, when they created a vision of a possible future and committed themselves to it, would be competent at changing the structures of their corporations to match that future. But this has not been the case. Returning to their jobs with a commitment to change, they exhibited little change and even less creativity in the redesign of their structures. (Most re-engineering initiatives flounder on this lack of ability and imagination, as do most consulting reports.) What they were demonstrating was their lack of understanding of structures.

Executives and managers are extraordinarily competent at *using* existing systems. (That may be the single most important qualification for the job.) By the very nature of what we consider to be competence, there is an inherent unconsciousness when it comes to looking at existing structures, not to mention considering changing them in any fundamental way. Not only does change reduce executives' and management's existing competence, mastery and the effectiveness of basic strategies, but it demands that executives and management invent something that has an existence and a nature beyond what they are typically aware of. This is like asking someone to reinvent the ground, or the air, that our survival depends on—and asking them to like doing it.

LANGUAGE IS THE KEEPER OF THE PAST

The first act in breaking free of the past is to understand its nature and that of the mechanism that maintains its grip. Looking at this in biological terms, the past must be wired in, or the future would continually break down into chaos and randomness, making the future beyond our capability for existence (at least as we know it). The past must in some way play an integral role in our present, or we would not survive. If the past had no meaning, or it failed to provide a structure of interpretation, then our corporations and society itself would break down immediately. But if we understand the past, the nature of change, adaptation, and the evolution of organizations, we are free to alter the design principles, structures, and purposes of our corporations so that they are able to emerge into something more than merely an extension of the past.

To gain access to a corporation's past and its design, we will need to consider them as linguistic phenomena. Linguistic phenomena are structures of meaning, interpretations, and understandings that we can easily access. Through language we have the freedom and power to access and transform our corporations. (Because language is a social phenomenon, we have access and power to the extent that we include the community. We cannot accomplish a transformation "on our own.")

The *meaning* of buildings, contracts, legal structures, etc. is more important than their physical existence. When I worked for IBM, I belonged. Those letters meant something to me and meant similar things to many people. The corporation existed for me whether or not I was in its buildings, whether or not I knew its legal structures, and whether or not I knew its agreements. I "knew" it as a set of values, although they were mainly from hearsay. The reality was unquestioned and yet the reality existed in language rather than material things.

Executives seriously committed to transforming their corporations, but who describe the process as painful and a struggle, are failing to realize the linguistic nature of corporations and missing out on the power that one has by understanding this. They also fail to see that the language patterns need to change more than the "thinking," "beliefs," or "commitments" of others. Their struggle is in trying to change things that aren't accessible rather than change language, which is readily accessible. Pain and struggle come from working against the nature of things rather than with it. And lastly these executives fail to see the social and inclusive nature of language as the source of change and end up mistakenly labeling people's efforts to understand as resistance.

There's one area in which individuals, groups, and entire corporations can break the bonds of the past and become free. That area is language in the form of speech, thought and dialogue. Let's make a series of assumptions to illustrate a point: let's assume that nothing happens in the world until actions are taken. Let's also assume that no serious actions are taken until decisions are made. Let's further assume that there is a regulatory and conservative structure for decision making and resource allocation, etc. So if nothing happens until action is taken and we have conservative structures (rules, controls, approvals, etc.) to ensure that actions are not dangerous, then why do we need any boundaries around our conversations or dialogues? We can only benefit from freeing our conversations, exploring possibility, and conducting thought experiments to our heart's content. We might even allow ourselves some creative freedom and poetic license.

THE COST OF BREAKING FREE

Conversation is an example of an activity in which the cost of *doing* is very low. The only real cost is the cost of learning how to do. No special budget in time or money needs to be set aside for such activities. Speaking, thinking and dialogue, which explore possible futures and free us from the bonds of the past, need not be time-consuming activities.

Conversation is cheap. Learning to be effective with conversation is only a little more expensive.

It takes no more time to engage in powerful, new, exploratory conversations about our future than it does to maintain past-based conversations filled with excuses, blame, justifications and reasons why something can't be done. Granted, it may take a little time to become powerful with this way of speaking and it may take some effort to unlearn the habit of killing off these kinds of conversations, but the investment is inconsequential in the face of the returns. In most cases, this kind of designed future-based conversation will be more valuable, creative and practical than any structured meeting for similar purposes

The payoffs are immediate when we break free of the past.

Breaking free of the past will take some effort and will require changes in structures, such as who talks to whom about what. Encouragement specific to this area is a must. But it will not take much more than encouragement and little, if any, extra time and money. The payoff is enormous. There will be an immediate release of energy as well as creativity. Dramatic increases will occur in the areas of responsibility, accountability and direct action.

When we alter our relationship to the past and end our unconsciousness in the area, we stop draining our energy and resourcefulness. The new release of energy and creativity brings up a new cost, because management will have to confront two things. The first is its inability to deal with anything beyond what is controlled and directed. The second is the need to deal personally and organizationally with the fact that some of the earlier ideas created at lower levels could have been acted on long ago and may have been of enormous value.

BREAKING FREE EXPANDS THE SPACE OF POSSIBILITY

Leadership by going first must demonstrate challenging the past and breaking free.

The most critical factor in the transformation of a corporation is not new systems, but rather leadership in challenging the past and breaking free so that possibility can be explored. In biology, the *space of possibility* is defined as the full range of what is available to be explored, without concern for whether or not it has been, or will be explored. It is this space of possibilities that our corporations need to access if they are to survive and prosper. The limited range of options that can be seen by an elite group of executives, managers, and professional specialists is not enough. This limited range of options is only a small fraction of what can potentially be accessed in the space of possibility.

A corporation can explore the space of possibility in the course of life itself, in the same way that a species within an ecological realm goes through its process of evolution. It is not necessary to pursue possibility as a special venture, although it may be profitable. Sufficient gains will be realized for

I have never worked in a large manufacturing or contracting operation in which there were not unspoken yet mutually agreed-upon rules about who shouldn't speak to whom.

In one specific British trades-based construction operation, the middle management all agreed that they couldn't talk to the guys working on the job. The guys working on the job in one trade couldn't talk to those working in other trades. The managers of one particular trade couldn't talk to managers in other trades.

Not only did they not talk about many important things, but they had established routines in their communications that were ineffective to an extreme. Their communications involved far too many people, great time delays, and almost complete uncertainty as to a response. And this company was recognized as one of the "best yards" in the industry.

As part of the consulting process, we brought them together in mixed groups and gave them an exercise. In the exercise they were to tell each other about their problems and get advice or coaching from the others.

They all were certain that it would be a useless exercise because, "What could a person from another trade or department possibly know about their area or contribute to them?"

By the end of the exercise, they were amazed at the understanding and help they'd received from others and surprised at the increased level of respect they now had for each other.

The most difficult challenge in this exercise was for management to see that its own lack of communication—in order to protect boundaries—was the source of the problem. Management had to confront that the immediate savings—in this case a million pounds annually—could have been made years earlier. It also had to let lower levels have more responsibility to realize the savings. Both took some effort to accomplish.

the corporation through the actions of breaking free of the past and designing itself as an intelligent entity operating within a rich and varied ecology. The activities of our everyday working lives will provide as much innovation as is likely to be needed for some time.

The process of breaking free begins with a leadership that is able to understand the nature of the grip of the past, is able to grasp the nature of possibility, and is willing to lead by example in the effort of keeping the past firmly in the past. A new leader coming on board has a certain advantage because that person doesn't share the past; however, a new leader must still be responsible for the past irrespective of the fact that she or he was not there for it. And that's a difficult task. New leaders do not start with a clean slate even though they're new.

An existing leader, however, is actually in a better position because she or he doesn't need to reject or ignore the past, but instead can retain, honor and acknowledge the past without being bound by that past. In either case, it will take courage and clarity to be aware of one's self and one's speaking.

QUESTIONS FOR THIS CHAPTER:

- What structures of your corporation can be accounted for by *frozen accidents*?
- What processes, beliefs, rules, etc. are thought to be necessary, but are not obviously useful?
- What does everybody know, but nobody say?
- When was the last time you created an opportunity to be challenged – and then did something with the response?
- What are the five oldest policies or procedures that have remained largely unchanged? (Change them.)
- What forum does your corporation provide for challenging the way things are done?
- What support is provided for those who want to challenge things?
- What are the current practices in your corporation that create opposition for those challenging the current interpretation of the past?
- Do people get offended or defensive when ideas or practices are challenged?
- Does the language used to challenge reflect curiosity, or righteousness and attack?

5 Intelligence by Design

"At any given moment in the unfolding of a sequence of patterns, we have a partly defined whole, which has the structure given to it by the patterns that come earlier in the sequence."
CHRISTOPHER ALEXANDER
THE TIMELESS WAY OF BUILDING

Prelude

To be a good architect requires that you understand design principles at a profound level. To understand architectural design at the level of design principles, one must be able to consider an entire context—and at the same time understand countless relationships between material and non-material elements within that context. Included in this broad gamut of elements are steel, wood, glass, electricity, light, temperature, culture, aesthetics, and life style—to name only a few. Changes in technology, education and life itself are constantly creating new principles and transforming old ones.

Developing an understanding of the design principles of corporations is not part of a traditional education. Their understanding may not include the most fundamental level—that out of which the principles of design emerge.

Rapidly occurring changes are altering the context of the world in which we live and work. We are now being asked to take on the challenge of redesigning our corporations to meet the onslaught of new demands. The executives and management of our corporations are poorly positioned to do so because they have grown up with an automatic competence in a design that is no longer workable. Unless they are able to get at the very source of organizational design, it will remain next to impossible to alter the course of what is occurring.

ORGANIZATIONAL DESIGN = HIERARCHY

We have inherited the design of our corporations. The design is so old that we think the way we see things is the way they should be. We don't even question the basic design of our corporations and those who do question it are misunderstood or rejected. While many in management talk about networks, distributed systems, etc., there are few who take such ideas seriously. We unknowingly assume that the hierarchical way of organizing is the way things must be organized. For nearly all of us, everything we know about organizing tells us to organize in this way.

Even though most of us have tinkered with organizational design, it has been mostly at the edges. Our tinkering may have included the introduction of some teams, group accountability, special projects, and certainly some different organograms. But all of these have retained the basic design *principles* of the corporation as it currently exists. Few executives and managers have contemplated major changes in the underlying principles at the source of how our corporations are designed.

Our persistent tinkering is the result of knowing something is missing in the way in which we are organizing and managing. We know something more is possible from coordinated human activity than what we are getting. The problem is that we have never been introduced to the idea of organizational design itself. We are comfortable and competent with the designs we have been given and few of us have any experience or education in the principles of design. Understanding these principles will be crucial if we are to transform the intelligence of our corporations into entities capable of meeting the new demands of the Information Age.

Frozen accidents account for the specifics of our current designs.

Every existing corporation is the result of a mixture of theory, values, and intentions that are being expressed through a largely inherited design. In this process, the particular organizational design is an individual expression of a common theme. The design is a result of unexamined culturally accepted principles of the times—all based on hierarchy as the overriding approach.

Any current corporation has become what it is today through a series of historical events to which ad hoc responses were made. Each response became the newly adjusted form of the corporation. These adjustments are referred to as *frozen accidents*. The longer a corporation exists, the more *frozen accidents* determine its current form.

DESIGN PRINCIPLES COME BEFORE DESIGN

Let's explore design principles, rather than the particular expressions of design. Design principles are being distinguished as the language, thinking, and linguistic structures that generate particular designs. To illustrate this distinction, let's take Walt Disney as an example. If he were transplanted into another era, or if he had started in another industry, the particular form of his corporation would probably have been different. However, his design principles would probably have been the same because design principles are phenomena that emerge from the philosophy and principles of a single person or a group of people. Design principles are not acquired by applying a logical linear formula to a situation.

Intelligence has design principles. The specific design purpose we are concerned with in this book is that which generates "intelligence by design." Intelligence implies the existence of an entity which is self-organizing and self-sustaining and that exists within an "ecosystem" of some kind. In this case, the intelligence could be said to exist within what Michael Rothschild, author of "Bionomics," refers to as an "information ecosystem."

In order to measure the degree of intelligence in a complex system, we look at its computational ability. This is particularly important when the nature of the system is that it is a coevolving system within an ecosystem; within that system every action of each entity affects the whole. Said another way, each entity is part of the environment of the other entities; each action affects the environment of the actor as well as the general environment of others in unknown and unknowable ways.

With these concepts in mind, let's explore the design principles for intelligence. Intelligence is a function of:

- The total number of internal connections of the system.
- The number and variety of connections to the external environment.
- A variety of loose and tight coupling with elements of the environment and the internal system, and the ability to alter the degree of that coupling.
- The number of internal and external connections of each element along with the combinations required for a complete piece of information to be stored, formed and accessed.
- A complex system composed of a limited set of principles which are strong, with many and varied possible inputs and a grammar which determines an order of events, which has impact on possible combinations.

- Communication operating freely within a structure, but requiring accumulation of other free communications to achieve meaning or relevance in action.
- Guidance by patterns rather than detail—the guidance is directional rather than absolute.
- A balance of reliability and randomness (mistake, experiment, trial, etc.) which maintains system integrity (identity) while allowing maximum flexibility.
- Attention at the boundaries and at the center with little concern for the "middle"—that is, a design that handles routine and limit checks while keeping values strong and information at a maximum.
- The amount of redundancy in a system that is a match for the ambiguity required for the existence of possibility beyond extensions of the past.

These are common elements in any system of intelligence. When occurring in nature, these elements are essentially "wired in" to living systems that have intelligence. It is the combination of these elements and the grammar, or possibilities of sequencing and combining, that transform the energy inputs into a recognizable identity or form.

The unique feature of our corporations is that they are subject to alteration in the design itself. When we have theory and principles from which to design, we can begin to have something to say about the design and intentions of a corporation. We are then able to impact what is created. We are never in control unilaterally and are not able to do absolutely "anything." We are not capable of creating something that is inconsistent with an organizational history, or the history of the elements that are functional parts of a whole. We are not able to be something for which there is no fit—no use—in the ecology in which we operate. We must continuously look both outward and inward and maintain connection and balance between the two. This Janus-faced view of corporation is an important approach to understanding design principles, and ignorance of it will end in unnecessary struggle and pain.

DESIGN IS A PROCESS OF UNFOLDING

During the formative stages of a corporation, the design principles may remain constant, but the design itself and the forms it expresses unfold as the corporation grows, meets new challenges and becomes a larger company. The unfolding or emerging is a result of the design principles interacting with the energies, circumstances and actions of life itself. As complexity theory suggests, a rich variety of expressions is possible from a simple set of rules or "attractors" when energy is directed or expressed through them. In the case of corporations, the "attractors" can be thought of as values, or operating principles. When looking out into the future, the exact form that a corporation will take cannot be predicted. We can, however, know that the general form will be consistent with the past and recognizable as having developed historically.

Design becomes more difficult when we are dealing with a corporation that has an existing identity. It has become something particular over time and because the process of becoming is already underway, the identity will try to preserve itself. Inherent in an identity is the tendency to maintain its own existence. An identity is organized to succeed at maintaining its existence using ways that have been successful so far. Just as a human body's immune system is designed to reject everything that isn't recognized as part of the existing organism (identity), so too a corporate body has mechanisms for rejecting what is not consistent with its view of itself. The few transformations that have succeeded so far are often described as having been painful, a great struggle, and involving the exit of a significant number of executives and managers. The struggle was probably the result of a design attempting to preserve itself, not a personal battle of executive will. We are attempting to create a process of transformation that is more natural and occurs as development, rather than as an intervention.

The General Motors NUMMI plant in California is a place in which new design principles were created by their association with Toyota and a new organization was created.

Through the conversion of an old factory, a "greenfield site" was established without having to move to a new location.

The old plant was closed, everyone was fired, and a process of rehiring and education was initiated. Productivity increased dramatically over the old business, without major changes in physical plant or personnel.

Jaguar started an auto body manufacturing plant by entering a joint venture with GKN. They provided extensive education, including outdoor challenge courses for *every* employee.

In each of these two situations, new design principles of organization were at the heart of the change. The source of new design principles, as in these cases, is likely to come in the form of a partner, a new leader, or input from sources which remain external.

During a start-up or the establishment of a "greenfield site," there tends to be more awareness of principles or founding ideas and less concern for the specific way growth will unfold. As time passes, a corporation gets increasingly concerned with its identity and less concerned with what it might become. Whether your corporation is new or old, the design principles are the same; what will vary is the application of those principles and the ease with which they can be implemented.

From design principles and varying circumstances emerge unique results.

The starting place for design, if it is to be anything more than imitation or surface alteration, is at the level of abstraction. What makes the process of design difficult is this beginning point. Implementation of a design is not difficult; difficulties arise from our unfamiliarity with the high levels of abstraction required for understanding the process of design. The first step in designing is to create the design principles from which the rest will develop. Design principles emerge out of an interplay of the theories of corporation, people, management, the marketplace and the business you are in. Their uniqueness will be in the many small variations in expression and emphasis, and the historical conditions they need to "dance with." Their expression in practice will be unique and unpredictable in specifics. Complexity theory leads one to expect that minimal variation in principles or fundamentals, when given different historical accidents and different energies as input, produce a rich and varied array of forms. What particular form will result is not predictable.

The design principles for the development and emergence of intelligence can be derived by combining the design principles that have emerged out of the interplay of the theories of organization, people, etc. with the history of the industry and the specific corporation that is being redesigned. Having survived to this point, a corporation has established a niche, a fit in the ecology of the marketplace, and the participants in it have acquired profound knowledge of what is important and central to the business. Profound knowledge is abstract, implicit and difficult to discover. However, it can be discovered by looking deeply into the current organization and the history of the company and its industry. What makes profound knowledge difficult to discover is that it is hidden by the practices, habits and automatic responses that are the everyday repertoire of behavior. Profound knowledge is also concealed by ordinary, everyday language that has obscured the intention and understanding that generated that language in the first place. By listening to and questioning the language and expressions used by everyone, the profound knowledge will reveal itself. But that task is not the usual practice of management and is one most managers have little patience for, or capability in, unless developed and facilitated in the process.

Profound knowledge is knowledge of the nature of the system.

Design is a matter of education and creation.

Emergent design is the only robust design.

W. Edwards Deming said that what management needed was profound knowledge. Profound knowledge meant knowledge of the system. If he were alive today he might say that he was referring to knowledge of complex intelligent systems—the kind created by human beings. He was introduced to this way of thinking through his initial training as a physicist.

Once the design principles are created, the next level of design begins to present itself. There will be two major areas to proceed with and they are best done together. One is to develop new ways of speaking. Allow a language to emerge that conveys the design principles in a way that has operational significance to those who are to be influenced by them. Remember: a design is implemented in the day-to-day actions of people coordinating their work. So begin to use a language that conveys the design principles explicitly as directional indicators for daily operations, settlement of disputes, decision-making, initiating new projects, etc.

The second area to work with is the intelligence of the corporation. Begin to engage others in the new way of thinking and speaking at the abstract level. From there, begin to develop some increasingly specific design parameters as the dialogue progresses. This is an educational project as much as it is one of design. Typically, we don't allow time to stop for thinking or dialogue; we feel we must get into action. In doing so, we miss the opportunity to design our own organization!

There is no way to separate the process of education from the process of design. While we can do it conceptually, in practice a natural unfolding of education and design in combination is the only way the design of a corporation can go through the process of transformation. We cannot direct a specific outcome because there is an infinite variety of expressions that might result. The process of transformation is one of emergence, rather than one of a specified direction, pathway, or intervention. Only a process of this kind will allow a corporation to survive at the same time as it is transforming. We can't know what specific design is "right," nor can we know exactly how to implement a specific design. What we *are* able to do is to learn and develop using our design principles as our foundation, and make full use of the existing intelligence of our corporation and everyone in it. If we accomplish this, we can expect remarkable results. At each stage of transformation, there are surprises to be dealt with. Some of these surprises come from the learning of earlier phases, some from the unpredicted development in application, and some from the unfolding of the ecology of the marketplace that has occurred since we began the process.

The process of transformation need not be long or involve suffering. Pain occurs when something is introduced that is contrary to the nature of an organism, or renders it unfit in the environment. So it is easy to imagine that there will be some pain involved in altering the current design or identity of a corporation. However, suffering and struggle are another matter. Suffering occurs as a result of holding onto something, resisting something, or not understanding something.

The CEO of one of America's large corporations recently described being 11 months into the process of transformation of his company in the following way: "Have you ever thought what it would be like to be a caterpillar in a cocoon being transformed into a butterfly when you had no idea of the existence of butterflies, or of the process of transformation? All you knew was that your body was disintegrating and that you were not going to survive." While the man's courage is admirable, the suffering was probably unnecessary.

An executive from a different company that has been in a process of transformation for 18 months declared, "This has been the best time of my working life!" Which one of these executives would you expect to succeed? Equally important, which one would you be willing to work with or for? This particular corporation completely transformed in 18 months, although the executive would say that the process is not complete because it is ongo-

---

In my second example, the executive had discovered some ideas in a book; the source of the ideas was a biological metaphor. He asked his management team to read the book.

He then invited them to a two-day meeting at which they would engage in a dialogue. On the first day, the managers stated what the ideas meant to each of them personally and then discussed the ideas as a group.

The second day was a dialogue about what the ideas meant in relationship to the design of the company. Within a very short period of time, the management team dramatically altered the company's design principles, put them into immediate action, and completely reorganized the form and structure of their business.

The following two areas indicate the scope of the transformation in this company. The company switched from competitive bidding to what they called "relationship contracting," in which they no longer submitted competitive tenders.

Also, the company removed the management hierarchy and replaced it with a project team-based system in which *nobody* retained their old job and each was "bid for:" a system similar to that of the annual pool system in American football.

The point here is not to assess the appropriateness of the company's particular solutions, because the marketplace has already rendered the judgment of their appropriateness by increasing the company's sales, assets, and profits. The point is to see that the company invented it themselves through a design process of thinking and dialogue derived from basic design principles.

ing. The company's financial results are significantly better than before the initiative, and they were already outstanding in their industry. No appreciable drop in results took place during the time of the transformation.

The issue is not the specific design, nor is it speed. The issue is success in the marketplace with the maximum of enjoyable, exciting challenges accompanied by minimum difficulty and suffering. An approach that is educational and developmental—*emergent*—will provide the best possibility. No one knows precisely what to do or how to predict the particular form of an outcome. There are guides along the way, but the maximum safety is to be found in intelligence, openness to information and ability to see patterns using an understanding of complexity.

Within the boundaries of the USA and their specific type of theme park, Disney has a great deal of intelligence. However, it has demonstrated a lack of design for intelligence in its move to Paris. Its design principles are sound but their specifically developed translation is American; its intelligence did not expand to recognize certain differences that exist between Europe and America. The design *principles* of its business are not at fault. The error is in the lack of ability to adjust to the ecology: in this case, the social ecology or culture. In the case of Disney's move to Europe, the structure they implemented was too rigid, thereby creating a loss of intelligent operation of the whole. Disney's business design principles will only work in other parts of the globe to the extent that they are supported by design for intelligence "in-the-world."

"In-the-world" is a phrase borrowed from the German philosopher Martin Heidegger; it emphasizes that those aspects of "being" such as intelligence, learning and knowing cannot be separated from existence in the world and all that is implied by that. Our operational definition of "in-the-world" is *"that condition where something which could be considered merely conceptual is made practical by full recognition of all the challenges and difficulties of working out its meaning in the context of a real existence in a complex environment."* Using this term is a way of recognizing that we are both influencing and influenced by the environment in which we live.

The Disney example reveals the distinction between design principles and a specific design. Their business design principles are robust and have demonstrated their effectiveness in both America and Japan. There is no obvious reason to expect these principles to fail in France. However, if one explores carefully the cultures or social ecologies of both France and America, it will quickly become apparent that an exact copy of the American application of these principles will not work in France. The problem was that the executives responsible for creating the theme park in France didn't work at the level of design principles; they worked only at the level of specific design. This resulted in a failure to take into account the context of a particular market and its social ecology.

Design is an unfolding process from abstraction to detail.

We won't cover in detail at this point how to create design principles for your specific organization. But the principles for approaching design that we have just explored should be sufficient to begin your work. To summarize, begin at an abstract level then move on to specifics. Involve as many others as possible in the educational and creative processes as they unfold; in doing so, you gain access to organizational intelligence. Apply the same design principles at ever-increasing levels of detail to allow for emergence and unfolding. Continual reassessment based on feedback should be included in the design process. By frequently using feedback to reassess both the design principles and the specific design that is unfolding, you will be developing organizational intelligence at the same time as you are altering design. Best of all, this same process will provide the greatest opportunity for marketplace success. In this way, the process becomes ongoing. This is not because "change" is constantly necessary. It is because intelligence and continual learning go together. When that is realized, there is no other way any person or any corporation would choose to be.

Change is not something to pursue—it happens. Increasing intelligence is something worth pursuing—and it doesn't just happen.

QUESTIONS FOR THIS CHAPTER:

- What does intelligence mean in the context of a corporation?
- What are measures of intelligence?
- How can we assess how the number, kind and quality of connections contribute to, or inhibit the growth of intelligence?
- In your corporation, what situations occur because of the application of an inappropriate or obsolete design?
- What are the design principles out of which that design emerges?
- What are the possible alternatives to these design principles?
- What new type of designs could be expected to emerge out of these principles?

6 Leadership

"Lead: to show the way by going first."
CHAMBERS' ETYMOLOGICAL DICTIONARY
EDINBURGH, 1912

"They all agree that no leader sets out to be a leader per se, but rather to express oneself freely and fully. That is, leaders have no interest in proving themselves, but an abiding interest in expressing themselves. The difference is crucial, for it is the difference between being driven, as too many people are today, and leading, as too few people do."
WARREN BENNIS

Prelude

What is leadership in the context of a complex intelligent system? In a linear command-and-control system, the personal qualities necessary for leadership and the nature of the process are clear to us because we are so familiar with them. In a complex intelligent system, however, the exercise of these qualities might actually do more harm than good. A system with its own intelligence is not missing leadership in the ordinary sense—so providing it may prove detrimental.

What is leadership in a complex system? What is leadership when everything is connected to everything else? What is leadership when co-evolution is the order of things? When what occurs is a matter of emergence, unfolding, or becoming, then the nature of leadership is transformed. Exploring the issues of leadership in an environment of complex systems will engage us for decades to come.

LEADERS HAVE THEORIES THAT GUIDE THEIR ACTIONS

Most efforts at organizational transformation fail. They fail for two equally important factors. The first is a lack of theory. The second is a lack of leadership. These two are closely related but must be distinguished clearly if we are to make significant progress in our ability to cause organizational transformation on a large scale.

Leadership without a distinct theory is merely a phenomenon of personality and will not survive the particular leader. More importantly, it will seldom have more than a temporary impact on a corporation. To be a leader implies the existence of something beyond ordinary thinking. Even if the leadership is one of integrity without a remarkable new theory, that integrity will come from some particular theory about life and will produce some unique thinking and distinct action.

Without a theory, organizational transformation becomes an issue of personal transformation alone. For a transformation to occur, a theory consistent with the emergent interactive self-organizing nature of human organization is required.

The distinguishing characteristic of leadership—whether it is an individual, a team, or a company—is to see the world in a unique manner and to be able to engage others in the development and pursuit of that view. In today's era of communication, computers and distributed intelligence, this is much more a matter of dialogue, listening and inclusion than a matter of individual effort and exhortation.

The idea of getting from "here" to "there" without an understanding of the process and a theory from which "there" comes, is a design for struggle, effort and suffering. Jumping in and starting such a journey without preparation (learning, theoretical work and integration) increases dramatically the likelihood of suffering.

Leaders have invested in development time; others have not. Leadership is not easy and requires courage. But let's consider the path that will generate the least resistance. A leader awakens to a greater possibility for her or his corporation. There is a series of events that make pursuit of that realization seem possible. There is a process of education and learning

---

Eleven months into an organizational transformation effort, the CEO of a $2 billion company said, "Can you imagine what it's like to be a caterpillar in a cocoon not knowing about butterflies? All you know is that the body that has served you so well, up until now, is disintegrating. That's what I feel like. It's a very painful process."

This executive is suffering the pain of being committed to a possibility without having a theory that will allow him or his organization to create what is needed. He's authentic enough. He's leader enough. Otherwise, he wouldn't be in the position he's in and he wouldn't be asking others to put themselves there also. But the pain and suffering is optional and will probably kill his initiative.

which suggests a way forward. And there is a time of development and integration of ideas before action is taken. The length and intensity of this period varies for each individual, but at some point one leaps into action and that leap is always taken without knowledge of all of the components of the path, or the exact outcome. Individuals must go through this process if they are to become leaders.

That same learning, developing and integrating time is seldom given to others once the decision is made to proceed. This is the source of the difficulties and struggles. The leader struggles because he or she is fundamentally alone, attempting to change a corporation which isn't fully understood and is doing so using an approach which isn't fully understood. The next group of people expected to lead, usually a management team, also suffers. They suffer because they have not been given the time for learning and integration that the original leader had. The process becomes forced at a very early stage. The *ecology of the corporation* makes itself felt and resistance is instantly triggered. To use a biological metaphor, the corporation recognizes the invasion of something foreign and mobilizes its immune system to defend itself—usually by attack.

Leaders come from anywhere and occur in action as "showing the way by going first."

It is important to consider for a moment who is being referred to when the term leader is used. Anyone can be a leader. A leader is one who "shows by going first" (the term is being used in the same sense as defined in the 1912 Scottish dictionary). Leadership is not a function of position but rather of having the courage of one's convictions. Implied in the definition is that

A chemical plant with long-standing severe conflicts between management and union was about to close its doors. The plant was now half its original size and it was supposed to be shut down in the next couple of years.

The current plant manager committed himself to a transformation, as had other managers of this same plant over the past few decades. This transformation, unlike the earlier attempts, began to demonstrate a new kind of leadership.

After a series of educational and developmental sessions, a small group of self-selected people started taking action—to show by going first. This group was made up of the plant manager, a few junior managers, a couple of supervisors, and a few of the direct labor force.

Very few of those exhibiting leadership had appeared as leaders previously. In fact, a few had been leading troublemakers. None of the other official leaders demonstrated authentic leadership in any way, including senior management and senior union officials.

Within six months, the transformation was complete and the decision to close was reversed. Within the year management began to install new processes at that location.

leaders have theories that determine and guide their actions. Anyone is capable of creating and utilizing theories. Anyone can "show the way by going first."

This is the kind of leadership that is needed for an organizational transformation. There must be a sufficient number of people willing to show the way by going first. It does not need to be the official hierarchy. It does not need to be an entire management team. It does not need to be the formally identified leadership of a corporation. In fact, in a large corporation it is often better if it is not the entire body of the official bureaucracy. Leadership is more effective when exhibited by people scattered throughout the corporation; people becoming leaders at different times. What makes this more effective is that there is no implied sense of force or coercion. Not "everyone" has to be on board at the same time. In addition, it is too much to expect or require that the whole corporation be on board in the same way at the same time. Such a sweeping shift would also threaten the existing hierarchy's ways, if not their very jobs.

THE SOURCE OF LEADERSHIP

Leadership is an emergent response and not a matter of personality or style.

The time has come to challenge the existing notions of leadership, such as the idea that there are styles or personalities more suitable than others for leadership. If we recall the numerous leaders and executives that we have encountered in life, it becomes obvious that leadership is a diverse phenomenon and not very personal or individual in nature. The leaders I have worked with are as varied in their personalities as we all are. The qualities they possess have much more to do with ideas and their relationship to those ideas than with style.

Let's consider the idea that leadership is a naturally arising phenomenon that occurs in a complex dance encompassing current conditions and personal history. At the moment that leadership occurs, it appears as though an individual is leading and that this action is a result of that person's leadership qualities. We see leadership embodied in a single individual. But if we look beyond the surface, we will see that this phenomenon has emerged, rather than "always been there." It is also not an isolated event—but rather an interaction.

Although certain people seem predisposed to leadership, there are few instances where we can say that they have always led no matter what the circumstances. These people may have gone relatively unnoticed or been considered troublemakers in other situations. The leader who emerges is often someone already in a position of authority who has been the official leader but has exhibited little of the qualities that we are now referring to as "being a leader."

Leadership is a continuum.

Consider leadership from the perspective of being a continuum. At one extreme end, which requires the maximum in leadership, there is an individual who appears to be standing alone against a large force. People exhibiting this type of leadership are showing the way by going first and they are clearly alone, staking their careers and reputations on their convictions. At the other end of the continuum, which requires minimal leadership, are people who decide to take action consistent with the new direction or approach just before it becomes "the only way to act." They are exhibiting leadership by making an independent choice to act before it has become the socially accepted system. At the moment a new system becomes the guide to action, when independent choice ceases to be required, that is the moment at which the occasion for leadership disappears. It can also reappear for those who are willing to stand alone in a place that is not in alignment in direction or degree with the new direction or approach.

The existential choice we all face at many times in our lives is either to be authentic and become a leader, or to suppress what we believe in and go along. Many of us manage to avoid choosing and thereby make *that* choice.

Leadership is a phenomenon that emerges from the interplay of circumstances external and internal to a corporation and the individuals who are part of that corporation. Occasions for leadership will occur constantly. Leadership will emerge when individuals from various parts and levels of the corporation come forth to meet challenges. To the extent that leadership is called forth and supported, it will flourish. To the extent that it is demanded and forced, it will become manipulation and generate suffering. Our theory of leadership must transform to match our theory of organization and human action, if we are to succeed at an organizational transformation. One of the theories that we can profitably get rid of is the idea that leadership must come from the top and that the whole top team must be aligned. Another is that everyone must be on board.

PERSONAL AND ORGANIZATIONAL TRANSFORMATION

Popular opinion suggests that if organizational transformation is to occur, then personal transformation of leadership is also necessary. While this is likely to be valid in the sense that one will seldom occur without the other, let's see if we can distinguish organizational transformation in such a way that personal transformation is not the cause or even a necessary prerequisite. To begin, let's start with the assumption that transformation is an emergent phenomenon. That is, there is no such thing as transformation by decree, by decision, or even by any planned linear process. Rather, transformation occurs or emerges from a rich interplay of many factors and forces. When these factors and forces go beyond a certain threshold point we say "transformation has occurred." At no time before or after that point will it make sense to say that certain events, actions, or conditions *caused* the transformation or were the pivotal factors. At best, we will be able to identify a significant portion of the total forces and conditions and be able to approximate where the threshold point was. And even that will occur only after the fact. (We will probably find such an analysis of little interest once we have crossed the threshold, and of little value before crossing it.)

Transformation is a rapid change in identity without a change in entity.

What is a transformation anyway? What are we attempting to define or represent when we use this term? What are we intending when we speak in favor of such a thing? What qualities, goals or actions are we seeking to represent by the term transformation? Let's focus on two qualities or intentions inherent in this term. One is that a radical change is involved. The other is that the change occurs rapidly, when compared to what is thought reasonable or even possible. Transformation can be viewed as a nonlinear result—a result that is not achievable by extending the past forward into the future. It is a result whose detailed causal factors cannot be methodically traced after the fact. A gradual change, even though significant, is seldom what is being pointed at or proposed. A rapid, yet minor shift is not transformation, either. The term generally indicates significant change to the whole, accomplished in a remarkably rapid manner. When comparing the resulting state to the beginning state, the nature of the change is so significant that it calls forth questions of identity. The change is such that the old is almost unrecognizable in the new.

The leader's reputation is fully at stake.

By defining leadership as "to show the way by going first," we bring together personal and organizational transformation. If the current leaders are to demonstrate authentic leadership in the matter of transformation, they will have to put such factors as their reputations, their jobs and their identities at stake. This is not as threatening as it sounds because these factors are at stake for leaders at all times and in all cases. The fact that leadership is being exercised in relationship to a transformation changes nothing. The only factor that is different in a transformation is that there will initially be less agreement for the direction the leader is heading. The leaders will be operating at the end of the continuum in which the maximum expression of leadership is required. It may appear that for some people, personal transformation is necessary if they are to generate this type of leadership effectively. However, it is more an issue of development than one of transformation.

In biological terms, a transformation occurs when something changes form or structure as a realization of the possibility that was inherent in its design. That is, something cannot become what is not already within its space of possibility or within its fundamental nature or design. Likewise, an organizational transformation is the kind of change where a greater realization of the existing space of possibility is actualized and where that influences the future space of possibility. It implies an alteration that affects the whole and is significant enough to be noticed. The time frame must be sufficiently rapid, because a change over a 50-year period would be considered merely evolutionary. Yet the time frame cannot be more rapid than the full process requires. So, while urgency is a factor, it is no more a factor than for most other competitive business activities. That life takes place in time is not a new element. A successful transformation will appear to have been rapid not because of the amount of time it took but because it happened at all.

Organizational transformation is a function of the development of new theory and education and the integration of theory into the policies and practices of the corporation. It is a process of learning and development rather than a process of intervention. It is a process of dialogue and experimentation, not one of decision and decree. It is an inclusive process rather than one of directed expert design.

Personal and organizational transformation are interdependent and emerge together.

The transformation of leadership will occur in conjunction with the transformation of the corporation. Similarly, the transformation of people within the corporation will occur simultaneously with the transformation of the whole. In some cases, the personal transformation will occur first and in some cases it will follow. In all cases, it is the corporation that should be the focus, because our responsibility is the design and functioning of the enterprise. In addition, one cannot go through a transformation on one's own, except within an environment that nurtures the process. Transformation is an emergent process and it cannot be accomplished by a corporation unless it is a coevolving process between the corporation and the participants. When an outside agent is brought in, she or he provides that environment as well as a theoretical base and learning structures.

Leadership is not a matter of being in control.

Leadership by "going first" is not the same as leadership "completing the process alone." The tendency of existing leadership to get ahead of the process is a reflection of the need to remain in control in the previously established ways as much as it is anything else. This can be one of the major sources of pain and suffering. It is authenticity that is being called for, not superhuman acts of unfailing competence and omniscience. All of the psychological and mystic clap-trap gets swept away in this approach to leadership and transformation. The old Scottish definition is so clean and accurate in this respect. Leadership needs personal support, education, coaching, and structural support in the early stages because people will be in the uncomfortable position of learning while they are leading. The fact that leadership is so consistent with the process of emerging allows for the possibility of little pain and no suffering. Suffering is a created relationship to pain when it becomes extended over time. The source of pain and suffering is a failure to appreciate the nature of the phenomena with which we are dealing and the unwillingness to alter our perceptions, interpretations, and responses to our current identification with a particular competence set. That is, we struggle as a result of our own attachments.

IDENTITY AND LEADERSHIP

Leadership opportunities are more often provided for you, rather than created by you.

Leadership in transformation begins with the realization that we are part of a complex intelligent system and not separate from it. If an executive considers that he is *the* leader rather than an executive and *a* leader, that person is thinking of himself as separate from the corporation. It is essential to see that our position and our opportunity for leadership are given largely by the corporation, not just created by us.

A position of formal leadership provides the privilege of more opportunities to contribute to others than typically are provided to most people. In a corporation which has no space of possibility for leadership, people will not express leadership—no matter what their position. In a corporation which creates the space of possibility for leadership, anyone can seize the opportunity irrespective of who else does or does not. There are positions from which it is easier to be influential in creating and nurturing this space of possibility, but the "ease" is relative and never easy.

Transformation does not occur from the top down, or the bottom up. It is from inside out.

The idea of "top down" or "bottom up" loses its meaning in the phenomenon of transformation. To the extent that transformation requires leadership (which is to a very large extent) it is a function of "inside out." That is, what is thought, felt, imagined and desired within ourselves must be expressed into the social world of the corporation through our speaking and actions. It then becomes an act of leadership, regardless of the level from which it is expressed. Because the corporation is a complex intelligent system, that expression will emerge from an ever-increasing number of places in ever-expanding areas of the corporation. Frequently, it will not be obvious where it started historically, but usually the formal leader gets the credit. Once the transformation is well underway, it will not be obvious who the most important leaders were initially. Heroes will emerge at all levels and it may be the ones right at the workface who will be the most important. "Middle management," who constantly suffer from diminishing choice, title and power, will also be a major force in the transformation. Unless leadership is allowed to emerge in increasingly complex ways and is not restricted to the top of the existing hierarchy, the transformation will flounder and fail.

Leadership, in a complex intelligent system, is the ability to exercise fully the possibilities available to that system. The nature of effective leadership is one of self-expression without attachment to identity. The kind of self-expression needed will come from those who see themselves as part of a complex system—a system in which they are both influencing and influenced by that system.

Authentic leadership is present when there is a connection to the whole, coupled with a willingness to be responsible for one's part in it, without sacrificing one's creative expression. Leaders in this type of system are in communication and are willing to be influenced by that communication. They will trust the results of dialogue, encourage dialogue in special ways and practice it regularly. They will tend to mistrust decisions and actions that are not the result of dialogue that includes the expression of others. Their touchstones will be theory, dialogue and feedback from outside the system. The role of the formal leader will be one of providing structures of interpretation, balancing internally and externally generated information

John Neill of Unipart led his company through a turn-around which transformed a manufacturing company, on the verge of closure, into a worldwide, top-quality automotive supplier.

He is often asked to speak about the process. When he does speak about it, he portrays passionately and intimately the human aspects of the journey and does so whether he is speaking to a large group of people, or talking amongst friends.

One of the unique things about listening to him speak is that it is easy to hear the theories that were used for the turn-around as well as those currently in use to continually improve the company and keep it at the leading edge of quality and productivity worldwide.

What you hear little of is anything about John himself. His powerful speaking comes from his passion for the theories, ideas and processes rather than any personal identity as the source of the ideas.

A further demonstration of the lack of personal identity attached to the ideas is the establishment of Unipart University which provides continuing education and development to Unipart employees. Leadership of programs is contributed to by many employees as well as outsiders.

and demonstrating the willingness to show by going first. A profound respect for awareness unclouded by personal identity will be one of the qualities of the effective leader. Integrity of speaking and action will be the basis for the effective relationship of a complex intelligent system to the leaders within it.

A complex intelligent system doesn't need "strong leadership" from a single person but a basis for the integration of its various independent agents. The following chapters will introduce the structures that will support that integration. Leaders will need to pay attention to these structures if they are to succeed within such a system. A successful transformation will almost surely include an unwavering leader—irrespective of personal style—or a leadership group that operates as a very effective team. (There seem to be even fewer of the latter than the former.)

The trappings of formal leadership often get in the way of authentic leadership.

Transformation requires courage at many levels. Those who are to lead must have the courage to step out on their own initiative. They must confront their own past and future, challenge their own behavior and style, and risk their jobs and possibly their careers. The very existence of the corporation is at stake when such a process is undertaken. The next best thing that can happen to a corporation on this path, after full success, is quick failure. An effort that has coalesced sufficient strength in leadership and launched the process must continue to move forward and cannot turn back without cost. A caterpillar can delay the process of transformation to a certain extent, but once begun the process is not reversible.

The personal challenge to those in formal positions of leadership is to see that others have been given an opportunity, a space of possibility—and no more. The issue of leadership is not one of self-importance or personal aggrandizement. We become attached to our positions and the social benefits that come with titles and power. We become attached to our beliefs that we are leaders just because we have titles. We become unwilling to alter the structures that surround these positions and we hold on to the identity that we have created in our own minds about "being a leader."

These attachments prevent us from showing the way by going first and they support the kind of thinking in which others need to change but we are fine; or these attachments deceive us into believing that we can create all the required change on our own. The worst outcome of this attachment is that we think we are able to know what to change and how to change it without including the rest of the system. We think as though we were outside the system. We forget that we have been granted the possibility of leadership by the corporation and the numerous interactions that occur between people. We may be able to retain the trappings by force or fraud but we cannot achieve the satisfaction of authentic leadership unless we rise to the occasion that was created for us. To be authentic demands acting and speaking in ways consistent with that offer and the nature of organization itself. Positions of leadership provide unique opportunities to face the challenges of being human and protect us from none of those challenges.

The singular challenge to be met in an organizational transformation is to continually be the source of leadership emerging until there is no need for leadership because the new "way of being" is the accepted way of being. Leadership will not disappear at this point but instead will be a commonly demonstrated attribute of people throughout the corporation. Individuals will exhibit leadership in the small and everyday affairs of life. Each challenge and each moment of work will be an opportunity to exhibit leadership. The challenge remains richly alive to reconcile the continual differences between who we currently are with respect to authentic leadership and who we can become in the face of that possibility. These challenges will provide occasions for expression that will be the source of the continual growth and development of ourselves and our enterprises.

QUESTIONS FOR THIS CHAPTER:

- In what ways does your current corporation invite or urge leadership?
- Are these requests aimed at specific individuals who would be leaders or do they enable leadership to emerge in many places?
- In what ways does your corporation suppress the possibility of leadership for those not included in the formal hierarchy?
- Review those whom you consider to be leaders in your corporation that are not within the formal hierarchy. What qualities do they exhibit that make them stand out as leaders? Do these qualities emerge as a response to circumstances calling for leadership?
- Review your organizational practices for generating leadership and ask how appropriate they are to a complex intelligent system populated by independent intelligent beings.

The Learning Loop

"What is needed is a view of production as an enterprise of unlimited potential, an enterprise in which current arrangements are but the starting point for continuous organizational learning.

"Only when grafted onto a production system dedicated to ongoing learning and communication can new technologies realize their potential as competitive weapons."
W. ABERNATHY

"A firm's efficiency is constrained only by its technology, and its technology is limited only by its members' ability to work together as intelligent creative participants in a learning organization."
MICHAEL ROTHSCHILD

Prelude

We have organized our companies for maximum productive capacity. Our orientation has been to create the simple loop of transforming input into more valuable output which in turn generates revenue that is returned to the corporation. This loop perpetuates a self-recreating game, thereby leaving itself only with itself as a scorekeeping measure for the game. For decades the name of the game has been production, measured in money, and we have organized ourselves and our corporations to succeed at that particular game.

As we leave behind one era and begin the process of transforming into another, the rules of the game change. The shift from Machine Age to Information Age brings with it one particular change that is of utmost importance: *intelligence*, both of an individual and a system, will move to the forefront and assume greater value because it is becoming the key to success.

As this shift occurs, the *production loop* must be expanded: what must be integrated into the *loop* is not only the intelligence of the people of the system, but the intelligence of the system itself. The result of this integration is what we will refer to as the *learning loop*. The rules, methods, practices and structures for this *loop* are unique because they are based on information, communication and the theory of complex intelligent systems. In the *learning loop*, knowledge is the name of the game: its accumulation, its use and its unique way of keeping score.

THE LEARNING ORGANIZATION

Among all the management fads that have paraded through the business world, those endorsing quality have been the most effective. Quality provides enduring value by demanding constant renewal, rethinking and adjustment to the current environment, irrespective of the form of quality being referred to. It is always worthy of attention and pursuit, even though much of TQM has missed the point—both in theory and in practice. Even with all of this going for it, quality has still been turned into just another fad and its value has been diminished—not because of what it is but because of how it is related to.

Learning and historical forms of organizing don't go together.

"The Learning Organization" is following the same course as TQM and is already beginning to suffer a similar fate. This is mostly a result of the fact that the management theories presently active in our corporations are not consistent with current demands. Consequently, information that is useful and essential for emergence into the new era is not recognized and has no way of being integrated powerfully into existing organizational design and management practices. Because the term "the learning organization" sounds as though it might have value, it is being propounded by management without a foundation of understanding or practical integration. Continual ungrounded use of the term will undoubtedly turn it into just another popular phrase in the parade of fads.

Similar to quality, learning has a fundamental enduring value that will return profits for effort invested in its continual rediscovery, renewal and adjustment to the times. Learning is even more fundamental than quality; it is the basis of survival for any entity that has the power to adapt to its environment, generate information and knowledge, alter its environment and be responsible for its own health and survival within a coevolving ecology. Given the nature of corporations and the competitive environment within which they exist, organizational learning and the accumulation of knowledge will be the source of immediate health as well as long-term survival.

Corporations do learn. The questions are, "How?" and "How fast?"

Let's begin by distinguishing learning in the context of corporations. Before creating an operational definition, it will be useful to set aside the numerous misinterpretations that surround the term "the learning organization." First, it is not about schools or other isolated ways of learning. Next, the phrase implies that there is such a thing as a corporation that doesn't learn. Impossible. By its very existence, a corporation can and does learn. A corporation is a complex intelligent system and it is constantly adjusting to its environment. The level of learning in a corporation may be low but there is nevertheless learning.

As we begin to develop the distinctions of learning in corporations, we become interested in ways of increasing the ability of the organization to learn: that is, how to increase its "IQ." We will become engaged in design questions such as, "To what degree is a particular organizational design capable of learning?" and practical questions such as, "To what degree is it actually learning compared to what is possible?" Then we get interested in, "What are the practices that promote learning and what are the ones that inhibit it?"

DISTINGUISHING LEARNING

Corporations and intelligence are both emergent phenomena. They arise when a certain complexity of design occurs concurrent with a threshold level of variety of input. If there is insufficient variety in the environment, or insufficient variety in the constituent parts of a Corporation (or an organism), then ability or opportunity for learning are not available. If there is not

William Stern, creator of the concept of IQ and the basis for its measurement, clearly stated that intelligence was not static and could be increased. Even so, opposition arises frequently, insisting that IQ cannot be altered.

Whatever the case may be for individuals, IQ is clearly not a static quality of a corporation (an entity in which we play an influential role in determining its design). Motorola, Unipart, and numerous other companies have clearly demonstrated that they can dramatically increase their "intelligence capability" and thereby increase their capacity for organizational learning.

sufficient complexity in structure, then ability and opportunity for learning are also not accessible.

In the kinds of organizations that concern us, complexity and variety are well past the threshold points; therefore, it is valid to say that organizational intelligence exists within them and that organizational learning is taking place. Once these distinctions are clearly understood, pressing new questions arise. These questions involve issues such as the degree of intelligence, the possibility available to that intelligence, and the actualization of that possibility.

Adaptation is a small part of learning.

Our major challenge is to distinguish learning in a dynamic powerful way: one that warrants our attention and provides directional indicators for actions that are most likely to pay dividends. To streamline the process of creating an operational definition, it will be useful to look at and set aside some of the unexamined assumptions we have about learning—assumptions that severely limit the possibility of learning.

The most common misconception is that learning and adaptation are synonymous. This is not the case. Adaptation refers to only a small part of learning. Adaptation is an action taken in response to the environment in order to produce a similar result from dissimilar circumstances. Adaptation is one of the results of learning but adaptation also can take place when no real learning is occurring. For example, plants adapt to their surroundings by manifesting pre-existing programs with no evidence of learning.

Adam Smith, a fountainhead in western economic history and currently a popular target, is constantly accused of being one of the originators of the kind of mechanistic thinking that has held western production captive to inhuman or unintelligent systems.

Perhaps those making the charges fail to understand the thinking of the Scottish Enlightenment group of which Smith is now the most well-known member. The group's thinking focused on the distinction of self-organizing systems and something we now refer to as *emergent phenomena*.

The famous "pin factory example," which promoted specialization of work tasks, is often cited as the source of reductionist approaches applied to production challenges. Instead, it is actually a declaration of the value of learning.

The particular form of specialization focused on in this example was appropriate to the times.

The message repeatedly overlooked in this example is that continuous learning is the source of ongoing growth and declining costs in production.

Adam Smith was keenly aware of the intelligence inherent in human organizations and valued it greatly. This has taken us centuries to realize.

Learning from experience represents a small part of the possible learning spectrum.

Another limitation that is placed on learning is implied in the statement "learning from experience." It is this type of learning that gets the attention, study and research funding. In the natural world, excluding humans and their institutions, learning by experience appears to be the only type of learning. While there is much to learn by looking at information regarding learning from experience, much is lost if that becomes the main meaning of learning.

The learning curve theory, developed decades ago and still largely ignored, is a powerful tool for those who use it. However, its foundation is in learning from experience and it views learning as a mechanistic phenomenon. This renders the theory somewhat dated and limits the breadth of what it includes. The learning curve's major contribution rests in drawing attention to the existence of continuous learning.

The active part of learning precedes experience and is distinct from it.

As we continue to clear away whatever assumptions we have about learning from experience, we are not excluding it as a way of learning, nor are we saying that learning can take place totally independently of experience. In the learning curve theory, units of experience are distinguished from units of time in order to understand learning—that is, learning takes place over time, but time is not the determining factor. In the same way, we can understand that learning does not occur as a result of experience, even though experience is involved in the process. In the theory we wish to articulate about learning, we want to capture the idea that learning does not occur *as a result of* experience, but occurs *before* experience in ways that multiply the learning that occurs later from a great variety of experiences.

Knowledge is not to be separated from action potential, or from pragmatic concerns.

The result of learning is knowledge. There are various distinctions in the area of knowledge that are useful in developing a theory and operational definition for learning. Before going into them, let's consider an operational definition for knowledge. *"Knowledge is information that is integrated with the entire system in such a way that it is available for action at potentially appropriate times."*

Knowledge is always useful; information and data are not necessarily so. Knowledge is available at both implicit and explicit levels.

Learning can occur in a totally implicit manner and always remain outside conscious awareness. It can also occur in a totally explicit manner. Even though it is learned with awareness, it may become implicit and unconscious. When knowledge that results from our learning is used, it becomes more fully integrated—more connections are made—and it will become more implicit and unconscious with use.

Learning occurs through use of knowledge rather than through experience, as such. This distinction reveals the potential value in making knowledge explicit, particularly for purposes of teaching or sharing it. There turns out to be a great payoff for sharing knowledge, both organizationally and individually, because in doing so more learning takes place in the original possessor of the knowledge.

Theory provides the context for learning when experience occurs.

Learning occurs ongoingly in our lives through experience or the mere passage of time. But a more dynamic, diverse and innovative kind of learning occurs when a theory is present to interpret and organize the experiences as they happen. The mind will view all new experience through the lens of theory and will integrate new and varying input into the wealth of knowledge that is already there. It will "force fit" experience if at all possible and will tend to reject the rest of the data as noise. *Noise is a technical term from communication theory that refers to anything that is not part of the intended message but instead acts as interference with the message.* Theory provides the standard of what the intention of the message is. When a theory includes the intention to test, learn and create, then experiences offer extraordinary possibility for use and learning that far exceed the automatism of our standard cause/effect learning.

Our operational definition of learning is *"the phenomenon that occurs when a novel internal state (structure, information, representation, etc.) is created by combining input (from external or internal sources) in ways never before combined, and this information is stored in such a way that it is accessible for future use."* Learning is a creative act.

CORPORATIONS AND LEARNING

It may be exceeding the boundaries of credibility to say that corporations have minds, ideas, internal states, and things which could be said to be previously unthought, but we can go so far as to say that they have memory. This memory lies in physical forms such as writing, computers and artifacts. It can be found in verbal forms such as stories and language and it can be found in action forms such as practices and habits. Memory can also be found in structural forms such as reporting and reward systems. It can be distinguished as memory because it provides information that is available for interpretation within that organization for use by its participants, independent of their intention or attention.

Any addition to that memory is considered learning. We can say that organizational learning is *"the phenomenon that occurs when any new in-*

formation is added to the available memory of the organization (whether an individual or a system), thereby making it accessible for future use by the system." This, incidentally, includes changes to the structure of the system itself.

Individual learning is the lowest level of organizational learning.

It is important to explore the relationship between individual learning and organizational learning. Questions relevant to the area include: can organizational learning occur independent of the individuals involved? If all individuals are learning, is the corporation learning? These questions remind us of our ability to create distinctions and the importance of distinguishing a corporation as an entity not only composed of individuals, but with an identity of its own.

If an individual learns, but does not make the result of that learning available to the corporation by integrating it into the structures of the corporation, has organizational learning taken place? One argument could be that organizational learning has taken place, at least at the lowest level, because as long as the individual is working there the corporation has access to that learning via the actions of that individual. Another point that could be made is that individuals are part of the structure of the corporation; therefore their knowledge is the corporation's knowledge. These are valid points, but individual learning on its own is a very minor part of the potential of learning at an organizational level.

Compounding knowledge is the source of great wealth.

Learning occurs at different levels and has varying degrees of quality. There are two important aspects of learning: the content of learning and the availability of what has been learned. Although specific uses for what is learned can be evaluated, its total value in the future cannot be known. The greatest value will arise from compounding it—continual building on the existing knowledge. In the pursuit of knowledge, there's no such thing as useless learning. Negative results may be produced in the process but the knowledge gained from that will also be valuable learning. Great value may be found in what seem to be today's "useless ideas." These will be part of the compounding base of knowledge. Because we are dealing with a complex phenomenon, tomorrow's breakthroughs may depend on today's "useless ideas." An extreme example of this occurred in 1993 when the Nobel Prize in biology was awarded for a discovery that took place twenty years earlier. The discovery was essentially ignored because its significance could not be seen until later when other developments had occurred in physics and biology.

The prize was for the discovery of strings of apparently random sections of DNA chains embedded in those that contained known and "useful" information. It took an understanding of complexity, cross-over and other recently identified phenomena to see the significance for adaptation of these

Action is the source of information.

random chains. With the development of the theories of information, chaos and complexity—upon which our approach to organizational design is based—the earlier biological discovery makes sense and becomes important.

The complex nature of organizational intelligence and organizational learning calls for methods of design and assessment other than the linear approaches that we have used for production. Organizational intelligence is a function of the number of connections, the intricacy of those connections and system design. Organizational learning is a function of the quantity and originality of the knowledge and information that is available for integration and formulation of new ideas. The quantity and originality of available information is a function of the variety of available actions. These design principles are profoundly relevant to the actualization of organizational learning through what we will distinguish as the *learning loop*.

The pursuit of organizational learning does not necessarily imply a significant direct investment of time and money in an activity called learning. An initial investment may be necessary if significant velocity is intended, but continued success in the area occurs in the process of the actions of the corporation. A demand for more investment in learning may occur as you proceed with implementation, but the demand will come from success, increasing returns and a commitment to velocity.

Contractors point out that clients aren't interested in having learning time included in their costs when a bid is made.

If work is done on a cost-plus basis, learning time can't be included in costs and any immediate gains would be forfeited. Work done on a project-performance basis is likewise restricted in charging clients, so any investment in learning must be absorbed from the contractor's direct profits. The potential payoff from learning is seldom seen to be greater than its costs.

In the process industries, process demands are built into the design of the system and cannot be interfered with. In production line systems, units per hour produced on the line affect the measure of performance and therefore cannot be interfered with.

In the service industries, the customer is first and foremost. Plus, customers are not good "test cases," or an appropriate opportunity for learning.

All of these examples point to unexamined assumptions that obstruct access to fundamental principles about learning. One principle is that learning and knowledge are the source of both short- and long-term profit. Another is that the corporation's learning creates its future possibility. And the final assumption is that the costs of learning do not need to be borne by the customer, even though the customer benefits.

THE PRODUCTION LOOP

Understanding organizational learning supports its actualization. The best place to begin the process of understanding organizational learning is with the actual operation of the production process itself. After all, it is the production enterprise that is both demanding the learning and making the learning possible. The learning that we are interested in is learning that will increase productive capacity in the future. These two, learning and production, are meant to be fully aligned and concurrent.

We have organized around production. We have designed to take every bit of available energy, money and attention, and focus them on producing more (or better) of whatever we are in the business of making and selling. And we have succeeded beyond the imaginations of our forebears. This kind of focus perpetuates the thinking patterns of our specific task, corporation, or industry that don't allow time for learning. These are the source of the justifications for our failure to embrace learning and reap the rewards of compounding knowledge.

The diagram of the production loop shows how most organizations are organized for production. Even though learning takes place within the organizations represented by this model, it does not include a particular element or focus that supports learning occurring at a rate faster than the competition.

The production loop of most organizations provides the limited perspective of a linear feedback loop. We have designed feedback loops into our sys-

TRADITIONAL MODEL OF ORGANIZING FOR PRODUCTION

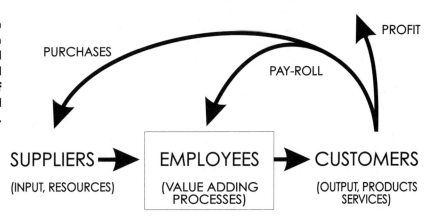

The production loop is focused on material flows and these are limited by issues of ownership and engineering.

PURCHASES

PROFIT

PAY-ROLL

SUPPLIERS → EMPLOYEES → CUSTOMERS

(INPUT, RESOURCES)   (VALUE ADDING PROCESSES)   (OUTPUT, PRODUCTS SERVICES)

tems to inform us when correction is needed. That correction is usually applied from outside the system by expert or management intervention. The only learning or innovative changes that can impact the system must come from outside the system. For the most part, the system is a closed loop that is altered from time to time by the intervention of experts or management.

It is not surprising that "covert learning" is a part of most people's working lives. Everyone wants to learn and develop while working, but along with that learning most people figure out how to keep what they learn out of the suppressive reach of the formal organization. In recognition of this, Xerox has begun to experiment with designs for production that support informal learning developing and spreading throughout systems without official interference in those systems.

With information and knowledge now being the greatest source of marketplace advantage, the production model alone is insufficient. There is just not enough information, knowledge, or learning available in a production-based design. The answer is not to throw out production-based design. In

A company, beginning its career in the manufacturing of disk drives, had 18 months of losses on its books since going public. Production graphs posted on the lunchroom walls indicated the production level required for break-even. Not a single day's statistics touched that level.

When our consulting firm was invited to work with the company on its inadequate production, we began by interviewing the company executives.

None of the executives could see how employee learning (beyond learning to do what they were told) had anything to do with the gains needed for the company. The executives were certain that profitability would occur as soon as the engineers got the new processes right and all independent thinking of the production-line employees was set aside. After all, the engineers were the experts.

The company agreed to work with us on a learning experiment. We requested that members of the management team not be involved at the onset of the experiment. The following month was the first month that the company showed a profit. Production was not only over the break-even line but it was off the charts and onto the ceiling!

With one month of success under their belt and the old production processes still in place, a new problem entered the picture: shipments of parts from Japan failed to arrive and employees had to make their targets by reconditioning parts that had been rejected earlier.

By focusing on learning, systems learning and generating ideas from production teams, production breakthroughs were accomplished without input from the engineering staff.

The single change that took place was that the production teams were taught how to dialogue effectively. They met very briefly on a regular basis to discuss what was needed and what could be changed.

MODEL OF ORGANIZING FOR LEARNING

The learning flows are recursive and limited only by the artificial boundaries which are created by ways of thinking which focus on control and attachment.

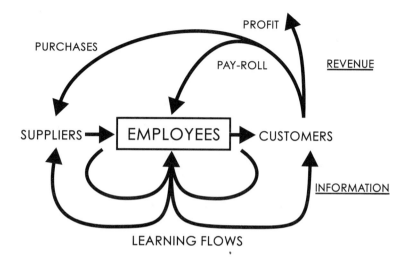

Accounting desperately needs to transform to meet the needs of a world of information. Fortunately, those needs can be satisfied by the technology that created them.

Systems that provide information regarding time cycles and costs and make that available to those doing the work will provide a breakthrough in accounting to match the breakthroughs in organizational design being proposed here.

An even more powerful approach, which would then create the demand for costing information, useful for both improved production and learning, is to invest the time and energy now used for re-engineering studies into processes in which those performing the work experiment with better ways of working while they analyze the processes.

Western businesses have attempted to "optimize" by opting for immediate low cost, and thus removed all possibility of redundancy, ambiguity and learning. Here we can see that the structures of accounting, which are deeply embedded in linear materialist thinking, are a part of the source of our problem.

The nature of "accounting" is revealed in the term itself: it accounts for the physical parts of an operation. Accounting can only measure. It cannot predict and is not designed to support the accumulation of learning or knowledge.

Many of the required activities and even results of learning will appear to be uneconomical when based on standard accounting systems. These accounting systems are as much a culprit as the hierarchy in inhibiting innovation and learning. They must be changed.

fact, creating a learning-based design is best accomplished by combining it with the existing production-based design, because the learning that is critical will be applied in practical ways to production. Even learning aimed at long-term intentions is best carried out in close conjunction with production processes. What is required is an appreciation of learning, operational definitions for practical application and a structure for the actualization of learning.

The diagram on page 89 illustrates how a self-generating process continues to create knowledge as well as revenue. Each unit of experience, which frequently will not be the same unit as the standard unit of production (i.e. finished product), is shown generating learning opportunities and knowledge as a result. One of the keys to success with the process lies in ensuring that the accountability for knowledge generation is as strong as the accountability for profit generation. There is nothing inherent in this representation to suggest that learning is a separate activity from production—they both occur during the same process.

CREATING THE LEARNING LOOP

Activities of learning are distinct from, but not separate from, production.

The learning loop can be displayed as an extension or elaboration of the production loop. An accurate representation of the learning loop shows it occurring simultaneously with the production loop.

The activity of learning is not separate from production. Unfortunately, the coemergent nature of the process is impossible to capture in our two-dimensional representation. The distinction between the activities of learning and the activities of production is a mental one, not a physical one. Learning is occurring simultaneously with work when a little attention is given to the fact that learning is being captured in the process of work. Production activities begin to transform when this distinction is made. The transformation results in an immediate increase in productivity.

During many of my consulting engagements, I have spoken to many people whose ideas produced early major savings during an organization's learning initiative—the kind of ideas that eventually resulted in savings of millions, year after year.

When I asked these people how long they had their idea, the most common response I heard was, "I've had it for years." When asked why it wasn't suggested before the initiative, they almost always responded with some version of, "Because no one was listening," or "They didn't want to know," or "It was too risky to speak up."

When the distinction of learning is employed, production is undertaken differently and learning is an integrated part of production. Learning occurs within production and is then integrated into production and this fosters more learning, integration and production refinements. When this happens the phenomenon of the learning-production loop converges with the world of complexity. That is to say, a simple set of principles generates a rich variety of results.

There are two major areas of understanding that must be developed if the learning loop is to become operative. One is an understanding of the meaning and value of learning and the possibility inherent in learning. The other is an understanding of the design of work processes and structures that will demand learning and accountability for the creation of knowledge. Our designs must encourage and allow learning to occur. These designs must include rewards for learning so that learning is continued and knowledge is accumulated. The initial difficulty with this designing process will be accessing individual learning and individual intelligence, because until now they have been almost entirely suppressed in our corporations. (Remember when workers were referred to as "hands"?)

Other great opportunities for learning that have been suppressed are team learning and intergroup learning. The barriers created in the areas of communication and teamwork and the boundaries established between departments, specialties, and so on have been so strong that creative dialogue across artificial boundaries has been prevented—if not forbidden. Fortunately, almost insignificant beginnings that open up this dialogue will produce immediate significant returns. The long-term gains are more difficult and far more significant than the initial gains for the unfolding of our future. The source of the difficulty lies in our cultural heritage within corporations: personal matters are almost always allowed to interfere with organizational matters.

A corporation's knowledge base and total learning capacity are its greatest resource for success. The building of this resource will take time and must be developed in conjunction with individual and team learning. The knowledge base and the overall learning capacity provide the context for learning to occur in individuals and teams. Commitment to organizational learning will provide the strength and direction needed to overcome obstacles and conditions that could defeat smaller initiatives unsupported by higher levels of management.

Enhancement of both a corporation's knowledge base and its learning capacity can be managed largely by changing structures, systems and processes so that they not only allow for learning, but require it. These include simple changes in time structures, reports, meetings, reward systems, communications, etc. If all a corporation's systems are reviewed from the perspective of the learning loop, many things will stand out as being barriers to learning, and new ideas will emerge for structures that will enhance learning.

During the reviewing and designing process, bear in mind that augmenting learning into the current production loop does not increase overall production time and does not require significant time away from the work site. Motorola, a leader in quality and innovation, requires two such weeks per year per employee and accomplishes the rest of its learning during working hours. It takes a little imagination to design the minimum requirement for knowing that learning is occurring and that knowledge is being accumulated—but no more than it takes for good measures of breakthroughs in production. (At worst, designing this will be part of one's own learning process.) Arguments that will be obvious obstacles in this process will be that any change will cost money and any time spent on learning will reduce production. Such obstacles are easily hurdled with the simple response that the challenge is, after all, to design learning into the loop and still maintain the most productivity over time from the expenditures of effort and resources. Remember, a significant part of that productivity is the production of information and knowledge.

The argument that learning costs money and that we can waste our resources pursuing it is no more valid than the argument that we might not make the right choices for any resource allocation including IT and new

Our consulting firm was invited to work with a heavy-equipment construction company. We started our association by doing some basic development work with one of its teams which included shop floor specialists.

The team began to develop ways of working that could create major savings for the company. Throughout the project, the shop people made comments such as, "When we make this presentation, we will probably lose our jobs."

When the presentation was made to the head of production, the source of the fear became readily apparent. The head of production's first comment was, "This is so obvious, why didn't you guys fix this years ago?"

Next the new procedures and the names of the members were mentioned to the senior executive group and a number of the executives said, "This idea won't work. This team is just a bunch of troublemakers trying to stir things up. You should have selected another team for the consulting project."

The courage of the employees won out and the company increased productivity by 50% in the first year. The employees regained a sense of pride and contribution through their work.

technology decisions. To avoid making the wrong choices we need maximum intelligence and systems that support economic returns. As a recent bumper sticker said, "If you think education is expensive, try ignorance."

The single greatest challenge lies not in organizing for learning but in creating an environment that is conducive to learning. Environment refers to much more than physical surroundings, although some attention should be given to the meeting space, cleanliness and external display areas. The major element for creating an environment conducive to learning is relationship. Relationship is an environment of respect, trust, lack of fear, openness and generosity. When relationship is pursued, it creates an increasing spiral. When it is neglected, a decreasing spiral ensues.

The qualities of respect, openness and generosity are universal, and when they are pursued in group or individual conversations, virtually everyone is in favor of them. The barrier to the emergence of these qualities is embedded in the designs of hierarchy and bureaucracy that exist in our corporations. These barriers work against the values that are at the heart of being human. Attachments and designs for control destroy the relationships necessary for learning. Not only have we inherited counter-productive structures but we are also heirs to the cultural mood that goes with these structures.

The learning loop embodies so much potential power because it is completely compatible with the nature of human beings and human institutions, both of which are major energy resources. As soon as we realize that continuous growth and learning are a natural way of life for ourselves and our corporations, then we will begin to design for those and be rewarded with success. We can now design our corporations so that they complement people as human beings, rather than force structures on people that are unnatural. The alignment possible between individuals and corporations by using this point of view for our working and designing is something that could light up the world. Those who are first to move out onto the frontiers and pursue learning intelligently will reap major competitive rewards. Those who are late to make the move will eventually be forced to do it anyway. A latecomer's only reward will be survival.

When interfacing learning into our production loop, the greatest challenge will be in realigning individuals, not structures. Individuals will have to be willing to give up some of their own comfort, acknowledge a certain lack of understanding and notice their attachment to the way they currently have their work designed. In this process of letting go, the issues will be emotional, not logical. Rewards will follow if the process is pursued with integrity—that is, we will begin to expand our own intelligence and learning, as well as become the designers of organizations that are more fulfilling to all involved. Although we do not have much experience in organizing for learning, we understand it well enough to begin.

QUESTIONS FOR THIS CHAPTER:

- What are the theories, practices and structures in the production loop of your corporation that are barriers to effective pursuit of learning?
- What initial changes can be made in the theories, practices and structures to support the integration of learning into the loop?
- What are the most common personal attributes persisting in your corporation or industry (attitudes, levels of expertise, moods, etc.) that are barriers to the kinds of relationships necessary for learning?
- What personal attributes are missing in your corporation, the presence of which would foster the development of relationship?
- How much executive and management time is currently spent on learning?
- Is learning time effectively integrated into your corporation so that it creates value for others, and if not, what organizational practices would create valuable utilization of the resource?
- Are there any agreed-upon, measured levels of accountability in your corporation for the accumulation of knowledge; and if not, what designs do you see possible?
- How is that accountability currently distributed and what designs do you see possible?
- What monetary value does your corporation delegate to knowledge assets?

8 Freedom

"Being on the tightrope is living; everything else is waiting."
KARL WALLENDA

"The word upon which all adventure, all exhilaration, all meaning, all honor depends. In the beginning was the word and the word was CHOICE."
TOM ROBBINS
STILL LIFE WITH WOODPECKER

Prelude

Every living thing is a complex adaptive system. Such a system is self-organizing and self-generating. No outside force or source of energy can make a living thing live or function. At the same time, every living thing is influenced to a greater or lesser degree by its environment, its community and other living things.

To the extent that the existence of a thing is dependent on its organization as a complex adaptive system, that part of its existence must be free to operate. What requires freedom are the operations that are complex and adaptive.

Because of their linguistic ability, human beings have the maximum need for freedom. The linguistic ability and the particular range of intelligence that is part of it means that almost every area of life operates more effectively in a condition of freedom. When control is applied in areas where the intelligence of a complex adaptive system is intended, the results are negative.

Our job is to determine how to allow freedom to operate effectively where it is being restrained. In this chapter we will consider the meaning of freedom as well as determine its methods of operation.

THE WAY IT IS: LESSONS FROM THE POLITICAL CONDITION

Numerous observers have remarked that companies in the countries that value freedom and individual expression are operated in a fashion more similar to that of the former Soviet Union than to their own democratic systems. Is this a plea for democracy in the workplace? Not at all. It is perhaps an indication that both the Soviets and Western managers may think that the way to get things done is by control, planning and direction from the top. It may also be an indication that the free flow of information is not valued and in many cases is considered to be a threat that is best avoided. Rather than a plea, these observations are statements about our lack of understanding and confidence in the area of self-organizing, intelligent systems.

In the workplace we seem to equate freedom and freedom of expression with anarchy and chaos. Quite the contrary, freedom is a condition essential for learning, innovation and creativity. Freedom is also a condition necessary for the full expression and application of human initiative, energy and intelligence. We must define clearly the operational meaning of freedom in an organizational context if we are to tap into its power.

The value of freedom is based on pragmatic concerns.

The principles that are the basis for the assumed value of freedom in organizational terms are those of information, communication and the evolutionary possibilities of independent intelligent agents. When we inhibit the expression of intelligence where it is a natural phenomenon, we generate peculiarities of mood and action that cause destructive disturbances in the system. Individual expressions come out in distorted ways. We cannot expect individuals to contribute fully when their basic nature is suppressed.

The rise and fall of communist states in this century has provided a vivid display of the role of freedom in the organization of coordinated action of human beings. At the apparent peak of Soviet power there were very few people, grounded in a theory of human beings and their institutions, who said that the communist system was weak and would collapse. Immediately before the actual collapse, there were only a few who could predict the extent and nature of that collapse.

Freedom is a condition of effective coordination of action.

It is not democracy and capitalism that have demonstrated an undebatable superiority over dictatorship and socialism. While it is probable that democracy and capitalism have been key factors in the success of the West, it may turn out that they will both undergo dramatic changes over the next few decades. This prediction, which is based in complexity theory and observation of technological advances, will be explored in a later chapter and is not central to our theme here. What is central and has been demonstrated is that freedom is a condition necessary for the effective coordination of human action. Although the political case provides us with a particularly vivid example, we are concerned with organizational principles.

In ordinary social discourse, the word "freedom" is loaded with emotive significance. We will need to create an operational definition that redefines freedom if we are going to use it effectively in our thinking. We cannot expect success in the area we intend to apply it to if we use the ordinary social meaning of freedom. The ordinary meaning has far too many contradictions and emotions built into it. Once it is distinguished, that distinction may be useful in the political domain; however, we are concerned only with applying it to the domain of organization of productive activity and its more pragmatic relevance to organizational and management concerns.

DISTINGUISHING FREEDOM

What is the most fundamental thing that we can say about freedom that will be of maximum use to us in the design and maintenance of a corporation? We are not concerned here with moral qualities, preferences, or beliefs about the social condition and what it "should" be. What we are concerned with is maximum effectiveness in the design and operation of corporations for productive purposes. Our operational definition of freedom is *"that condition in which the agents in a social system are unrestrained in their ability to act except by rules or principles that apply to the organization of a system as a whole—including those responsible for the rules."*

Freedom can be said to exist in a system in which there are no rules or controls designed specifically for individual agents or designated groups. Freedom is a term of degree. In total freedom there are no rules or controls designed for the individual. In minimal freedom, actions of particular individuals and groups are managed by special rules for those individuals based on situations, degrees of trust and other specific factors. Note that freedom refers to the domain of action that is a publicly identifiable phenomenon and not to private areas such as thought and feeling.

TRANSITION DEMANDS FREEDOM

There is a group of actions that is of particular significance for our purposes. These actions are in the domain of communication and are concerned with information, learning and expanding knowledge. They demand freedom and a recognition of the nature of human beings when they are in ventures requiring coordinated action. This group of actions may not have been very significant in the past, but for our purposes it is of great interest and shows the altered condition in a dramatic way.

The fall of the Soviet empire reflects this dramatic shift. It occurred during the change of an era, when we shifted from the Machine Age, in which physical matter and its organization were the principle factors for productive success, to the Information Age, in which communication and the mental component are the principle factors for productive success. It was a lack of freedom in information, learning and sharing of knowledge in changing times that was the death blow to the Soviet system and is making a mockery of communism in China. It is also this lack of freedom combined with the era shift that may explain the surprising collapse of major corporations and the fall of the Berlin Wall.

Between rigidity and chaos is a robust area of complexity.

To state our operational definition of freedom more simply, it is: *"that condition in which the agents in a social system are unrestrained by special privilege or constraints in their ability to act."* Agents are governed only by rules or principles that apply to the system as a whole. Freedom that is most significant for productive purposes, learning purposes, and purposes of accumulating knowledge is in the area of communication. Freedom does not mean support, but rather a lack of particular kinds of controls.

The larger the corporation and the longer its history, the less freedom that corporation usually manifests. IBM and other declining giants are examples of companies having rigid yet unwritten rules about what can be expressed and to whom it can be expressed. Other companies that do not *yet* show such a dramatic decline are also examples of rigid suppression of expression.

Some of the large oil companies are models of unskillful practices in the area of expression. When the conditions of the competitive free market finally catch up with them, surprises almost equal to the fall of the Soviet Union should be expected. Decline in the oil industry will probably be blamed on conditions in the energy market, the global situation, or other external causes.

Few will appreciate the fact that it was a lack of expression, communication, and allowing freedom for their employees that was the source of their inability to adapt.

The oil companies' isolation from the marketplace makes them prime candidates for this type of criticism.

There are numerous examples similar to those mentioned and it will be very useful to investigate the factors discussed here before risking too much of your company's future.

It may be useful at this point to ask the following questions. What is it about the nature of human beings, human organizations and information that makes freedom a fundamental necessity? What is the nature of this freedom?

There are many places where freedom can be designed into an organization, but we are talking about designing it in for purposes of maximizing intelligence. The freedom that is being called for lies within the area between chaos and rigidity. The expanse of this area is between the minimum requirement for a flexible response to the maximum possible for innovative and creative success. We are referring to the area required for the survival of a corporation.

THE NATURE OF HUMAN BEINGS IN ORGANIZATION

Our theories about the nature of things give us our actions in relation to those things. Similarly, our views about the nature of human beings determine how we relate to people in our corporations. Human beings are the most critical factors in the success of a corporation. In most corporations, we are captive to a view of human beings and organization that takes away our effectiveness as managers and dehumanizes the workplace.

Our views about the nature of human beings that are commonly implicit (or very occasionally explicit) in our approaches to organization and people in corporations are completely useless for our purposes. While consistent with the earlier theoretical basis for the human sciences, they do not work with any great effectiveness in corporations. These views are mecha-

Imagine yourself as a manager of a winery. One of your responsibilities is the quality control department.

A condition for the effective operation of this department is that the people who work in it have a nose for wine. After all, bouquet is significant in determining quality and price.

It turns out that one of the people in the department has no sense of smell. What will you do?

Now consider that you are in charge of another area of the winery that requires teamwork or some particular form of cooperation.

One of the people in such a position turns out to be unable to cooperate with fellow employees. What will you do?

The point of the exercise is to illustrate that everybody has a nose, that each nose functions and looks slightly different from other noses, and that it is not a personal matter that we are dealing with.

What is the difference when we are talking about personality or ways of being? Excluding choice, which can hardly be a mitigating circumstance in this situation and may not be accurate anyway, there is no difference. There is merely something that doesn't work in the situation.

The actions you take are not personally directed but derive from the requirements of the job.

nistic and reductionist and fail to take into account that human beings are complex, intelligent beings. These views may be useful for analysis of individuals but are not useful for creating theories about human beings in corporations from which effective action can be taken. An analysis of the source of responses in individuals and difficulties of individuals does not yield material for understanding how people behave, think or act within human organizations. Individual human beings and their individual problems are not a corporation's primary concern. As a human enterprise, the concern is one of a social institution existing for the well-being of its members and the communities within which it operates. As individuals, we have a natural concern for others and this will influence the way that we respond in handling each individual case.

EXPLORING SOCIAL SYSTEMS: GROUNDWORK FOR UNDERSTANDING FREEDOM

We are creatures of our social context, which occurs in language.

At this point in the distinguishing of freedom in corporations it is important to understand the context of those corporations and the individuals in them. Let's provide a background for ourselves before we discuss how freedom can be designed into corporations.

The new thinking that is redefining the world we live in suggests that human beings occur in a social context and that more is to be learned from exploring that context than from all the analytical theories of history. There are two major areas to be explored. The first is the role of language.

We are socialized into a world of language—a world in which sense is made of things by means of language. The language of the culture that we are born into, whether it is German or American, urban or rural, upper class or lower class, socializes us. The behaviors, personalities and social ways that we develop as individuals have far more to do with the offerings and acceptable alternatives of the cultures that have socialized us than our own individual creation. It would be more accurate to say that they were selected from the menu offered.

A complex intelligent system cannot be understood except as part of other complex systems.

The second area to explore in social contexts is the nature of human beings as complex intelligent systems operating within larger complex intelligent systems. Complex intelligent systems are beyond our power of explanation and understanding at the level of detail and individual events. They are more poetic, more a "Gestalt," or more a response to the whole. They are constantly adapting in unpredictable ways to influences beyond our vision and understanding. The social system in which we live is a complex intelligent system and each of us is a complex intelligent system within that system. We are unable to understand ourselves in exactly the same way that we are unable to understand the complex intelligent systems of which we are a part.

We cannot understand others at the level of individual without reference to the culture and circumstances in which they are living. In the same way, we cannot explain or understand ourselves without reference to our circumstances and cultural history. We cannot predict accurately what our responses will be, nor can we know the full effects of our own actions upon ourselves and others.

Actions automatically self-organize in relationship to attractors.

When looking at corporations and the people in them, we notice that it is in the nature of human beings to seek to maximize their individual payoff from the system. The nature of what is considered a payoff and the time frame that is thought to be important will both vary by time and individual. The payoffs and the time frames will tend to be within socially determined boundaries. Notice the patterns of complexity here. Human beings are *structurally coupled* to their social environment. This means that the actions they take, and the values or payoffs they seek, tend to be within the principles that are the *attractors* or values of the social system they find themselves in. To use the term *invisible hand* from the 18th-century Scottish Enlightenment, self-organization will occur without any agent intending that it organize. This is amazingly consistent with the latest complexity theory.

CORPORATION AS AN INDEPENDENT PHENOMENON

A corporation coordinates the activities of individuals for productive purposes and can be seen to have as its main objective its own survival. A corporation is a phenomenon that has emerged out of complexity and now has an independent existence. It is not merely a collection of individuals. Organization is a complex system that is concerned (or not) with its individual components in the same way that your body is concerned with its individual cells.

A corporation exists independently of its members. If a corporation is said to possess intelligence, it is not the intelligence of the members that is being referred to—although that may be included—but something independent of that. If a corporation is said to communicate, that communication is not the sum of individual members' communications. The vision of a corporation, if such a thing exists, is not the vision of its leaders except to the extent that, as part of the organization, they share the vision. An intention to survive may be shared by all a corporation's members but it is independent of each of them.

Possibility and redundancy balance for survival.

The central feature of a corporation is its computational ability. A corporation must be able to send, receive, make sense of and act on information in a nonlinear, complex way if it is to survive. It must be able to create, test, generate feedback and continually process all the information that it generates. A corporation must also be able to generate a wide variety of possible interpretations that are independent of the original communication or source of information. The design of such a system must have a maximum degree of possibility in the number of connections and interpretations combined with the necessary degree of redundancy to ensure that the various interpretations do not take control until they have demonstrated their survival value. The ability to generate a wide variety of possible interpretations must be present in every part of a corporation, including the executive level, as well as in any individual within it.

Communication and information are nonlinear complex processes.

The nature of information may be the most difficult distinction to grasp and the most important for our purposes. The currently acceptable definitions are inadequate because they are generated from a linear and mechanistic understanding of the world. Not only are communication and information treated as mechanistic and linear phenomena, but so are human beings and corporations that are the agents of the communication and information production. Words such as "messages," "receivers," and "senders" exemplify this way of thinking.

We need to create a new operational definition for information that goes beyond this mechanistic model if we are to become powerful in this arena. An initial definition is: information is *"a change that makes a difference."* Information *value* is dependent on the entity that is processing the

Before the turn of the century physics was in a state of "no possibility" and appeared at a dead end. Most thought the science would die because it could no longer solve its problems.

It was transformed by the arrival of Albert Einstein, who was not restricted to a classical education as a physicist; nor did he get his ideas from the "used up" body of knowledge that was then physics.

In his own later writings, Einstein indicated that he was able to transform physics because he was not bound by its traditional language, definitions, or computational restrictions.

change, not on the nature of the change. Information does not refer to the content of change, nor does it imply that change will be interpreted in any particular way. All information is the result of a processing event and an interpretation structure that is independent of the "message," "sender," or "signal." An important part of the transaction is the "receiving" activity within the system of the processor. The most important part of the receiving is the interpretation.

The transmission of accurate data without possibility of difference in message is a very small part of the whole spectrum of information or communication. The areas of information and communication that have the most value for survival, innovation, computation and flexibility are concerned with systems that allow maximum unpredictability to be combined with minimum necessary redundancy.

Our mechanistic approach to thinking is only of use with systems in which detailed control is possible and desirable. Therefore, it is essential that we develop a new, powerful vocabulary in the areas of communication and information; one that is not currently the norm in corporations and society at large. Effective thinking tools are needed, such as those used in the fields of radio, computers, and code-breaking. The industries developing these tools are already developing distinctions that provide effectiveness in innovation and creativity as well as effectiveness in message passing, where certainty between sender and receiver is necessary.

Information is the result of possibility rather than certainty.

Information is not the result of predictability, but the result of the range of possibility—a rich variety of stimuli being processed through a structure. Both input and results are unpredictable. What gives rise to the possibility of information theory is that there is a vast amount of the unknown to explore. The realm of possibilities is beyond what is known and makes theory of information both possible and pragmatic. This calls for increasingly effective theories, distinctions and operational definitions that extend our reach into what is possible. If that realm appears to have an end, either falsely or not, then growth and innovation cease.

FREEDOM AND ORGANIZATIONAL DESIGN

Having laid the groundwork by distinguishing social systems and information, we are now ready to look at freedom in the context of organizational design in a new light. The nature of human beings, organization and information suggests that a large degree of freedom will go a long way towards producing intelligence and survivability. There is now an irresistible case for building into our corporations the maximum freedom. It is clear that we will have to reconstruct our corporations and design our structures so that the actions and choices that emerge from the condition of freedom are contained by something. We will have to create a structure through which information will operate. Complexity suggests that redundancy and principles that are simple and function as *attractors* can be the source of that containment.

"Contained" is an unfortunate word to use here, but we don't yet have a language which provides a better one. When *attractors* are operating or when self-organization is occurring, there is something going on that maintains an identity without there being any sense of containment or even restriction. It is the robustness of identity that we are seeking to focus on.

The area of predictability necessary for production contains the least information.

Due to the unpredictable, unknown, and largely unknowable nature of all three phenomena—humans, corporations, and information—it becomes clear that we cannot design for direct control. *What* to control is unknown. What will constitute valuable information is unknowable in advance. The space of possibilities is too vast for any direct control at all. The area where control is possible and where it has value will be near the area in which everything is already predictable. In this area, everything of value is known. While it is important for repetitive productive activity, this small area has little value for development, learning, innovation or survivability in an uncertain world—that is to say, its place is limited.

All the theories that we have been examining can be tested for their pragmatic value in our ways of thinking and acting. They are of course not the only theories that can be used for organizational designing. They may not necessarily be the best theories for every application. Very different theories might be needed if we were concerned with religion or medicine. However, it is the best possible set of theories that I have found for organizational concerns. Research has provided evidence of the pragmatic value of these theories and shown that they can be worked with successfully in the context of human institutions intended for productive means.

An uncertain future may make our current strategy a threat to longevity.

Research on complexity has revealed a phenomenon that is interesting in relationship to this conversation and is important in strategic thinking for corporations. Numerous studies and simulations have produced the same result. That is, when a system is stable there is a significant degree of predictability. And when one of the agents that is part of the system fails, or alters in any significant way, or the environment changes, the whole system becomes unstable and completely unpredictable. The reliable qualities of stability turn into chaos.

This principle also applies in industry and corporations. In an industry where one of the major players goes bankrupt, or makes a major change in its operations and/or relative competitive position, an entire network, including suppliers, competitors and customers will be disrupted. The previous leaders may even be losers in the order that eventually emerges. A company's previous competitive position will no longer be valid and the relative effectiveness of its competitive qualities may change dramatically over a short space of time.

What will have maximum survival value will be competence in communication ability, availability of information, and computational ability. What will have minimum survival value, maybe even negative value, is a design which pursues prediction and/or specific visions of a future.

THE DESIGN OF FREEDOM

From the interplay within a system emerge guidelines for coordination of independent action.

There are always internal design constraints. There are always external constraints. To expand our operational definition of freedom within human-generated organizations based on the general scheme we have now developed, we might say: *"Freedom is the system where the actions of an individual agent are generated largely by the interplay of internal factors, which is shaped by an external environment. The system has no concern for the individual in the matter of this interplay."* The "shaping system" is designed by human beings to coordinate the independent actions of individuals in an environment of maximum communication and independent action within the context of required redundancy for survival.

Freedom and chaos are not the same thing in this approach. For our purposes, chaos refers to a condition in which there are no discernible patterns and no information can be gained from the stimuli being received. Chaos refers to a condition in which there is no design or the design that does exist cannot be understood or recognized in any useful way.

Freedom as we have distinguished it here does not imply absence of design or structure. Freedom implies a condition that consists of simple but fundamental principles. It is inconsistent with detailed control, minute levels of design and structures of suppression. Free agents in the latter systems will cause breakdowns that may very well lead to chaos and destruction (recall The People's Republic of China.) Freedom designed with an understanding of complex intelligent systems and their self-organizing nature will lead to positive results beyond our imagining.

QUESTIONS FOR THIS CHAPTER:

- Does your corporation value freedom for its own people in their work environment?
- How is this expressed?
- What is the nature of the limitations on freedom in your corporation?
- How do those limitations manifest themselves in practical terms?
- How much of the formal organization is focused on controls that inhibit freedom?
- Where can redundancy be built in to take the place of rigid rules, specific controls and micromanagement?
- Are you able to distinguish the operational definition of freedom clearly enough to be understood *as you want it* by those to whom you are explaining it?
- Are there any areas in your company where there is too much freedom and where there should be more control?
- Should that control be on action or communication?
- What can be designed to maximize intelligence?

III Organizational Application

This section develops the theory by applying it to the major questions concerning strategy that are confronting corporations today. The new theory of organization, based on complexity, provides insight into how to meet the challenges of rapid change and increasing competition, how to continually expand what is possible, how to create structures that match fast-moving markets and intelligent action, and how to capture the drive and intelligence of every human being in a corporation.

9 Strategy

"Regaining competitiveness will mean rethinking many of the basic concepts of strategy."
GARY HAMEL AND C. K. PRAHALAD
STRATEGIC INTENT, HARVARD BUSINESS REVIEW

"All of us have the need to look for answers in new and different places. And the categories by which we have thought of things—whether it is by disciplines or functional areas of business—are simply too limiting."
MEG WHEATLEY
LEADERSHIP AND THE NEW SCIENCE

Prelude

When change is slow within an environment, when conservative forces predominate and when we are secure in our predictions, strategy is reduced to planning. The fundamental issues have been effectively determined. During such times goals are clear, targets are easily defined, and the actions required for their accomplishment are predictable.

In contrast, when change is happening at an accelerated rate, when technology and its applications are unpredictable and when competition appears around every corner, strategy takes on a major role; there is an unprecedented demand for thinking in new ways and distinguishing new levels of abstraction. The fundamental issues of the times have not yet been determined.

When rapid changes are occurring everywhere in areas seemingly unconnected to us, we can be certain that they will soon affect us. When well-informed, intelligent people are being surprised by new developments, we can be certain that it is time for a new level of strategic thinking. The longer that we rely on inherited strategies that are mere technical functions, the more we will have to learn when it is time for new depth in strategic thinking. It is time now (for some it may be too late) to take on the challenge of discovering what strategic thinking really can be.

A NEW DEMAND FOR STRATEGIC THINKING

For most of the twentieth century, our corporations have only required planning. Because of the impoverished demand in the field of strategy, planning has been mistaken for strategy. Strategy and planning, however, have no more to do with each other than deciding to get married and planning the wedding. Strategic thinking attempts to understand the nature of things. It creates the opportunity to respond to current circumstances and actions in such a way that the future created far surpasses any future that would have been created by the mere continuation of what is already in existence. To be considered effective, strategic thinking must be shared with many individuals in such a way that action can be independently coordinated throughout an organization.

The first and most important task in strategic thinking is to provide a theory by which an uncertain and constantly shifting world can be approached. Whether or not a theory is workable can be determined by examining the following criteria: it can be tested, it will provide the right questions, and it will lead to the information necessary for the next iteration of the original theory or for the new theory that will replace it. Once a theory is clearly articulated, it coexists with strategy and strategic thinking and it is used to generate actions and responses in our everyday working activities. It is important to note that strategic thinking and strategy are distinct from the execution of strategy—except in those cases where the manner of execution is itself strategic.

Once strategic thinking is underway, planning can then begin. Planning is a practice in and of itself. It is concerned less with the source of the idea than with ensuring that action is consistent with the original intention. Planning is a design methodology and practice that creates structures for fulfilling ideas. The challenge of planning is to create structures that are perfectly aligned with the principles of the original intention.

SEPARATING STRATEGY FROM EXHORTATION

Extraordinary results over long periods of time are extraordinary occurrences. They are so rare that they are considered accidents not worth pursuing. A recent study, spanning decades, has shown that there are big winners

DISPLAY OF LONG TERM SUCCESS

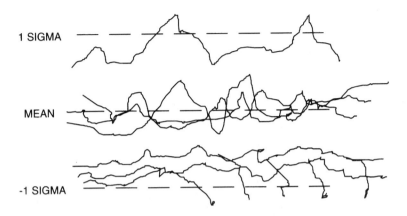

1 SIGMA

MEAN

-1 SIGMA

for short periods of time but never for extended periods of time. The best cases were found to be those companies that measured a little above average for their industry and did so for long periods of time. The study disclosed three distinct groups: those that do a little better over time and seldom leave that category, those that float around the mean and seldom leave that category, and those that do worse than the average and whose members come and go. Very seldom does a member of the third group become a member of the first group. Theory supported by models of marketplace competition developed by Christopher Langton at the Santa Fe Institute provide a similar result which can be represented by the above diagram.

Expressions of strategy demand integrity.

This rather startling research suggests that the language used by leaders of corporations who seek to "be number one," "dominate the market," or some variation on that theme has no value other than exhortation. Exhortation is detrimental to the functioning of a corporation and therefore may be part of the condition that keeps a company from moving to higher levels of success. Given the complex nature of the thinking and speaking that is required, executives would be of greater service to their corporations if they were more thoughtful in their declarations of intent. Exhortation lacks integrity and authenticity. Its main use is for "motivation" and is usually seen as such by those it is intended to motivate. It should not be surprising that such declarations of intent frequently cause disbelief, loss of respect and eventual failure. Exhortation frequently replaces the hard work of strategic thinking.

STRATEGY FOR COMPLEX SYSTEMS IN A COMPLEX ENVIRONMENT

Survival is a function of fit with the environment—now and in the future.

These ideas are designed to provide a sobering effect before we consider what strategy might be. Evolutionary and ecological biology have some things to say about complex systems in complex environments that are even more sobering. For instance, no species of any kind has ever become so successful that it dominated the landscape of an ecology. That is true whether or not the ecology is a planet, a rain forest, or a small pond. This same phenomenon holds true in economics; similar patterns are visible whether it is a global economy or a local marketplace. Only legalized force has managed to dominate for long periods of time—and this too is subject to failure like everything else. Ecologies offer no guarantee of survival, nor a possibility of sustainable excess. The long-term winners in complex ecologies are those that fit with an environment, compete within a context of cooperation and create systems that become increasingly complex while remaining extremely flexible. Entities such as these prosper because they are able to continue functioning over long periods of time in a wide variety of circumstances.

Most of the executives using exhortation, disguised as strategy, fail to demonstrate any changes in behavior or resource allocation that are consistent with their declarations.

In contrast, British Petroleum executives created a strategic intent that has resulted in over $1 billion being cut from their operating costs over the three-year period following the announcement of their new strategy.

To succeed, BP had to discover what it would take to increase its competitive position, even though its main source of oil (large fields in the North Sea) was rapidly being used up. BP innovatively designed a new scenario in which many small dispersed fields became its main source of oil.

The company quickly realized that the way in which all of its systems were currently set up would not work in the new environment.

Slashing costs was only a small part of the shift that needed to occur. The company realized that it needed to invent new ways to bring oil from discovery to market.

BP also realized that the entire supply industry needed to be reinvented. Included in their strategy was an understanding that every employee and every supplier was responsible for applying their own intelligence to the challenges of the industry as a whole.

The strategy went on to include intensive education for all executives and management, extensive educational program for all staff, and even programs for the entire supply industry.

Strategy is for creating a future, not merely adapting to one that is happening already.

Corporations and business schools have displaced the generative aspects of strategy by approaching it in an analytical way. Most corporations consider strategy to be a matter of selecting from options and adapting to the environment. Those few who realize that strategy is a process of profound original thinking about their company and its relationship to an evolving landscape of ecologies are gaining an enormous marketplace advantage. For these corporations, strategy generates the future as much as it predicts it. In a complex adaptive system, such as an economy or an industry, the actors in the system are as much influencers as the influenced. The future emerges from the complex interactions of the players and is unpredictable in detail to them all because of that.

Complexity theory was developed from the idea that simple rules (structures, principles), with a design or grammar, are the source of the greatest variety and flexibility in the universe. The theory has been demonstrated and further developed by experiments made possible by very elaborate computer simulations. The message is quite clear: survival is contingent on a design that balances the forces of an ecology in such a way that a stable base identity is created—an identity with enormous flexibility in its specifics and applications.

The challenge for a complex intelligent system—a corporation—is to continually develop both the ability to *adapt* to the competitive environment and the ability to *influence* that environment. Mastery of this iterative and seemingly paradoxical ability determines who dominates the game, who merely survives and who goes out of existence.

THE LANGUAGE OF STRATEGIC THINKING

How large is the space of possibilities for a corporation? How "grand" can a strategy be? What constitutes appropriate expression of a strategy? These are the kinds of questions we should look at before we begin to work with content for our specific strategy. Our current inherited vocabulary, ways of speaking and practices are bankrupt and obsolete at this point in the game.

Every corporation either has an explicit statement of strategy or is berated for not having one. In my experience, only a very small percentage of companies have a strategy that is understood and respected by employees or the public. Most are faulted for lack of originality, lack of clarity, or lack of understanding of the business and marketplace. In a great majority of our companies, employees say that management doesn't know what it is doing. Management is also frequently faulted for a lack of match between action and resource allocation with regard to what is said to be the strategy.

Strategic statements coordinate the actions of independent agents with the intention of the whole.

Strategy is *for* the future but it is *about* the present.

Every executive, board, and analyst knows that both strategy and its expression are critical. Statements of strategy provide reference points or foundation for the thinking and actions of each person, so that they can coordinate their actions. Strategy is not only needed by employees to guide their day-to-day choices but it is also what interests intelligent investors as they look to see if there is a match between a corporation's statement of theory and its approach. What is strange about this phenomenon is that rarely do you meet an executive who is willing to tell the market makers their strategy or is willing to be tested on how well it is being carried out.

Because of a peculiar Western understanding of the nature of the world we live in, we fail to see the interconnectedness of all things. We also misconstrue time and imagine that the future is somewhere out there in front of us and that, through effort or waiting, it will unfold more or less as predicted by our current thinking. This notion can be found in our language. We say we live in a world of goals and targets and that these extend all the way up to our vision. These days "everyone" knows that vision is important and most people have designated it as the source of success in the present and the future. However, this way of thinking may fall into the category of what Will Rogers, the American humorist, was referring to when he said, "It's not the things that we don't know that are the problem; it's the things we *do* know that ain't so."

For every leader who says their success is a result of having a vision and moving toward it in a determined and planned way, there is a converse example of someone equally successful who had no vision whatsoever.

Larry Risley, founder of the successful Mesa Airlines, set up his business on a very small scale by using other people's planes to transport passengers. At one point he took the risk of buying his own plane. His investment proved successful, which led to another plane, which led to an airline.

When he talks about the process he says, "There was never any grand plan." And he seems surprised at his success. The success story of Mesa, like most others, is one of carrying out an idea well—a strategy—and then simply continuing to act in accord with that idea when the next opportunity arises.

The challenge facing any large or small company with a successful history is to design for continuous development in which strategy generates success and in turn new opportunities unfold.

The idea that we imagine a future and move toward it is a useful fiction for some and a disadvantage to others. It is not a necessary approach and can be detrimental.

There is no conclusive evidence that we create an image of the future and live into it. There is also no evidence that creating a vision and goals is a necessary or even effective condition for success. There are as many reports of failure as there are of success when individuals or corporations have engaged in these practices. The best we can say is that it is a technique that, when developed, produces positive results for some people in some circumstances. That it has any necessary value as a corporate activity has never been shown.

CHALLENGING MECHANISTIC APPROACHES

The predominant theory about who we are as human beings, woven through our entire Western culture from as far back as Aristotle, is largely responsible for the ideas of goals and visions. This theory sees everything as having an external cause. The mechanistic nature of this way of thinking has reduced humans to automatons that must have goals to function effectively. The methods for achieving such goals are also mechanistic. The creation of a vision, the establishment of goals, and the existence of a "strategic plan" are all part of the approach emanating from this theory.

The problem with approaching the challenge of strategy in this way is that it is based on assumptions about human beings and their motivation that do not match how things actually occur. Being conscious of a past and clearly able to imagine a future is not a necessary condition for operating effectively. Being able to imagine a future has its benefits, but the day-to-day affairs of business are not one of them. Imagining futures can be a rich source of creative input for action. However, imagining a *particular* future provides very limited action. Creating a future, as something to work toward, will often be more detrimental than useful, especially when you consider that we do not know what is going to happen. We have demonstrated beyond a doubt that we are very bad at predicting the future!

Yet, there is some gold in here somewhere, because all of us have experienced ways of thinking and operating that are in accord with "strategic intent," and the power in them has been obvious. To mine for the gold, the tools we will need are an understanding and language that will allow us to break free of our inherited way of thinking and approaching things.

GOALS IN A COMPLEX SYSTEM

The idea of "goals" has spread to include all kinds of nonsense.

Evolutionary and ecological biologists provide extremely useful insight into the role of vision in the scheme of things. Their theories point out that when things are simple it is not necessary to have our actions motivated by goals or a vision of the future. In fact, actions emerging from immediate responses to what is occurring, internally and externally, are quite sufficient without the addition of ideas such as goals or a vision. The "magical incantations" of our culture have taught us to think in terms of goals even though it is an unnecessary complication. We continue to apply this approach even though no consistent pragmatic value has been demonstrated, and many instances of its use have failed. We do not need to think of "goals" to imagine hunters and gatherers and even farmers successfully going about their daily productive lives. We can imagine that they had visions without making the visions a necessary cause of their success.

We don't *need* to think of goals to make sense of action. The complexity of life can easily be imagined as merely an unfolding of the inherited patterns and learned actions necessary to survive in a particular environment. Management theories and practices have added this extraneous way of

Many transformation efforts gridlock on the issue of vision. IBM executives argue about whether or not a vision is needed. If one is proposed, they argue even more fiercely about whether or not this is the right vision. DEC executives have been pilloried because their vision was wrong.

Countless managers are berated because they don't make their goals and, as a consequence, managers create goals that aren't worth having in order to avoid "beatings" in the future. These same managers impose goals on employees to manipulate (sorry, "motivate") them into working harder.

The Wall Street Journal ran a series on corporate surprises in the '70s that revealed losses from fraud and stupidity in various companies. For example, a large corporation and its senior management charged with falsifying financial statements said they did it "because they thought the executive wouldn't tolerate lower results."

In each case, there was a very strong use of goals and rules. The behaviors that caused the negative surprises were a direct correlate of the system of goals and the pressure used for meeting those goals. The goals were generally within the corporate vision statement.

In contrast, A.G. Edwards is one of the most profitable brokerage firms based on return on capital. They have no mandatory budgets and no pressure to perform against arbitrary targets.

Working with this company was a delight because people were always interested in what would enhance performance rather than in artificial pressure created by vision and goals. Their simple operating principles and general intention to succeed seem to be quite sufficient.

thinking and speaking to our day-to-day work lives and, in doing so, they have hindered the effectiveness of people and their organizations.

THE FLOW OF LIFE

Things move from simple to complicated. If they are to succeed over time, they must continually return to simplicity, but at a more complex level than the original.

Many of our corporations have started out producing things in a relatively simple manner with the use of machines and systems. As the businesses have unfolded, things have become more complicated and because we have failed to understand complex adaptive systems, we have made "patch" adjustments. By making many small adjustments, we complicate the system. (This happens even with inanimate systems. The jet engine started with only a handful of moving parts. It now contains 22,000.) When a complicated system takes too much energy to maintain, some very pragmatic tools can be acquired from complexity theory that, when applied, will allow the system to become workable again. Simplification is a function of understanding principles and ignoring detail.

The point at which a system becomes complicated is the point at which complexity theory has the most to offer. By creating a few simple rules or principles that will act as a structure, all information and input can be moved through it or be influenced by it so that a system that would otherwise be considered complicated is seen as simple. These few simple rules are likely to be reformulations of the rules that were applied initially when the game was simple. Through the process of rethinking, reinventing and renewing, these rules will be "denser" (contain more information) than they

Complexity theory sheds new light on many of our activities by giving us insights into rich, robust phenomena that result from a few simple rules or principles.

In biological terms, complex phenomena can be seen in the simple structures or codes of DNA. In the world of language, these same phenomena are seen in the limited set of sounds, grammar, and syntax. In economic terms, they are represented in a few simple laws and an exchange medium.

A corollary of this theory is that by providing a few simple principles for independent agents,

they can develop actions based on their own interests and interpretations. A self-organizing phenomenon will naturally occur, that is, a marketplace, a language, or a species.

The robustness of this theory is seen in the fact that animals always reproduce offspring like themselves and not like other creatures.

It is the possibility of variety, beyond prediction, occurring within robust boundaries that makes complexity theory attractive for organizational purposes. This same approach can be translated into values and structures of accountability.

were initially. These rules will contain more ambiguity and demand more creativity from the system. The system itself will have to contain sufficient redundancy to manage breakdowns caused by that ambiguity.

Information theory, developed in the early part of the century, provides insight into the way communication and information work in systems. The balance between redundancy and ambiguity determines the robustness of a complex intelligent system. Without ambiguity and uncertainty, information value is low. But with it, there will be mistakes and breakdowns. Redundancy provides the facility to make sense of what might otherwise appear random or chaotic and to limit its potentially dangerous effects. Human language systems are redundant for this reason.

THE POWER AND USE OF STRATEGIC INTENT

A strategic intent is a statement of the future in present terms.

A statement of vision becomes a simple statement that embodies values or principles that represent the most desirable qualities for the present, which are expected to endure as we move into the future. A statement of strategy becomes a statement of design through which principles and practices (the "grammar" of the organization) are developed. These statements provide a perspective from which to think that represents the whole as seen from any location within the corporation.

None of the features of a statement of strategy mentioned above imply anything about the future even though they provide a blueprint (DNA) and conceptual schema from which the future will be created. That future will be of the sort suggested by complexity theory—unpredictable in detail, un-

It may be that the value of vision statements and strategies has been to make sufficiently explicit the code against which individuals can organize their own actions, and which are sufficient to provide the basis for self-organization. The value of a vision statement may not be the vision itself but rather the reference point that it provides for thinking and conversations.

If this is the case, then we would design our statements differently and make them far more powerful. Being "number one" provides little information for daily operations or larger strategic

questions. A broad but specific statement of intention, such as Disney's "provide a quality entertainment experience," and a set of operational principles will allow strategy to emerge and continue to evolve.

Hamel and Prahalad have made a significant contribution. By providing a new expression—*Strategic Intent*—they have focused attention on an area that is more fundamental than analysis or planning and they have invited us to consider strategy as connected to intent.

predictable in specific content, yet rich and varied in particular expression. The most that can be said about that future (and only when looking back from it) is that its pathway of unfolding or becoming makes perfect sense within the context of the strategic intent.

The purpose of a strategy is to provide a theory, an understanding, a structure of interpretation, or an orientation to the world. Each person, on hearing a particular strategy, will look into the immediate occurrences of her or his everyday environment and be able to make choices that are coordinated with the choices and actions of others, even though they are removed from their sphere of communication. Each individual will be able to count on others to take actions that will result in a self-organizing coordination.

A powerful statement of strategic intent embodies sufficient ambiguity to generate creativity and enough clarity to evoke common understanding.

Every individual or organization shares the common intention to survive and continue or extend itself through time and space. What expression of *strategic intent* will result in the fruition of this intention? "To survive" will not provide sufficient information to generate intelligent action—that is, we cannot expect effective self-organization to come from such a simple expression. In the same sense, "to be the best" or any variation of that only provides a stage for exhortation. To replace that kind of strategy statement with a long list or a specific list of plans and intentions will then produce an expression that is complicated and will result in chaos rather than the self-organization of complexity. The nature of a statement, which I believe *stra-*

Disney has created a statement of a vision of quality service that is very consistent with complexity theory. The statement is backed by a set of operating principles that make it immediate and consistent with present commitments. If pursued with intelligence, which its form allows, it will also serve as the source of a future consistent with the present.

The strategy can be said simply: "Keep it clean, keep it friendly, make it a real fun place to be—and make sure that it is that way for employees as well as guests."

Doesn't sound like much of a strategy, does it? But what has made it such a successful strategy for Disney is not the words but the fact that

it operationalizes the strategic intention and trusts that the resulting actions will take care of the future.

The strategy gets operationalized into practices and processes following the formula: Quality Cast Experience + Quality Guest Experience + Quality Business Practices = Future. They have also harnessed the power of language by referring to employees as cast members and customers as guests.

John Hench of Disney says, "We'll probably be explaining this to outsiders throughout our next two decades." Why? Because the strategy is perfectly balanced in simplicity and complexity. Executives and management have not yet grasped the power of that distinction.

tegic intent indicates, that will produce sufficient information and sufficient ambiguity is one that contains only a few elements and requires active interpretation to make sense of it. Yet, it is simple enough to relate to at an immediate level. Hamel and Prahalad's *strategic intent* is pointing to a statement that will provide sufficient information and sufficient ambiguity to require active interpretation and yet remain simple enough to be translated into immediate action.

NEC's statement of strategy, "to develop communication and computers," was a powerful and effective statement of strategic intent at the time that it was introduced into its field. The Rouse Companies combined strategic intent and values into a statement that led the company to outstanding and continuing success:

"That the lives of people and communities for generations to come will be affected by what we do; that the surest road to success is to discover the authentic needs and yearnings of people and do our best to service them; that people seek warm and human places with diversity and charm, full of festival and delight, that they are degraded by tacky, tasteless places and are oppressed by coldness and indifference; that they are uplifted by beauty and order and made significant by the creative caring which that demands; that we believe everything matters, that all detail is important."
—*Jim Rouse*

A STRATEGY STATEMENT MUST PROVIDE INFORMATION

The power of a strategy statement is determined by its information value.

There are few statements of vision or strategy that pass the test by providing sufficient simplicity and sufficient information value simultaneously. If a statement is too simple, it will be lacking in possibility and it will not demand creative interpretation. If it becomes too complicated, it will fail through lack of use. Information theory tells us what kinds of statements will provide maximum power. Complexity theory offers us valuable insight into how to design a statement so that it captures the intended thinking and expression.

For a statement to be effective it must call forth extraordinary thinking.

It's not a better vision of the future that is needed but rather information so that we can make meaning of things as they happen. Our ability to interpret and act will be the source of our success both in our immediate world and our long-term future. This computational ability is enhanced through internal communication structures rather than the external activities of information gathering. Most corporations are designed to gather more than enough information. The challenge and rewards lie in organizing internally in such a way that information continues to flow and develop into ever more creative interpretations.

If an executive is authentic about becoming an extraordinary leader, extraordinary thinking leading to extraordinary resource allocation and use will be required. For an organization to be extraordinary, an extraordinary increase in information, freedom and creativity will be required, along with a structure that can be counted on to organize all of that. Anything else will be too costly and too short on intelligence, and will probably collapse. It will be self-organization or nothing.

An example that clearly illustrates this phenomenon can be found in the current ways in which large computer systems are being managed. This new way of managing systems is called "distributed processing." The design principles of this process are derived from the observation that independent agents will automatically self-organize for productivity when operating in a marketplace-like environment. In a centrally controlled computer system, as much as 30% of the computing time can go to managing the system itself. By creating simple algorithms that allow many independent machines to allocate their own resources and bid for parts of projects (rather than all allocations coming from the center), the overhead for managing the system itself can be reduced to less than 15%. This design works because it recognizes that beyond a certain threshold point of complication (associated with size or number of units), it is much more efficient for communication and management to be self-generated than centrally controlled.

In his research into complexity theory, Stuart Kauffman (an evolutionary biologist from The Santa Fe Institute) has made some interesting observations about environments (landscapes), an organism's relationship to that landscape, and the evolution of that organism. He notes that there is a pathway of development—an organism develops in ways that move it in the direction of getting more of whatever it is seeking. This development he calls *hill climbing*; and in this process an organism goes from less complex to more complex. If the pathway being pursued yields continually increasing benefits, the organism continues to specialize until it is unable to return to its earlier ways. It has often specialized the earlier forms away and it can no longer go back "downhill."

This observation has interesting implications for both corporations and human beings. We should be able simply to retrace our steps, but the further we move along a certain pathway the less freedom we exhibit in our ability to do this. The longer we pursue a certain pathway that has provided rewards, the harder it is to give up that pathway to return to an earlier one or create a completely new direction. This is partly because what is required of us is to "go downhill." More significant than the retracing of steps or regression is the forfeiting of the rewards or success of our current practices. To give these up is contrary to the fundamental thinking and design of corporations. Aspects of complexity theory offer insight into the size of the jump from existing behaviors best suited to generate the most information and still maintain the best chances of success. These strategies depend on where you are on the "hill."

STRATEGIC DESIGN

Complexity theory suggests that a sufficient number of teams acting as largely independent agents offer maximum creativity and information.

Complexity theory articulates the design principles of organization. Some of the pioneering work being done at The Santa Fe Institute involves computer simulations that illustrate this phenomenon. A grid of lights acting as individual agents is designed to turn on or off automatically depending on the differing intentions and surrounding circumstances programmed into each agent. When an agent is programmed with instructions only to be concerned for its own state, the lights either quickly go into an inactive death state of all-on or all-off, or they go into a state of chaos in which the lights flash wildly and show no discernible pattern for as long as the program is running.

In another series of simulations the grid is broken up into only a few large units (or teams), and interesting patterns begin to form and repeat themselves. But soon the repetition settles in and there are no new patterns

Examples of hill climbing can be seen in small successful machine shops that continue to increase the amount and size of their equipment in order to meet the demands of bigger jobs.

Their employees adapt to the requirements of large jobs, their overhead expands, their systems change so that large complicated projects are manageable. Before long they discover that they can no longer succeed at the small jobs that were the source of their initial success.

If the marketplace turns around and demands a return to small job efficiency, this business is more likely to go under than to be able to "go back downhill" and succeed again at smaller

jobs. The longer that it has focused on large jobs, the less likely the turnaround will be.

A larger scale example of this can be seen in the steel industry. "Mini mills" are taking an increasing share of the market and US giants are going out of business. So why not just copy the mini mills? They have no impenetrable cache of technology.

What makes it almost impossible is that the steel titans have developed scores of complex systems that have become so *tightly coupled* through lengthy historical development that they cannot be separated *in the minds of those responsible.*

(or new information). However, as the parameter size of the units is re-established into a smaller, more favorable size and each individual agent is programmed to maximize its own unit (but not the whole unit) and each unit is programmed to maximize the state of the whole—patterns begin to appear that are interesting and contain maximum information. These patterns never settle into a repetitive state of no information, nor do they go into a state of chaos. Self-organizing principles appear to be at work and they offer indications of how to *strategically design* work groups and company divisions that will provide maximum flexibility and information without central control. These principles suggest there is an optimum unit size and that there is little benefit in making the units concerned for the whole as long as they are bound by certain values or conditions.

What is revealed by computer modeling and the theories that have been developed in the light of them is that strategy is a matter of information and computational ability. Strategy is not about a vision of a particular future that is to be generated. Models can be created to explain the successes of the

---

When approaching quality, re-engineering, or time-based initiatives, many companies express concern about having too many teams doing too many uncoordinated projects.

To keep the teams under control, they create hierarchical structures and, in doing so, violate the *strategic design* principle that goes with the intention of teams.

The transformation of a corporation will fail if the responsibility is placed in the hands of a few focused teams directed—or favored—by management.

A team-based approach has inherent in it the possibility of anarchy. Too many teams without an alteration in organizational design cannot be tolerated by the old system. Too few teams will fail to produce the necessary energy and creativity.

What is required is a set of principles that will guide the formation and operation of teams as well as minimally integrate those teams for interaction. Each team's immediate conditions for continued success remain local.

A small scale version of this *strategic design* has been accomplished by Broken Hill Proprietary (an Australian company). After a short series of education sessions, one of its off-shore oil field projects previously operating with a "team" of over 1,000 people broke work down into small integrated teams. They came to see it as strategic to form many small teams within the larger project—including subcontractors in the teams. A substantial increase in project productivity resulted.

The same has been accomplished on a massive scale by VISA. Currently one of the largest companies in the world, it is comprised of many teams that are interrelated but not centrally controlled—or even centrally understood. Their independent teams are coordinated through flexible robust communication networks.

past and yet more models can be created to explain processes that are currently succeeding; but all of these are *after-the-fact* models and they were not the source of the success. Following them may destroy the very thing that they are designed to create. How many companies have turned the sources of their success into the millstones that prevent them from keeping the very thing they are trying to preserve?

The future is not knowable and prediction is not the source of success. Instead, the source of success at any given moment is fitness for the *landscape, ecology, or culture* in which one finds oneself. The way to build future success is to design oneself to be maximally effective in three areas:

● Adapting to current circumstances
● Influencing the circumstances one finds oneself in
● Increasing ability and flexibility in order to achieve the above two more effectively and in a wider variety of circumstances

The strategy of a corporation should be focused on what can be done in the present to increase its ability to operate in the future. These activities will be related to the existing external environment and may include prediction; but they will be equally focused on the internal structures, existing abilities and self-generated creativity that are largely independent of the current circumstances. These actions will be related to, but not determined by, the specific history of the corporation.

A small but very successful computer company invited our consulting group to work with its management. Because of its escalating growth, the company had hired many new people and the velocity of expansion now exceeded its management abilities. The spirit of the company was disappearing and new product development had come to a standstill.

The company's management only saw two choices initially: one was imposing standard management practices across the board, thereby losing the innovative culture that had created its success. The other was keeping the culture and watching profits decline because of lack of coordinated action.

After some design work a resolution emerged. The resolution was to develop a statement of strategic intent and then create a *strategic design* to implement it. The design was one of creating "cells" and designing communication between cells instead of between individuals or in a hierarchical pattern.

This design not only retained the culture but it also improved the communication and information flow.

A corporation's specific expression of a strategy will be a combination of theories that have general application to people and organization, are specific to an understanding of the corporation's area of business and have been tailored to match the historical organization which has developed. The process of creating this expression is not analytical but one which can only be accomplished through dialogue between the internal and external environments.

QUESTIONS FOR THIS CHAPTER:

- Can you state your strategic intent in such a way that people are able to get a sense of it and how it is unique to your corporation?
- Can you express your strategy in a few simple statements, so that anyone in your corporation could make sensible everyday decisions based on those statements?
- When was the last time your strategy was changed?
- What was the occasion for that change, and was it received with a positive response from employees and the financial community?
- How much time in the past year has the leadership team of your corporation spent working with strategic thinking as you now understand it?
- What displaces strategic thinking and strategic conversations from your agenda and that of your team?
- To what degree does your strategic intent demand that you change external circumstances and to what degree does it demand that you change yourself?

10 Innovation, Creativity and Flexibility

"Security is mostly superstition. It doesn't exist in nature nor do we as human beings experience it. Avoiding the danger of life is no safer in the long run than outright exposure. . . . Life is either a daring adventure or nothing."
HELEN KELLER

"We'd better learn that from now on we're making it up as we go along."
BERGER & LUCKMANN
SOCIAL CONSTRUCTION OF REALITY

Prelude

Animals, human beings, corporations and society all exhibit some degree of flexibility, adaptability and innovation. These qualities are not brought in from the outside or added on, but can be found within the design of the entity itself. If you see innovation and flexibility as gateways to marketplace advantage, then the exploration of the natural phenomena from which they arise will provide rich rewards.

High levels of innovation and creativity are at once exciting and dangerous in their possibilities. Exciting . . . because of the potential of leaping into a future far beyond what our current circumstances seem to allow. Dangerous . . . because our survival is at stake. How can we ensure that successful and adaptive innovation emerges? And how do we recognize adverse innovations before they endanger us? How can we ensure that the structures that minimize the danger of innovation, creativity and flexibility do not suppress the very thing we want?

Human beings have a unique capacity for creativity. We can form organizations that have a far greater capacity for creativity than our individual activities. This capacity is the source of great possibility for social well-being.

ORGANIZING FOR INNOVATION, CREATIVITY AND FLEXIBILITY

Innovation, creativity and flexibility are the qualities most highly valued by executives and yet these qualities are more likely to be exceptions than the norm in our corporations. This is not surprising, since we seldom see evidence of these qualities in the executives who are demanding them in their corporations. We continue to remain brutally impoverished in these areas because we fail to understand the source of these qualities—especially as organizational phenomena. Innovation, creativity and flexibility are all different aspects of the same thing.

Our current theories, ways of thinking and methods of organizing for production all belong to the *either/or* genre: it is *either* innovation *or* reliable production. Our task is not to make a wise choice between the two but instead to balance challenging systems with strengthening the very systems being challenged. What remains obscured because of our lack of under-

---

If you are going to do business with someone in a contracting industry, you want innovation and creativity to be a part of the package you buy.

But people in a contracting industry will have a litany of reasons as to why they cannot spend the time or money to develop innovation and creativity. The list will go on to include a transient workforce; the nature of subcontracting; their contracts, which have no provision for the time or money needed for innovation; and the efficiency that has already been built up in the midst of a competitive industry.

People in the manufacturing business also want to reap the rewards of innovation and creativity, but they claim that the very nature of their business prevents them from spending the time and money to do so. They cite the relentless demands of the production line, the time pressure of each and every moment, the necessity to keep costs down, the lack of space and time to experiment, the need to keep "the machine" running at peak efficiency and the belief that the manufacturing process is already engineered in a specific way.

The design and structure of manufacturing businesses have been developed for production, not for learning, and not for innovation, creativity, or flexibility beyond what occurs naturally.

The justification for not changing anything and the claims of difficulty have their origins in the existing design and structure of the corporation. Once this is acknowledged, it is easy to see what changes must be made in order to nurture the emergence of the qualities of innovation, creativity, and flexibility.

The breakdowns that occur in the pursuit of these qualities are a result of the new approaches conflicting with the old structure.

The resolution of these breakdowns lies simply in creating measurable and reportable accountabilities in regard to the qualities being pursued and in supporting the system in making those changes.

Innovation and creativity occur where information from the chaotic "external world" meets the structured information of the "internal world." Creativity is the process of making new meanings in the combining of these two domains.

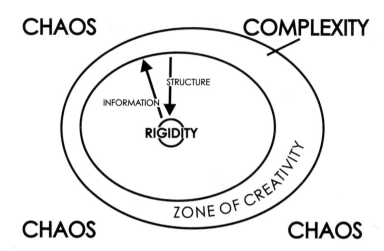

standing is that there is a design or structure that is the source of creativity, just as there is for production; these designs or structures need not conflict with each other.

Every human being is capable of creativity. Our corporations suppress the creativity inherent in people and it's an invitation to problems: One of the biggest problems is a reduction in productivity. The capacity for creativity of every corporation is beyond that of the individuals within it. The problem is that our lack of understanding of systems, combined with the mechanisms of control, has created a monster that swallows the vast majority of attempts at creative expression. Eventually, people become so resigned as a result of suppression that they no longer try. It's easy to see that a design that releases this potential pays immediate rewards.

It is the match between intention and how we organize that produces results.

Japan's Sony and the USA's Merck and 3M are among the few companies renowned world-wide for their innovation. Each company carries an extensive portfolio of new product creation. These companies have intentionally developed their ability to create new products and have designed ways to continually measure that ability. We know them as leaders because they both organize themselves to be innovative and let themselves be known for innovation.

Many companies would like to be known as innovators, but their invested time and money are ineffectual in that pursuit. Even more companies are looking for fame as leading innovators, but are inauthentic about their stated intentions. In truth they actually direct little time, money or attention in that direction. The former type of company can transform its intentions into success by understanding the nature of innovation. The latter might make a move toward authenticity when it better understands the phenomenon it says it wants.

The distinctions that have been made thus far in the areas of learning and intelligence will be cornerstones for the work ahead on innovation, creativity and flexibility. Even though flexibility seems a little less sexy than innovation and creativity, it is a useful place to start because it moves us away from the perspective of solving our innovation problems through locating a sufficient number of creative people. When we consider flexibility, it's easy to see that although individuals in a corporation may be lacking in the area, flexibility is much more of an organizational phenomenon than an individual one. People's lack of flexibility in a corporation has much more to do with the power structures, controls and inaccessibility to information and responsibility in the corporation, than it does with personal idiosyncrasies.

Our consulting group is repeatedly approached by executives whose companies have undertaken TQM initiatives in the last few years.

The common theme in their statements is that the initiative had an exciting and promising beginning but now has little life and is not much more than a bureaucratic burden. They wonder how it happened and what can be done.

The CEO of a government-financed education center in Australia was traveling around the world in search of answers to the question, "Why do all our initiatives for quality begin to lose effectiveness in the second year?"

When our paths crossed, my response to his question was that anything can be started with enthusiasm and that the initial interest comes from both new ideas and action.

The problem is that not only is action seductive, but we get pulled in even more because of business's focus on results. Once drawn in, we fail to take the necessary time prior to the inception of the initiative to develop an understanding of the process. We also neglect the cultivation of ways to perpetuate the development of that understanding.

Strangely enough, one of the worst fates of such a program is immediate success. Everyone thinks that they understand what is being initiated and that all there is to do is to put it to work.

Try this test if you think you don't fit the description: Write down the main principles of a quality program or any other program that your corporation is currently pursuing. Next make a note of the success of your efforts in each of the principles. Then refer to the source of your theory or approach to see how many items you have right.

My experience has been that most people miss many of the points and that even fewer of these principles are actually operational within people's corporations.

Worse than that—even fewer are being authentically pursued.

FLEXIBILITY

In order to be able to understand "flexibility," we must begin by looking at the conditions of survival, growth and success within which our corporation must operate effectively. Theories from the world of evolutionary biology and ecology offer interesting perspectives that allow us to see a corporation as a co-evolving system within a larger complex system and to see that this system, as a whole, is also an adaptive system. Although some of the system's elements are physical or material, the system as a whole is complex and adaptive.

The precondition for flexibility is an environment of constant exchange—getting what is needed and giving back what is needed.

The very nature of a corporation is to generate the actions that will acquire from the ecology whatever is necessary to continue its existence. At the same time, something of value must be returned to the ecology. What is critical to see in this illustration is the robust dynamics of the entire system. This self-organizing complex exchange evolves constantly and it does not occur in a linear, back-and-forth direction. The exchange includes not only physical material but also a rich variety of information.

THE MATRIX OF FLEXIBILITY

Our operational definition of flexibility is *"the capacity for a variety of responses and the speed of changes in response to both similar and different circumstances."* Flexibility refers to the variety of actions that can be taken in the face of identical circumstances, as well as the variety of circumstances for which there is at least one possible response. The tests include:

- For any one circumstance, what variety of actions can be employed?
- For any one circumstance, what variety of responses can produce the (same) desired result?

Coupling refers to the varying ability to form complex systems by combining flexibility and the cohesiveness of attachment.

Tight coupling refers to a condition in which the identities of the elements become so closely connected that they may require each other to survive or may even be seen as one entity.

Loose coupling refers to a condition in which the identities of the elements remain clearly distinguished and interact with each other with a great deal of choice or flexibility based on convenience and circumstances. After interaction they may separate or even cease to interact again.

The loosest coupling is one in which the "choice" of whether to interact or not is unpredictable, but recurrent.

- For how many circumstances can a single action or process produce a single (same) result?
- For how many circumstances can a single action or process be called upon?
- How many unique combinations of actions (complex processes, behaviors) can be created from the individual elements that will result in an increase of any of the above measures?
- How long does it take to switch from one action, process, or behavior to another?
- How much energy is required to make such a switch?
- How quickly can the choice to change from one action or behavior to another be made?

The above matrix is useful when exploring an organization's "core competencies" (a distinction developed by Hamel and Prahalad—see *Harvard Business Review,* May–June 1990), that is, those capabilities most amenable to combination, rapid change, and the widest variety of applications most likely to contribute to a corporation's flexibility. The greatest possibility is available through the "core competencies" that are capable of combining into complex systems and those that are capable of *coupling* with other complex systems. This kind of flexibility provides the greatest value for survival and growth.

STRUCTURES FOR FLEXIBILITY

Flexibility emerges out of a structure. Specifically, it emerges out of a complex adaptive organization that can be enhanced or inhibited by design. The elements of this design and structure are:

- *boundaries* intentionally created that are meant to be temporary and changed regularly
- *accountabilities* for structures that are outside those structures and therefore only have a pragmatic interest in their continuation
- *communication structures* to cross boundaries that come into existence with every creation of a boundary, as well as the ability to demand such communication outside the structure
- *measures* of speed of change in relationship to registered or perceived changes in circumstances
- *practices* of variations and *practices* of changes to those variations

- *continual simplification* (measured) of processes in conjunction with an increasing variety of circumstances that they can handle and results that they can produce (the rule of complexity, which says that rich variety can be produced from a few simple factors)
- *mechanisms of feedback* that are increasingly rapid and designed to discover changes in the environment

The principle behind the above structures is to move away from small parceled activities that are rigid in application, lack flexibility as to order and demand detailed control; and to move toward processes that can be loosely applied, carried out in a variety of sequences and demand a profound understanding of a few simple principles. Most corporations still have processes parceled at just the wrong size for complexity. They are generally formulated as parts that are large enough to develop rigid structures but not large enough to be independently self-sustaining.

If they were smaller they would have the flexibility to combine for effective complexity. If they were larger, they could be complex intelligent systems in their own right. Instead, we have broken them down in our attempts to make them simple linear systems and lost the best of both worlds!

Unipart has undertaken a program of intensive education and continual change in work processes, which has transformed production facilities that "the City" recommended be scrapped. It is now one of the best manufacturing facilities in the UK.

It has also ushered itself into the top 10 companies in the UK regarding profitability. And all of this in the space of five years.

The later stages of Unipart's accomplishment were made possible through creating teams and "cell" approaches. Even though teamwork and personal factors are usually given most of the credit for Unipart's success, there may be other more important factors at work that are going unnoticed.

It may be more advantageous to look at the dynamics of how processes are created and interfaced. A process can become more effective as a self-organizing unit if its boundaries are either decreased or made more complex, thereby creating a more favorable size for developing flexibility.

The boundaries of teams and processes will reorganize over time as the demands for flexibility increase as a result of interaction with other processes.

INNOVATION

Innovation is a matter of design. As with intelligence, learning and flexibility, the most effective perspective from which to look at innovation is in the context of a company as a self-organizing, self-maintaining entity living in an environment that for the most part embodies those qualities itself. Every corporation already has some innovative capacity and is exercising at least some of that capacity. Corporations that are known for their innovation are specifically designed to create occasions for innovation and support innovative activities. They include reward systems, communication practices, investment, blending people and ideas and appropriate reporting structures.

In corporations not specifically designed for innovation, the innovative capacity is mostly displayed by individuals who are sufficiently powerful and competent to get their ideas accepted. Given the lack of design to support such activity, the relative organizational innovative expression in such corporations is quite low.

A construction company in the offshore oil platform industry was trying to set up an "initiative for innovation." Our consulting group was brought in to facilitate the process.

We began coaching a self-selected team on the processes of innovation. The team chose to focus on piping as an important area of productivity.

The team was allowed to develop approaches of its own at the level of theory only. The team designed and articulated a very simple theory that was mentioned (not even in a formal presentation) to the steering committee. Its idea was dismissed as insignificant.

However, the team was allowed to continue, based on the commitment to empowering the process of innovation.

The team's simple theory, "Think pack order" (that is, from start to finish of the process continuously think about testable packages of work) was further developed and put into practice. It reduced costs by over 25% in its first application, which was only partial because the theory was applied in mid-job.

This simple theory has produced even higher rates of savings ever since.

Encouragement of group communication between people who ordinarily do not communicate and group thinking time, for those not normally expected to create theory, created the breakthrough.

INNOVATION IS A FUNCTION OF COMMUNICATION

Organizational innovative capacity is a function of communication for the purpose of innovation. If innovation is viewed as an individual phenomenon and the corporation wants innovation, then it must design practices that encourage and support that. This is difficult because, as an individual activity, the pursuit of innovation is risky and it may disrupt production, service and image.

The management and engineers in companies looking for innovation very frequently express a fear about the possibility of people doing things that will mess up the system and as a result they themselves stop the processes initiated for developing innovative ability. Those few who have managed to develop a level of trust with the "powers that be" are entrusted with innovative efforts and all other efforts are suppressed. The vast potential for innovation available through a group of people actively engaging in a co-operative, productive venture thereby remains untapped.

Innovation occurs only where there are complex intelligent systems operating.

Innovation is an intentional activity. Our concern is not to develop the ability to make an accurate assessment of innovation after the fact but rather to enhance our ability to develop the capability itself and the results that will follow. Our operational definition of innovation is *"that activity which results in a change that has usefulness beyond a current application and that alters the ability of the system as a whole."* Innovation increases the flexibility, complexity, or computational ability of the larger system.

Innovation is a creative act that is not merely an adaptation to circumstances but is an independently initiated activity that generates novelty with respect to pragmatic concerns. Novelty refers to something new, something that has not been thought or done before, or something that is not merely an extension of the past. Innovation takes existing circumstances and redefines and utilizes them in novel ways, thereby altering the capability of the larger system. It is this pragmatic element that distinguishes innovation from other forms of creativity.

ORGANIZING FOR INNOVATION

Innovation requires designated time and space.

We limit the possibility of innovation with our concern for immediate costs and risks. To realize the benefits of innovative thinking, the system must provide an opportunity for experimentation and some minimum protected time for it to prove itself. While much of the innovative process occurs in thinking and dialogue, an innovation must be given sufficient protected time and attention for its gestation into practical terms and its integration into the whole in order to test its contribution and survivability. Without this integration, novelty and successful experimentation will die out, or remain isolated from the whole.

At a minimum level innovation is a continual improvement in processes, products, or services. At a maximum level innovation will lead to surprising new applications of existing processes, products, or services as well as brand new products, or ways of doing things. The continuous effort required for maximum innovation will not occur without the development of pragmatic ways of recording and measuring innovation so that continual intelligence, learning and innovation can be applied to the area of innovation itself.

To organize for innovation, disturbances must be designed into the regular processes of the corporation. Some of these disturbances might be:

- challenges that cross boundaries
- overlapping accountabilities
- planned redundancy with random factors injected
- artificial barriers designed into normal activities
- blending of ideas and people
- dialogue managed in ways that create diversity
- visual displays that invite different thinking or new participation
- exploration of apparently unrelated companies
- academic input from seemingly unrelated fields

If integrated as standard processes within a company, these ways of organizing will allow for an ongoing development of the innovative capacity. An investment in time, equipment, and money will be required. For maximum effectiveness the investment must be allocated without requirement of *individual* justification through results. The allocation must be accompanied by policies and practices that ensure that the overall investment in innovation is producing adequate results.

CREATIVITY

Much of the groundwork has been laid in order to distinguish creativity as an organizational phenomenon. Pathways have been cleared leading us towards new ways of thinking and approaching the issue and away from the perspective of looking at the caliber of creativity in the individuals of a corporation. Individual creativity aside, it is easy to see that groups, teams and corporations all have varying degrees of creativity. An investigation reveals there is no "group mind" or specific location of that creativity, so where is it occurring and where does it come from?

Creativity is an emergent phenomenon.

Creativity may arise as an emergent phenomenon—that is, it may be one of those phenomena that result from a complex interplay of other phenomena (arising from the interplay itself). A sufficient variety of connections and an appropriate design structure, all occurring at the same time, produce an emergent phenomenon. Other examples of emergent phenomena are language, marketplaces, law, relationship and love.

In a group or team, creativity occurs in dialogue itself. An individual may have originated and be identified with a creative idea. Yet, if an idea is a group creation, it is the result of the interplay of the participants, both for or against the idea. Each individual has contributed to the thinking, the creative process and the creation itself in ways that are not always obvious. We've all been in a situation where, at some point, an unforeseen resolution occurred as a result of dialogue between individuals.

A group of biologists, intent on displaying the theory of emergent properties as a phenomenon of complexity, developed a computer program that simulates the process. In the program, a simple set of principles causes lights to turn on and off. When the number of connections is low, the screens rap-

---

Our consulting group was working with the molecular biologists in the labs of a chemical company as they were pioneering a project that would put them into the bio-technology market.

The creative level of each individual researcher in the venture was very high, but they frequently failed to function effectively together to make decisions about creative matters. Our challenge was to ensure that the creative level of the division as a whole was high.

Simple yet critical problems remained unresolved: Which individual research project would receive resources? When was it appropriate to abandon a project? When was it appropriate to initiate completely new areas of research and testing methods?

The problem wasn't that each person didn't have ideas about how to resolve these issues.

Nor was it about the arguments for or against one's own or others' opinions.

The problem was that the group dealt with the individual ideas one at a time and the solution always seemed to be one that had existed in one of their minds before the meeting had started. Nothing was created *by the group as a group.*

The time it takes to arrive at a creative solution is often a function of how long it takes people to express their ideas and then leave behind what they *already* know.

They began to reach solutions when we were able to get across the idea that what constituted a successful creative meeting was the creation of ideas not in existence prior to the meeting and where meeting practices were established that prompted that to happen.

idly go either completely light or dark and stay that way. If the number of connections is high, the screen continues to flash random patterns and never settles down. But if the number of connections is at a "middle ground," beyond a threshold point but not far beyond it, the computer creates patterns that repeat with enough variety to be entertaining, yet never settle into a fixed pattern or spill over into chaos. The program displays a phenomenon similar to creativity. In fact, the patterns generated by these programs are not always discernible as having been computer generated and are often sold as art.

THE BRAIN'S DESIGN FOR CREATIVITY IS LOOSE CONNECTIONS PLUS REDUNDANCY

Another illustration of creativity as an emergent phenomenon is the intelligence and creativity of the brain that is created by numerous varying connections between cells. Intelligence or "ideas" cannot be found in the cells themselves. All that exists is a limited variety of simple elements connected by a design that operates by means of a fairly limited "grammar." The brain's design structure includes a demand for redundancy, a demand for convergence and numerous unreliable system connections with many individual failures built in. It is here that the rich patterns of thought are created. The same is true of language. A simple grammar and a few letters (sounds) create an infinite variety of meaningful sentences. There is enormous redundancy and many possible misunderstandings. These same principles are being used to create new drugs, efficient computer programs and more productive production lines.

THE BARREN CORPORATION CASE

By imagining an organizational situation in which there is no more than the minimum individual creativity that goes with being human, we create a backdrop against which it is easy to illustrate and watch the emergence of a greater creativity. Further, by being able to visualize this situation, any situation that we are confronted with in reality will offer an increased likelihood of success. Imagine a "barren corporation"—a corporation with minimal creativity among its individual members. Each individual has ordinary intelligence and information, and ability to carry out activities in a co-ordinated manner. Each is limited to his or her own approach in each activity and never exhibits novelty in that approach. Each has her or his own unique knowledge. Each has a limited set of information and feedback to work with. Also, each individual is prone to random influences and makes mistakes. Now let's begin to work with the scenario—by merely increasing the connections between the individuals, creativity will begin to occur. By designing those communication pathways so that they favor certain kinds of communication over others, creativity will increase even further.

As long as a system is complex (any corporation producing goods and/or services is a complex system), there are factors operating within the system that are beyond the understanding and knowledge of any individual in the system. Any increase in communication between the individuals within the system will increase their knowledge, increase the richness of the content and demand creativity.

"Demand" emerges as a result of ambiguity and uncertainty caused by information being added which the original design did not require. In the resolution of that ambiguity, something new and unpredictable will occur. Creativity occurs when resolution is required and when paradox and ambiguity are present. To be able to assess accurately what kind of creativity is needed for a situation gives one no power in the matter; power lies in being able to create the conditions in which creativity occurs.

Fundamental design principles combine ambiguity with redundancy.

By designing communication pathways, by arranging meetings between individuals and groups, and by offering favorable facilitation, novelty can be expected to increase exponentially. As a result, creativity will also be on an exponential rise. It is important to remember that creativity requires a great deal of redundancy.

To put into operation what has been learned so far in the domains of flexibility, innovation and creativity, it is necessary to introduce the corresponding principles and establish appropriate accountabilities and reporting systems in your corporation.

Next, begin to implement the new designs, structures, and practices that are consistent with those principles. What you will encounter as you try to implement new designs will be justifications for why they won't work. This kind of conversation is a "red flag" indicating that people do not understand the principles.

Meeting the situation with an increase in education might move the initiative forward, but a more effective response would be to insist that management put into practice its accountability for flexibility, innovation and creativity in order to discover what is possible right in the midst of action.

As the process unfolds what will become obvious is that our previously established theories and practices in these areas are off track for the simple reason that creating an emergence of flexibility, innovation and creativity is not consistent with the production machine of the past.

If creativity is allowed to occur, structures must be in place that demand certain forms, limits, and "logics" be followed that will prevent unworkable ideas from getting too far. These limits should appear as "hurdles" rather than prescribed controls, so that creativity is not stifled too early. The creative process must allow error and useless ideas to occur if something useful is to emerge. It is the balance between limitation and freedom that is the constant challenge. There is no guarantee that novelty or creativity will produce positive results each time, therefore complexity theory has much to offer as we look for a starting point for creativity.

It is easy to see why there is such a lack of creativity in most corporations; typically they are organized to prevent disruption to the systems of production and regulate resource wastage. Organizational design has been refined to such a level that there is no longer room for creativity. By seeing that we are organized *against* creativity, we have a place to begin to change these conditions so that they are more favorable—or we can leave them as they are and be satisfied with basic production.

Dialogue is conversation that creates something new.

To be creative, an organization must be structured to promote dialogue aimed at and capable of producing something that was not in the mind of any individual participant prior to the dialogue. Our operational definition of dialogue is *"communication that has as its intention the creation of information that has a degree of novelty."* The dialogue may be oriented toward a practical level or the highest level of abstraction, but it must have novelty as its main intention. Other key elements for developing dialogue are use of analogy, promoting informal conversation among small groups with diverse areas of expertise, and solving problems that demand creative thinking.

ORGANIZING FOR INTELLIGENCE

Organizing for intelligence, organizing for learning, organizing for innovation, and organizing for flexibility are not only complementary but often virtually the same. The payoff is generally immediate and significant. The level of development within the personnel of a corporation as well as the corporation itself is a reflection of our ability to distinguish clearly processes for innovation and processes for production, combined with our ability to weave one into the other.

Although innovation and production are distinct, they do not function well when separated from one another at an operational level. Creativity divorced from production is distanced from the tests of reality. Production divorced from creativity becomes stale and lifeless and ceases to be adaptive. We do not learn to act, but act to learn. It is the balance of both creativity and production within an individual, within an operation and within the company as a whole that ensures a robust, healthy entity, capable of continued success within a complex, ever-changing environment.

QUESTIONS FOR THIS CHAPTER:

- Does your corporation have a specific commitment to creativity, innovation and flexibility?
- If so, how is it expressed? How is it measured? What specific structures, systems and practices are effectively in place to nourish that commitment?
- If surveyed, would your employees report that they are included in efforts at creativity, innovation and flexibility? Would they say that these qualities are requested of them and adequately supported?
- Are you willing to take the risks of the pursuit of creativity, innovation, and flexibility at the organizational level? What are your fears and concerns in the matter? What controls do you have to limit the risk? Are they also seriously limiting the possibility?
- What is your belief about the ability and willingness of the whole corporation to engage in activities consistent with creativity, innovation and flexibility?
- What specific amount of your resources is dedicated to attempts at creativity and innovation? (This includes efforts that have failed.) What is the return you are getting for that investment, if you are making one?
- If you aren't making such an investment, how do you expect creativity and innovation to flourish?

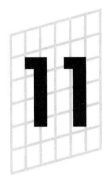

11 Exploring Possibility

"I am committed to the permanent possibility of someone having a better idea."
RICHARD RORTY

Prelude

What is possible? When asked this question, we tend to look immediately at our recent history and then begin to consider what's likely, what's probable and what's predictable. We consider the options that we might pursue and consider the most likely scenarios. We then proceed by extending the past into the future. The question "What is possible?" is a question about the future, yet it is not about prediction. It is about the present and our capacity for imagination and development.

What's possible is anchored in the past and in some way is an extension of the past, but what's possible is not determined by our understanding of the past, present, or future. Our interpretations of what's possible are staggeringly small compared to the space of possibility. Only a handful of people in the generations before us have managed to come close to imagining what we now take for granted. Even after people were told about these possibilities, very few were actually able to imagine them. Yet these once unimaginable things have become an integral part of our lives.

The field of possibility is so vast that we cannot begin to explore it all. Our greatest challenge will be to explore it with others, in dialogue, so that we can begin to move beyond the historical limits of our current interpretations. The level of development in the language abilities of our companies, teams and groups does not come close to what is needed for engaging in satisfying and productive conversation. Yet our future depends on that ability.

THE NATURE OF POSSIBILITY

In one breath we say "anything is possible" and by the next breath we've resumed living a life of no possibility. Almost without exception, executives and leaders recognize creativity as the portal to success and, at the same time, design their corporations so that they obstruct exploring possibility. Most corporations don't even provide a place in which to say "anything is possible," let alone provide avenues for pursuing actions consistent with even a small part of that expression.

Everything is not possible but possibility is larger than we can fully explore.

"Anything" is not possible. There are limits to what can happen in the world. Physics declares certain things not possible in its theories about a *cone of light*. These theories state that by definition information cannot travel faster than the speed of light and that a result cannot be caused faster than the time it takes the information to go from the "cause" to the affected entity. Theories in biology and evolution describe how what occurs is limited by its relationship to past development. While all these fields have vast unexplored possibility, they also instruct us in ways of thinking about the limits of possibility which are far beyond our experience. The parameters of what is not possible are determined by design. Design refers to the combination of factors that make an entity what it is and not anything else. The rules of relationship, grammar and historical accident and the interplay of all of these give identity and provide the platform from which future possibility will be realized.

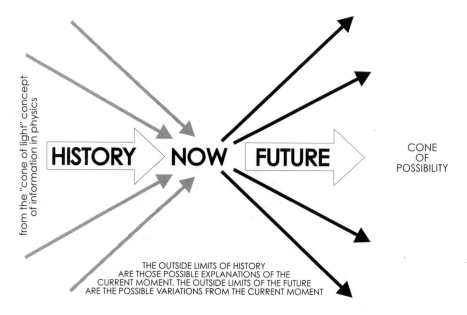

from the "cone of light" concept of information in physics

HISTORY > NOW > FUTURE >

CONE OF POSSIBILITY

THE OUTSIDE LIMITS OF HISTORY ARE THOSE POSSIBLE EXPLANATIONS OF THE CURRENT MOMENT. THE OUTSIDE LIMITS OF THE FUTURE ARE THE POSSIBLE VARIATIONS FROM THE CURRENT MOMENT

LOCATING POSSIBILITY

Human beings have the capacity for exploring possibility. The design of our corporations can vastly expand this capacity. To be fully human we must spend at least some time and energy on the exploration of the space of possibility; not only for ourselves, but for larger concerns. Not to do so leaves one at best unbearably boring and at worst seriously at odds with the world. When asked about their lives, criminals, members of youth gangs and other "in-trouble" people disclose that they see no possibility for their own lives and express a deep resignation about their future. They find no reason not to engage in acts that result in terrible consequences for both their own lives and the lives of others.

Possibility exists in language—not in physical reality.

The world of "anything is possible" resides in our thinking, language and imagery. Here we can play freely with thought worlds, creative dialogues and imaginary constructs. To the extent that we can clearly distinguish the domain of thinking and speaking from the domain of action, we are free to explore possibility. To the extent that we shy away from such exploration, we reveal that we have not clearly distinguished between the world of thought and language and the world of action. The basis of creative thought and a prerequisite for the continual exploration of possibility can be found in our capacity to engage freely in thought experiments, flights of

A particular individual's view of what's possible may be larger than that of some community *of which he or she is not a part*. However, if that individual is part of the community, the community view of possibility will include theirs and will always be larger than the individual view. If dialogue occurs, the community view will continually expand and be larger than the "sum" of individual views.

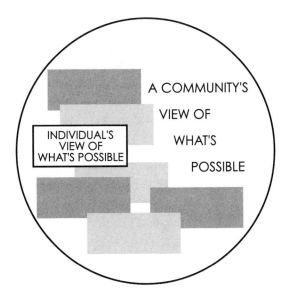

fancy and poetry. A part of this capacity is the knowledge that one need not act on one's thoughts.

Where does the ability to explore possibility reside in a corporation? It is insufficient to say that it resides in the individuals of the corporation, even though the act of exploring the space of possibility for the corporation includes individual effort. It is insufficient because even though individuals can be creative on their own, what can be created by effective groups, teams and communities far exceeds any individual efforts.

Reversing the well-known saying, "the whole is more than the sum of its parts," offers us a fresh perspective on the insight that it is trying to illuminate. "The whole will be reduced to less than itself, when reduced to parts." The transposed version brings to our attention the fact that we tend to look at things using a reductionist model in which things are made up of parts. The whole loses all its (living) qualities when reduced to parts. Complexity theory tells us that the whole is a phenomenon that has emerged from a rich and vast interplay of forces, or information with a simple set of principles. The whole is a complex phenomenon; reducing that whole to detailed analysis, even specific instances of the whole, will not even begin to reveal the complex phenomenon that exists.

The field of possibilities for a corporation is so vast that it lies far beyond the power of that corporation to explore. Even more, such a quest is far be-

A small, rapidly growing computer manufacturer was discovering that its current organizational form and practices couldn't keep pace with the changing demands of the marketplace.

Initially, the loosely formed organization had more flexibility and was able to resolve its problems in dialogue that occurred spontaneously between small groups of people. But at one point in their expansion, more space was needed and it was necessary for the company to move into three separate buildings.

Three distinct divisions were created—administration, sales and research—each in its respective building. Each division began to develop its own culture, and communication between them broke down.

The company's product began creating possibility faster than the company could handle it and, in search of a solution, teams were created representing each of the divisions. The research people proposed research-oriented solutions, the sales people offered sales-oriented solutions and the administrative people proposed solutions from their perspective.

The impasse was resolved by having each division work toward a resolution using another division's point of view. Solutions were found, and work began to keep pace with the possibilities of the marketplace again.

yond the power of an individual mind. A corporation has more information contained within it and more information potential than any individual can imagine, let alone tap. The field of possibility for a corporation is limited by its history, its design, and the design of the social environment(s) in which it finds itself.

If you designate a team which is comprised of one individual from each of the different divisions of a corporation and you ask the team to transform the business, the solutions that each individual proposes will be those that reflect the interests and understanding of each person's respective division or specialty. It is not until each member of the team begins to understand the other's historically based perspective and engages in dialogue that transcends everyone's own individual understanding that team members can begin to approach the challenge differently.

Our imaginations are limited by our experience and understanding. The practical field of possibility, available to most, is not "anything," but what is given by our history, which limits the next step in development. When we have access to our history but are not bound by it in our thinking, then we can be active agents in creating the future of our corporations and our industries.

Design for possibility is a design that calls forth dialogue.

The ability to explore the space of possibility can be found in a corporation's ability to engage in dialogue. Irrespective of its many forms, dialogue's sole purpose is to create something that has not previously been thought by any individual prior to the dialogue. Its purpose is not to share information but to create information, to explore *information potential* beyond what exists as "facts" and to let go of, or recombine, what is already known for what might be known.

As with any living organism, the ability to explore the space of possibility is distributed throughout the corporation (inclusive of all of its parts and operations). It *emerges* from *that distributed organization* rather than being located in some, or even many, of its parts. The exploration of possibility occurs within the complex design of all the operations in all of their various locations. The free, rich interplay of information and communication within the redundant structures of operational practices is the source of the exploration of possibility.

Synectics, a little known science, presents methods of approaching challenges through the utilization of creative thinking, analogy and informal conversation within a small group of individuals of diverse experience and expertise. Design elements that encourage synectic activity also increase the capacity to explore possibility. Design elements that limit the expression of actions keep evolution at a developmental level and maximize the chances for continuation of the current identity. Even though communicative (synectic) activity may be favored in various locations within the corporation, those engaged in the activity want access to the knowledge of the corporation, which can only be accomplished through the activity itself. In practice, this communicative activity must engage many levels, and these levels must vary from time to time to keep the information rich and alive.

The need for free play in dialogue is not to be confused with the committed conversations of accountability. Each kind of communication must be clearly distinguished: communication for possibility, communication for production, and communication for developing knowledge. The intentions, structures and practices that accompany each of these distinct types of communication will vary according to their purposes. The collapse of these distinctions is partially responsible for the hierarchical and bureaucratic limitations that have been placed on the generation of possibility. This same collapse in distinctions fosters statements like, "But you can't just let anybody talk to anybody about anything!" You can if it is about possibility. You cannot if it is about accountability and results.

A major chemical company, like so many other organizations, was not able to develop new processes and get them into operation fast enough to keep a substantial market share through its new products.

Our consulting firm was invited into the company to explore possible solutions. We began our work with a series of interviews and meetings.

Our conversations revealed that the functional departments in the company did not allow communications to take place between the various levels in those functions. Flattening the management structures had not changed the way work was organized and, worse, it did not change the way communication was conducted. Process development speed did not increase.

The way the executives spoke about the company's problems revealed their lack of ability to distinguish between conversations regarding spending decisions, conversations regarding production efforts and conversations for the development of possibility. (Ask yourself if you are clear about these distinctions.)

During the process of distinguishing the different kinds of communication, the executives involved saw that they could retain their functional control over resource allocation and that there was no need to limit the corporation by controlling other types of conversations.

The practices that had developed as a means of protection also dramatically affected unrelated areas. These areas were freed by clearly distinguishing the different types of conversation. Not hindered by unnecessary limitations, the process of development was unleashed and accelerated dramatically.

POSSIBILITY AND IDENTITY

A corporation has an identity, but that identity is not important to it in the way that an identity is important to an individual. A corporation exhibits no interest in the design of its identity. Many of the individuals within corporations have lost sight of this. In fact, most directors and executives are as attached to a specific corporate identity as they are to their own identity. (Both conditions are a threat to success.)

Corporations provide a multi-directional flow of value.

The purpose of corporations is to provide both a flow of value to their organizers and a flow of value to the community through the marketplaces of products, services and employment. There is greater concern for continuous flow of value than there is for whether or not what is valued changes. When the flow of value ceases, the entity will no longer survive.

It is the arrival of the fittest that is most important.

The space of possibility is determined by history and environment. Every entity is constantly *becoming* something; that is, every entity is in a process of realizing some particular possibility in its space of possibilities. Each actualization opens the door for some new possibilities and at the same time closes others. *Survival of the fittest* can only follow the *arrival of the fittest*. *Arrival* is a matter of creativity and innovation from experimentation, chance and accident. *Arrival* is not merely random for it is influenced by design and grammar. *Survival* follows because it fits with the current environment and has adaptability, or robustness in future environments.

The condition of hill climbing is easily seen through a sports analogy. Like all sports, the game of tennis has been transformed over the years. Topspin shots were not seen on the hard courts in the '60s, so none of the veterans or older players have developed these strokes.

When veterans are across the net from a younger generation of players and in trouble, we often attribute it to age. Many times, there is a much stronger factor at work.

Older players have crafted a certain set of strokes that have secured wins for them. As young competitors' games improve and include new strokes (complexity increases), seasoned players continue to practice strokes that they have already mastered—ones they know they can rely on. But using them now to achieve a victory requires more struggle and effort.

Time spent practicing new strokes would cause the performance of older players to suffer and defeat would follow.

A trip "downhill" would be a must before a player could begin winning again using the new strokes. And of course, there is the risk of not being able to come out on top using your new game. The reluctance to go "back downhill" is obvious in this case. (Bjorn Borg has spent the "downhill time" and is now a serve and volley player in the veterans' circuit with impressive results.)

The space of possibility is so vast that the challenge is not to search for the right space to explore but to explore the possibility that we are presented with in an energy efficient way. Energy efficiency emerges with a balance between redundancy and creativity, not through calculation or reduction of input. Sufficient allowance must be made for wide-ranging unpredictable explorations, while maintaining a design that will produce positive results. This will be unleashed through thinking and theory rather than economic balance. The design principles that accomplish this are based on complexity and patterns rather than linearity and analysis of detail.

Success at hill climbing can be fatal to further development of possibility.

There is a natural tendency for people and corporations to pursue specialization and become ever more efficient at what is already being done. This tendency, based on our identity, is the very thing that will prevent exploration of the space of possibility. Our natural inclination is to resist going backwards when in many instances that's what is necessary in order to explore the space of possibility. If possibility is seen as a landscape and specialization as a mountain, then the higher one climbs toward the top of that specialization, the more one has to give up to explore new possibilities. What has to be given up is reward, competence and one's own identity. The summit of any mountain has limited territory to explore, hence it has the least possibility. It is useful to locate where one is in relation to the summit of one's mountain and then generate an appropriate strategy of exploration. If we can see our location clearly, we will be able to expand the effectiveness of exploration.

For anyone projecting into the future, it is easy to see that the *creation and utilization of information* towers above all else. More profitable challenges lie there than in production, sales, or even finance. Because the major input, activity and output of a corporation is information, our interests should be invested in discovering the most effective way to access that wealth of information.

Zen koans are examples of concise, ambiguous expressions creating a great deal of information.

Present yourself with one of the most famous koans, "What is the sound of one hand clapping?" Notice how the search for an appropriate response leads through a field of possibility to the creation of a great deal of very creative thinking.

Information that calls forth thinking and dialogue and requires effort to "unpack" or resolve is rich in information value.

Organizational input, action and output are information.

The value of information is measurable. At one end of the spectrum, information carries with it complete predictability. For instance, if you receive a photocopy of a letter that you have already read, the photocopy carries no information value. Or if you know exactly what I am going to say next, what I say will have no information value.

At the other end of the spectrum, information carries almost total surprise, unpredictability, uniqueness, and little recognizable form or pattern (no possibility of compression). Each expression is a moment of surprise. Information carries maximum value just before the point of total randomness. At this point a great deal of ambiguity exists, a great deal of possibility is present, and it is resolved only when the whole is present. Information that is not fully understood but provides insight or increased understanding carries the highest information value. Maximum information value emerges by creating designs and practices that keep us at the end of the spectrum closest to ambiguity.

The center of the diagram, which is a location in possibility not a specific location in space, represents an area in which almost everything is predictable and communication is mostly redundant. When things are working at the center, the only message we get from such a point is the same message over and over again. When things are not working, we get a simple message

The space of possibility is a constantly moving zone where information exceeds the capacity of current structures. The zone begins at the edges of structural capacity and extends to where the excess information will almost spill the organization into permanent chaos and potential destruction.

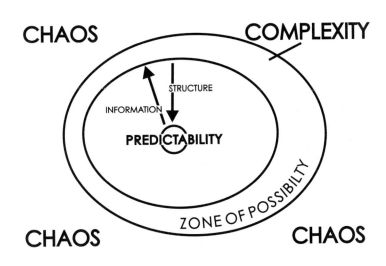

such as "stop" or "broken." The outer edge of the circle represents an area in which little is predictable but there is much to be explored, learned and created. At this outer edge the only thing that can be produced is new understanding, insight and knowledge. Only as we develop the information gained, provide structure, and reduce the information content (surprise) can we move it into usable production information. We must continually balance the dynamics of this process.

The *cone of light* diagram (at the beginning of the chapter) illustrates how possibility is related to information and time. As distance from the present moment increases, the amount of information possible and variation in actions and results also increases. The *complexity of information* diagram (page 149) illustrates the same phenomenon. In this representation, information value and possibility are equivalent and distance from the known and predictable is the key factor. One of the most challenging and powerful aspects of the *complexity of information* diagram is that it removes the field of possibility from time.

THE PLACE OF VISION

The concept of vision is our organizational attempt to fill the space of possibility. Most visions suffer from a lack of understanding possibility and the future. Most people see the future as a place to get to and live as though the future is waiting out there in front of us with an existence of its own. In these limited linear models of the universe and time, a vision as a goal makes perfect sense. At some level we all know that the future will not unfold in the way that we are imagining it and that a vision will not be accomplished as stated. But even so, there must be some value inherent in having a vision.

Exploring what's possible opens possibility. Codifying what's possible closes possibility.

Exploring what's possible and engaging in the thinking, dialogues, and actions that develop those possibilities are both of great value. The richness of the representation of the resulting future will depend on the amount of participation and dialogue that has helped create it. Then how we are to describe our future becomes the challenge. A rich representation of that future will be possible and valuable only if it can be expressed in poetic, metaphorical, or abstract terms. If these terms are able to capture the fundamental and enduring values of that vision, then something of power has been created. An expression that keeps a corporation's values bright and clear and at the same time remains abstract and nonrestrictive is a powerful way of keeping a space of possibility open. But even more effective than that, the space of possibility can be kept open by continually engaging in conversations that develop the very space itself.

Most vision statements and other such expressions are designed to motivate people. If these expressions actually carried intentions of including people in the development of the possibility of the future, then we would gain much more. But inherent in intentions to convince or motivate are notions of separateness that are counterproductive to the possibilities of inclusion and participation. To begin to integrate these intentions, we must realize that exploration of the space of possibility is the domain of each and every person. When we realize that people are interested in and capable of exploring possibility, then we will unreservedly include them and gain a wealth of information and creativity. When we recognize that possibility emerges from dialogue and that the broader the dialogue the richer the possibility, then we will have broken through into something exciting that remains alive and flourishing.

To develop dialogue in our corporations that is more aligned with our nature as human beings, we need a new relationship to language. We learned to use language as a way of describing or being functional within the realities of our culture. This is still valid, so replacing it is not the answer. We also need the ability to see language as a means of creating realities beyond those already in existence. We can use language to transform probability analysis into possibility creation, as well as to transform the mere selection of options into creation of opportunities.

The design principle for exploring the space of possibility is to continually move toward information that carries maximum ambiguity. Maximum ambiguity is determined by satisfactory resolution within the time allotted. The boundaries must be continually tested.

One of the reasons we fail to include others in exploring what is possible is that we have not learned the conventions of dialogue that support the creation of possibility in our conversations with others.

Most of us are masters in the domains of argument and assertion. We are brilliant with our analytical abilities and can effortlessly talk about the physical universe as we see it.

Few of us have refined the distinctions of creativity and synectics. We have failed to cultivate the speculative and generative aspects of language with which we can speak about what is not yet manifest in physical reality. We have also failed to develop our listening or our ways of relating to generative dialogue.

The design principle for maximizing realization (productive results) of the space of possibility is to continue to remove the ambiguity from the information until it is predictable and repeatable with very little information value left. It is here that efficient production takes place. It is the constant balancing of moving toward ambiguity and removing ambiguity, in conjunction with developing each, that is the source of maximum survival value to a corporation.

QUESTIONS FOR THIS CHAPTER:

- Does your corporation have a vision statement, and what specific value does it provide to your corporation? What is your evidence that it is providing that value?
- Does the statement of vision generate expanding horizons and remarkable actions?
- What is your corporation becoming in its current course of action?
- What might it become?
- What are the boundaries currently limiting the exploration of the space of possibility in your corporation?
- Consider the current information value in your meetings, reports, and communications; what can be done to maximize information value? What currently has little information value?
- How much organizational time are you investing in exploring the space of possibility in your corporation?

12 Structure

"New Beliefs in an Old House: The overthrow of beliefs is not immediately followed by the overthrow of institutions; rather, the new beliefs live for a long time in the now desolate and eerie house of their predecessors, which they themselves preserve, because of the housing shortage."
NIETZSCHE

"At any given moment in the unfolding of a sequence of patterns, we have a partly defined whole, which has the structure given to it by the patterns that came earlier."
CHRISTOPHER ALEXANDER
THE TIMELESS WAY OF BUILDING

"Community Learning is the key part of the learning process that enables a country to become wealthy. We are wealthy because we work in a society that has developed a culture and a system that supports high and growing productivity."
MAX SINGER
A PASSAGE TO A HUMAN WORLD

Prelude

Visible structures emerge from invisible structures. When we see the beauty, order and functionality of a building, we are looking at its surface structure. When we look beneath the surface, we find structures of steel, electronics and plumbing. When we go one step further and look behind those, we find the structures of design, plans and instruction that made all of that possible. And from an even more refined perspective, we see that there are languages of design, construction and use, which we tend not to think of as structure because we cannot see them. Yet it is these very patterns, information and practices that allow for all the visible and physical structures to occur.

153

During the Industrial Era, the understanding of nonmaterial structures was not considered important. Production appeared to be a physical and material domain. But in the dawn of the Information Era, information is the foundation, rendering the physical merely a result.

To meet current demands, organizational structure must leave behind a focus on specific forms and develop an understanding of the principles of theory, possibility and relationship. Out of these principles will emerge forms appropriate to today's rapidly changing environment.

Structure is at once the most powerful conservative force in human affairs and the most powerful productive force. In both instances structure is usually invisible to us. If our attention had to be diverted to structure, it would draw energy away from our intended actions. Our effectiveness results from our unconscious competence with the human structures that we have created (our intellectual and physical customs, habits and practices) rather than from our individual conscious effort.

It is startling to discover that those in charge of structure (executives and management) are usually incompetent at dealing with structure itself. They are generally incognizant of the design of structure and ineffective at initiating even minor changes to it. And yet, structure is the very source of intelligence and productivity for a corporation. Organizational transformation remains out of our reach until we have become masters in the domain of structure.

To accomplish a breakthrough in our understanding of structure, we will have to expand our view of structure to include linguistic and nonmaterial elements. Structure encompasses unspoken customs and rules. It determines what can be said and what can't. The language that is used to make sense of things (to interpret) is part of the structure. Theories, processes and practices are also included in structure. The organization of machinery as well as the machinery itself are components of structure.

THE INFORMATION NATURE OF THE UNIVERSE

Physics reveals that everything around us is substantially less solid than we think. Your sturdy oak table is a collection of moving particles and has no solid surface from a molecular point of view. Its smooth surface when looked at more closely is, in fact, rough. When looked at even more closely, a "surface" cannot even be found. If we examine the table at a molecular level, we see that the molecules are actually made of smaller particles in constant motion and with even closer observation, we discover that we cannot find a particle. Yet, there is still something there. The whole world appears to be made only of forces, or information—with no substance whatsoever. The development of science has been marked by these increasingly refined levels of understanding, each level going beyond the understanding that can be provided by sensory data, or the "common sense" grounded in that kind of data. When apprehended by an independent agent this progressive movement of "looking below" allowed for better predictions and wider applications, without disturbing the underlying cosmology of a physical universe.

Eventually a transformation to a new cosmology occurred in the sciences. It was a result of scientists thinking about what they were doing. In thinking about science itself, they realized that they were inventing ways of speaking about the world that were affecting how the world occurred for them. This transformation in view has completely altered the way in which the world occurs for us: it has changed from a material world that can be broken into parts, to one of energy and information that emerges from immaterial structures, which in turn create unpredictably rich and varied results—a world of complexity.

The transformation of the thinking of science occurred simultaneously with a transformation in philosophy. Both pointed to the new cosmology that puts information at the center and material structure as a coexistent which is itself dependent on information. Every field of study is currently being transformed by this thinking.

The creation of a new cosmology and the corresponding actions that ensue have influenced every area of human thought and activity. Those working in the fields of study which are transforming to align themselves with these new models are finding that they are able to solve problems and produce results that were either previously impossible, or demanded a more substantial input of energy. In the few fields that remain untouched (i.e. corporations and political parties), the lack of alignment with current thinking and technology is repeatedly felt via increasing energy expenditure for continually decreasing results. In the absence of a renewal of theoretical foundations, we witness either a proliferation of fads or a lack of intellectual and creative activity.

Theories of organization and management not grounded in the current cosmology, or the thinking and methodologies appropriate to that cosmology, are bound to produce increasing frustration and decreasing results. Organizational changes fueled by obsolete theories, such as those occurring in the reorganization of the struggling corporate giants, are bound for failure.

Mechanistic approaches will not produce results that will interact effectively with the new cosmology. Even approaches based on the newest management methodologies will not work if they are forced into structures based on mechanistic thinking.

The structures we have inherited are sufficient for a world organized around mechanistic thinking and material production. They are, however, insufficient for the demands of a world of information. The material world can be managed with little effort by individuals who possess the appropriate information. But even for the management of our material concerns, it is critical that we transform our structures so that they are appropriate to the dimensions of an information world. The shift proves difficult because the structures required for an information world are mainly composed of information; if we are distracted by the material forms of structure, we will fail to see what is occurring.

The executives of a large company in Germany began to educate their management at all levels in these new ways of thinking.

This particular company had been paralyzed by the requirement for decisions to be made at the top. Many decisions were not made at all, or only when it was too late to take effective action.

From the education sessions, teams began to be formed throughout the company. These teams addressed problems of quality, delivery and timeliness and began to produce breakthroughs in all areas.

More importantly, they altered the structures of the corporation and its communication. In the process, the formal hierarchical structure began to loosen its grip and new structures began to be created. However, financial recognition of prior mistakes, plus a broad economic downturn, produced poor results and the initiative began to be reversed at the level of organizational structures.

The executives were pleased that the educational sessions were of value for those in management but they thought themselves beyond the need of personal development or education. However, lack of thorough understanding of the new approaches on the part of the executives killed recent successful initiatives.

When management began to voice its dissatisfaction with a return to "old ways," it occurred to the executives that there were many aspects of the new thinking that they did not share.

The executives empowered the management to take the helm and to continue working with the new structures and the company turned around during the following year.

Grammar and the rules of relationship provide the possibility of meaning.

As we redesign our corporations to meet the needs of the future, it is clear that certain structures will inhibit the realization of our intentions and others will enhance that possibility. A favorable structure will be comprised of grammar rather than physical objects. Information will be the instrument with which we focus our considerations for structure and its design. Concerns relevant to the area of information will be its creation, flow, accessibility, use and maintenance.

Physical and material concerns will be seen as sources of information and will be organized for information purposes, while maintaining their material and productive ability; that is, we will maintain or increase our ability to produce as central to the processes of information. Quantum physics has replaced Newtonian physics in theory but there are still many instances where it is simpler and more effective to use Newtonian approaches. (But you will only know that by considering the challenge from the quantum point of view.)

In the same way, the transformation in thinking that replaces material concerns with information concerns doesn't demand that everything be changed immediately: but to make effective choices, you must be able to consider things from an information perspective. If an information perspective is not taken into account, then the resulting material organization will ignore the potential for information embedded in its processes, and the significant information value lost to you will be realized by competitors.

THE SURFACE STRUCTURE OF PRODUCTION

There exists a social stock of physical components for production and a matching grammar or set of processes for their operation. Operations that produce physical products are ordered in particular ways, that is, you never polish before you grind. The machinery required to do these operations is designed to match these processes and the ways in which we think about work. Capital, information flow, control, and so on are all organized according to the same design. The way in which we organize people is matched to the way we organize for production and the material things that go with it. Our internal organization (our thinking, approaches and expectations) also correspond to that way of organizing. We live in a world given to us by our culture, organized in a particular way. We have organized ourselves (our thinking, feelings and responses) to match that. Our corporations are structured as though people are production "machinery" and we accept this, though mostly unhappily.

The introduction of electric motors was supposed to increase factory productivity dramatically. It wasn't until 20 years after their introduction that productivity began to increase. Why? Because the organization of work flow and the layout of factories didn't change; electric motors were merely a substitute for steam engines in the existing structures. The surrounding structures of production remained unchanged and inhibited the potential of electric motors. (Michael Rothschild, author of "Bionomics," brought this example to my attention.)

The introduction of information-processing circuits (computers, robots and automation) is experiencing a similar and probably more prolonged delay in stepping up productivity. Why? Because we don't understand the importance of structures and therefore attempt to realize the potential of the new productive equipment within the hierarchical and linear structures appropriate to earlier methods of production grounded in physical flows.

Examining support structures is the key to productivity increases.

The existing support structures include: physical objects (such as machinery, computers, faxes and time-management books), personnel (such as secretaries and assistants), procedures (such as accountability and reporting arrangements, regular meetings, pay and reward systems, permissions,

---

A manufacturing company saw the potential for increasing its organizational intelligence by working in teams. It provided education and direct management that encouraged and enabled work teams to form and function effectively in their own processes.

The initial burst of productivity was sufficient reward for the effort; a payback was realized and the practice of forming teams began to spread. Then productivity leveled off and the total effort was called into question.

It wasn't until the company began to inquire into what kind of structures an organization composed of teams would require, that structural changes began to be made.

The company discovered that changing the physical shape of the production line (the work flow) would encourage each team to function more effectively as a team.

The company also began to look at communication structures (reporting, reward and control) as environments conducive to creating breakthroughs in production, rather than just small incremental improvements.

When the company acted on the approaches they had developed, they changed the production line to "U-shaped" and created policies, practices and information vehicles appropriate to team accountability.

Public and visual displays of information became a key element in the reporting structure; more people gained access to information which enabled them to participate independently and in their own unique ways.

One of the most important areas of transformation was linguistic—"team" replaced "individual" in the speaking and practices within the corporation.

authorities and schedules), the layout of a plant or production line, and the countless physical objects and routines that make all these available and reliable for supporting coordinated productive activity. And last, structure includes the language we use—every sentence that is uttered and all the definitions employed in our day-to-day activities.

The extensiveness of the list shows that we are embedded in structure. Structure continually reproduces itself as well as the results for which it exists. There is not a *single* structure of support, nor are there *isolated* items of support. Each structure and item exists within the complex system of productive activity, tools and coessential support structures. When the items or structures are considered in isolation, their significance is often overlooked.

It is difficult to awaken executives and managers to the potential value of developing the people who support them or others. The investment in support structures is generally very low compared to what would be most profitable, given the returns that they can provide. Consider for a moment how productive you would be if there were no support structures around you. Appreciate how much of your productivity is a function of other people doing their jobs, of things being in the right place at the right time and of information being available when you need it, in the form that's most useful to you. A full view of support structures quickly discloses their value.

THE DEEP STRUCTURE OF PRODUCTION

All the tools ready for our use constitute only the surface structure. At a deeper level, the whole of a cooperatively productive organization is arranged according to social conventions, understandings and relationships. Irrespective of time spent on making things work, on communication, or on explaining and training, we are dealing with everything at the superficial level. Each of these activities and the organization that makes them possible are a function of processes interacting with one another at levels greatly exceeding our detailed understanding, no matter how deeply we examine them.

We are embedded in structures that produce their intended results—and most of these results occur without effort, attention or awareness. A moderate exercise of our energies will produce the basics of our currently acceptable standard of living. (Those who are having trouble surviving in Western cultures are those who have failed to learn how to use existing systems spontaneously or in low energy–consuming ways.) The competitive adventure of business is to go beyond these structures continually and to invent new ones that are more efficient. The social benefit of this accomplishment is that the results are available to everyone and the game continues to improve the effectiveness of the application of our energy.

When considering structure, it is essential to remember that it is complex and largely outside the awareness of its users, so any change in it will have unpredictable results. An alteration in structure will affect people in unexpected ways and will even affect unexpected people. Surprising information is sure to result. Efficiencies beyond those intended and even new inefficiencies will occur. Any change also means that those who have become dependent on the existing structures will be discomfited in some way. However good the results that follow, a change will require that people become conscious (aware) and therefore temporarily less competent (less automatically effective) than they previously were. Any change in a support structure will have immediate and frequently unpredicted costs. And at the same time change will begin to payoff beyond what can be predicted, if the approach embodies the principles of complexity and if it emerges from an understanding of the simple structures that allow for maximum variability within the limits of useful performance.

To understand structure at a deeper level requires an understanding of language. The understanding of specific structures is rooted in language, in the relationship between ideas and in the ability for integration into the social structures, which are also created in language and accessible only in language. Grammar and structure are two aspects of the same thing and they all reside, for human beings at least, in language.

Complexity provides a way of understanding and working with deep structure. The way most current structures are designed, used and evaluated is based on logical linear approaches to physical entities. So the design and use of these structures tend to be hierarchical, bureaucratic and controlling, due to their tendency to focus on detail. While this supports a certain kind and level of productive activity, it provides no room for innovation, creativity, or even information.

The approaches of complexity have the capability of transforming most structures. By altering the structures to match information theory and complexity theory, we increase the usefulness of the structures. Transformed structures become sources of creativity rather than tools of suppression, and they call forth communication and information exchanges that lead to innovation. The relationships between production, people and structures are altered when structure is altered, so that everything becomes more adaptable and less "solid." Nonmaterial phenomena such as communication, information and knowledge all become more "solid" and available as substantial realities, as well as available as material for innovation and development.

Structure is generally outside our awareness, inherited and therefore taken for granted. When we use structures we are seldom concerned for their maintenance or continued existence. We ignore not only the structure itself but the people who provide that structure, or often *are* that structure. We give little and take all and, as with any system, that leads to breakdown. The "fallacy of the commons" is most evident here. The things or land that we own in common, for which no one specifically is responsible, are always overused and under-maintained. The "commons" of our corporations are the support people and the support structures.

We find ourselves in the most precarious position when we are so used to the structures we have inherited that we have no idea how to create structure. We have inherited structures that evolved during an era organized around material production and we are trying to use them in a time that is increasingly focused on information. It won't work. We must master the principles of design appropriate to the shift that is taking place all around us and begin to remake our enterprises. One of the best resources for approaching this problem is complexity theory and the corresponding theories and approaches outlined in this book. Continually ask the question, "What information is being generated or can be generated from this situation, activity, or process?" Then go on to consider what structure will increase the amount of information and what will increase its availability for those who might generate still more information.

AN INFORMATION VIEW OF ORGANIZATION

Introduce structure that promotes (temporary) ambiguity.

The design of structure includes interactions, processes and relationships. The major design function is to generate *kinds* of events or interactions, not specific events or specific results. When a complex adaptive system such as a corporation is operating within the greater levels of complexity of economies, states and ecologies, then there must be room for a great deal of ambiguity, creativity and learning to occur. The ambiguity of the rich, robust possibility present in information can then be resolved within structures that offer sufficient redundancy to be able to establish operational parameters regarding that information.

One of the ways to work with this design approach is to empower multiple teams to tackle the same problem. Inhibit their communication with each other in the beginning, but encourage communication once they have developed their own approaches. This is a design for process, information and innovation, as well as increasing returns. Ambiguity is created by not favoring any of the teams. Another way to work with the design of structure

161

is to create overlapping accountabilities through which participants have to work out issues that were ordinarily handled by the authority or rigid design of hierarchical structures. If these examples seem extreme or impractical, it is because they are being looked at from a point of view grounded in mechanistic theories, rather than theories based on complex systems and information.

The first design consideration is to examine the principles around which structures are to be built. After that, explore which areas of the corporation will be considered as candidates for the process of design and implementation; remember that each will affect the other. It is this interactive coevolutionary process that demands that the thinking, theoretical work and design work be done first. If the structures are changed before this, they are bound to conflict with the existing ones and a basis for resolution will not be available. If the basic design principles are not simple and few, then they will go beyond complexity into *complicated-beyond-understanding*, otherwise known as chaos.

The linguistic structures within which information is interpreted are perhaps the most important concern for the executives of a company. Because all people within a company are intelligent beings, their actions will be based on their interpretation of information. The overall coordination of actions depends on their understanding, or interpretation, of a situation.

The fact that reorganization efforts are rampant in countless aspects of corporate life appears to challenge the idea that we are incompetent at structural thinking and structural change.

During a six-month period my invitations to visit prospective clients revealed that each of these large companies was already undergoing, or was about to undergo, some kind of reorganization.

Each of my meetings was perfectly timed: it was either just the right time because they knew they needed help to implement their initiative; or the wrong time because they needed time for the change to occur and then "settle down."

This may be evidence of a lack of ability.

Each of these companies had undergone a significant reorganization in the previous two years and for most that was followed by a more recent reorganization.

For example, a company had received some education and coaching in how to approach strategy, how to reorganize to increase intelligence and how to match strategy and organization. During the process they clearly decided on the organizational changes they intended to make and these were consistent with their expressed intentions..

When I returned for follow-up sessions, I noticed that those on the executive team had shifted positions and two new members had been added. The names of departments and

Without an effective structure to support *integrative interpretation,* only rigid rules and fixed guidelines are available for the physical elements of production. A common illustration of this is the approach of "fool-proofing" which is based on the notion that the best way to handle any situation is to take the possibility of interpretation out of it. However, this includes forfeiture of the possibility of having intelligent beings doing the work.

If structural design principles, rather than the structures themselves, are the starting place for changing structure, important benefits are gained and burdensome problems are avoided. The problems avoided are those that arise when something is created without sufficient participation of those involved: a structure imposed from the top is not clearly understood by others; its mistakes will not become obvious until implementation is attempted. The benefits gained are those that occur when a change is developmental rather than an intervention from outside the system—including a change from above.

Implementation of structural changes by those involved in its design and those most affected by the change ensures better understanding of the changes and a more natural integration with the past as well as with the rest of the system that has not yet changed. All the benefits of complexity (creativity, intelligence, innovation, flexibility and variety) are realized, because the approach to installation is consistent with the intended operation of the

processes had all been changed but most departments were still being run by the same people. Ninety-five percent of the company was still the same.

Further examination revealed that the company had not followed through with its intended changes in operating style. Even more significant, the structures relating to operations (ninety-five percent of the company) were unchanged in practice.

From here their process could play itself out in one of the following ways: the shifts at the executive level indicate that the executives have indeed taken a developmental step because the process has shaken up their relationships and their ways of communicating and has provided new thinking capabilities—and the process will continue to make progress as their development occurs. This, followed by significant structural changes, would allow transformation of the business to occur.

The other (more likely) result could be that the business will adjust its old structure to comfortably accept the changes and it will carry on as before—continually losing intelligence and market share.

A change that doesn't focus on structure (relationships, reporting and practices) will not create lasting impact. A change of *surface structure* (titles, organizational charts and visual aids) will not affect the *deep structure* of coordinated activity.

structure being created. This type of implementation means that the intelligence that created something will be present for its use. (This approach is far beyond the motivation-based approach of pursuing "buy in.")

The approach that will provide the most power is one that continually balances *possibility, theory, relationship* (the subject of the following chapter) and *structure*. It is the dynamic balance between these four factors that keeps a corporation vibrant and alive. These four design factors are sufficient if any complex intelligent system is intended to develop and grow through emergence. When these four factors are maintained at every level of the organization (company, division, team, executive and individual) the phenomenon of self-similarity occurs, in which every part has a structure similar to the whole as well as to each other part. The principle of self-similarity suggests that each level should be concerned with all four of these elements at a level of detail and content appropriate to its accountabilities.

The interplay between structure and information gives rise to the rich variety of life, while at the same time maintaining the robust survival of the identities of the elements. Without structure, there would be no information. Structure provides the framework to make sense of data. Without the interplay of information with structure, there is only a lifeless reality with no variety, no movement and no concern for structure. The responsibility of management rests in the continual balancing, directing and focusing of the interplay between structure and information.

QUESTIONS FOR THIS CHAPTER:

- What structures in your corporation increase organizational intelligence?
- What structures decrease that intelligence?
- Where are things kept in place so that they reoccur, and yet the structures involved remain transparent? Discover this transparent structure by observing how nonmaterial or linguistic patterns occur. What is the design intention behind the surface structures apparent in your corporation?
- Do the structures of your corporation support the stated intentions of the corporation?
- What structures have been put in place to support new initiatives or projects? Are they sufficient to survive in the face of the existing structures—including existing habits and practices?
- Is there a "structural blueprint" for your corporation's major initiatives?

13 Hearts and Minds

"The answer rests in the hearts and minds of the people. It was not our numbers but our ideas which made a big difference."
GENERAL TEMPLAR
"WHO DARES WINS"

"We are going to win and the industrial West is going to lose out. There is nothing you can do about it because the reasons for your failure are within yourselves.

"The survival of firms today is so hazardous in an increasingly unpredictable environment that their continued existence depends on the day-to-day mobilization of every ounce of intelligence. For us, the core of management is the art of mobilizing and putting together the intellectual resources of all employees in the service of the firm.

"Because we have measured better than you the scope of new technological and economic challenges, we know that the intelligence of a handful of technocrats, however brilliant they may be, is no longer enough to take them up with any real chance of success.

"Only by drawing on the combined brainpower of all its employees can a firm face up to the turbulence and constraints of today's environment."
KONOSUKE MATSUSHITA
MATSUSHITA INDUSTRIES 1979

Prelude

When we are passionate about something in life, it is a great challenge to be able to engage in dialogue with others in ways that allow ourselves to be changed, while at the same time enabling others to generate their own passions. It is not our job in life to sell others on our ideas, or to get others to believe in something; but perhaps our responsibility lies in being able to express ourselves in ways that contribute to the possibility for all of us.

Within an organizational environment based on control, direction and authority, the challenge of engaging others remains beyond our capabilities. In our attempts to engage others, we delve into our own resources and those of the corporation. What we find, among other things, are force and manipulation—and we use them. Any effort to suppress forcefulness and manipulation constricts our potential for full expression and power. Any use of force or manipulation undermines our attempts at engagement.

To engage the hearts and minds of others, we must begin by recognizing every human being's ability and right to choose. This recognition is the source of our own ability to be engaged and of our ability to engage others.

In the area of engagement, there is nothing to do but forge ahead. Being responsible begins with our own full expression. The cost of doing so should fall on us. The benefit of doing so should fall to everyone. Such a process of expression and responsibility is the greatest source of growth and development available to us.

RELATIONSHIP IS THE FOUNDATION OF HUMAN INTELLIGENCE

If we are serious about the pursuit of results beyond the ordinary, we must become serious about the development of relationships that will allow those pursuits to take place. The relationships we have, both internal and external to our corporations, are mostly not on a level that allows for the questioning, challenges and coordination of effort required for the pursuit of the extraordinary. Relationship is one of the four fundamental elements of design for intelligent organization and it is the basis for accomplishment beyond what can be done by an individual. Creativity, intelligence, coordinated action, thinking, information-gathering and analysis all depend on relationship in order to produce results beyond the limited possibility of individual action. Relationship creates the context and environment within which we live and work.

Relationship must increase due to the demands of technology and possibility of the Information Age.

The great legacy of hierarchical command-and-control systems that underpin our social structures and corporations provides us with barren ground for the cultivation of relationship between independent intelligent human beings. These designs have intentionally excluded both independence and intelligence—the qualities most needed for the development of relationship. If we are going to engage the hearts and minds of each and every person in the changes we want to make, we must develop in ourselves and others the ability to create, deepen and strengthen relationship so that the necessary environment and context is created.

THE SPECIAL COMMUNICATIONS OF RELATIONSHIP

There is a very distinctive kind of communication required to create the context and the relationship needed for coordinated human actions and it is the kind we must become adept at if we are going to create something beyond what is already given by our current circumstances. This kind of communication is used by leadership, management and all other endeavors when extraordinary performance is wanted from someone or a task requires the participation of others.

Speaking that engages is missing from most transformation initiatives.

The source of failure involving TQM, re-engineering and other fads is rarely the program itself. Neither is it the more commonly attributed causes such as lack of leadership; lack of planning, preparation or funding; lack of in-depth understanding or insincerity at the management level. These reasons (excuses) for failure are cited by almost everyone. W. Edwards Deming was an exception in that a great deal of his efforts were indirectly focused on the larger issue. These elements may play some role in the failures; however, something else may be playing a much more significant role. It is something I have rarely heard mentioned, even though it plays a major role in most failures. It is a particular type of communication—one we will distinguish as *engagement*. It is a kind of communication that is missing in all failures and present in large measure in all dramatic successes.

Others remain unmoved in our interests because they do not share our private understanding or our personal history.

Since neither our people nor our corporations lack the intelligence to make something out of a good theory or methodology, then it must be that they are not interested. It is my observation that most corporations and people are not interested in most programs that are introduced. Sure, a few will always champion such an effort, and their interest will generally spread at least far enough for some pocket of success to be achieved. But corporations in general and the majority of the people in them appear not to be interested.

ENGAGEMENT—A NATURAL HUMAN CONDITION

Engagement will be missing when the leadership's capacity of dialogue is missing or when an organizational design inimical to intelligence, to the inclusion of new ideas and openness to influence, is present. What exactly is engagement? What role does it play in our corporations? And why is this natural capacity not better developed in the leaders of our corporations?

Our organizational environments are in desperate need of a particular kind of communication—one that includes a way of speaking that engages others and a way of listening that engages oneself. To articulate this, an interim operational definition of engagement is *"the process of communication through which we are able to express ourselves in ways that allow for the full participation of others in creating possibility—a possible future, a new theory, a new opening for action."* This type of communication will recognize the self-organizing and self-creating nature of human beings and their connection to the institutions and corporations of which they are a part.

People who interact with others in an engaged way are self-generating, self-organizing and self-maintaining. People who are "engaged" tend to be those who can be counted on to produce results, even in the face of great difficulties. The nature of a group is to be self-generating, self-maintaining and self-organizing. In our recognition of this, it becomes obvious that people need to be informed and communicated with.

Engagement does not emerge from intentions of manipulation or selling.

The difference between selling and engagement is like the difference between conscription and voluntary labor, manipulation and invitation, or dictatorship and leadership. These are not trivial or subtle differences—the results of each are significantly different and the impact on the people involved (immediately and in the future) is dramatically different. There is a vast dissimilarity in the quality of life and the quality of expression that surrounds each of these. Selling and manipulation, in the context of management, are dehumanizing ways of interacting with people; whereas engagement represents a respectful and humanizing relationship to those around us.

Given the predominance and acceptance of manipulation, force and authority in our general and corporate culture, most people are either unaware, or deny the manipulative nature, of their activities. Listen carefully to the current ways of speaking that surround day-to-day management activities. The language carries tones of getting someone to do something which requires certain manipulations—or at least it is easier with these manipulations.

When the intended result is participation and inclusion, and there is nothing hidden and no tactics, then a context for engagement has been created. When intentions for participation and inclusion are displaced by attention on an end result that we already have in mind, the communications and actions that follow will tend to be selling and manipulation. Engagement is characterized by openness and dialogue, rather than mere discussion, and by an intention to preserve and encourage full freedom of responsiveness and choice.

There is nothing inherently wrong with manipulation. There are times and places where its use may even be beneficial. It simply means "handling something to produce a specific result," such as manipulating the physical environment in order to produce desired circumstances, or using tools to meet specific ends. But when we are manipulating people, it implies that they have nothing to say about what is occurring, and most human beings tend to resist that idea. It implies that people are being related to as tools of some kind. To the extent that we understand the essential nature of human beings as having freedom to make choices for themselves, we tend not to like situations such as manipulation, in which that nature is violated. To the extent that we think and act in ways that resemble manipulation, we must view our current organizational designs as being inherently wrong.

There are few, if any, corporations designed to provide people with choice and responsibility as fundamental operating principles. Instead there are a myriad of controls, conditions, processes and practices that inhibit and work against our human nature and our ability to choose and be responsible. The question we must ask ourselves is, "Do these structures and practices work effectively in a human organization?"

In order to examine the different intentions and behaviors that are a part of the world of conversation, we can differentiate conversations into three distinct areas.

1. *Discussion.* During a discussion, the majority of attention is on sending. Receiving is done merely to provide ammunition for the argument being made. A discussion is the appropriate type of conversation to have when there is an either/or choice to make, when it is a win/lose situation, or when one person or side is intent on a particular outcome with no interest in any other outcome.

Discussion allows for manipulation, but does not require it. It is my observation that the majority of formal meetings and conversations in business are discussions.

2. *Inquiry.* The second type of conversation can be distinguished as *inquiry.* When inquiry is occurring there is attention on listening. The intention behind the listening is not for seeking ammunition or openings for attack, but in order to understand and interpret. Although inquiry often has a particular end intended, inquiry allows for change, discovery and learning. A conversation that unfolds as an inquiry deepens our understanding of an area.

3. *Dialogue.* This is the model of mutual creation and generative conversation. Although a dialogue may be in service of a particular end, there is no compulsion for the achievement of that end. In a dialogue, there is no demand that specific results be produced and manipulation is not used. The intention of dialogue is to produce a result that was not in existence before the dialogue and to create something that can only emerge from the process of dialogue itself. The process of dialogue is compelling and generates engagement.

ENGAGEMENT IS NATURAL

Engagement occurs when we realize that humans are intentional beings and that their intentions are self-generated in relationship to their environment. It is not a specific choice or the circumstances alone that determine subsequent actions, but instead a combination of the two. Dialogue is the medium that brings the two together and is thus central to engagement. Engagement isn't a concern, except in an environment in which intentionality is already recognized as operative. To make the point: there is no possibility of engagement with a slave as long as the individual to be engaged remains a slave.

What's interesting about engagement is that it has more to do with context and listening than with speaking. While manipulation can be done outside of awareness and without any willingness on the part of the subject, this is not the case with engagement. Engagement involves a conscious act of choice, or at least an opportunity for choice. The word engagement is only appropriately applied when the people involved have something to say about their intentions. Our operational definition of engagement is *"communication which engages the intention of another (or others) in ways that do not depend on force, coercion or covert operations of any kind but instead fully recognizes the self-organizing and self-creating nature of individuals."* Engagement does not have to involve choice; it is just that choice cannot be precluded or even attempted to be avoided in any way.

Engagement does not involve subtle coercion. Coercion by reason is excluded as much as coercion by force or manipulation. Engagement is a matter of context and approach rather than a particular thing to do. It occurs as a result of our way of being and our intentions rather than from particulars or goals (narrowly defined intentions). If engagement is to occur in relationship to a specific program, it must first occur at the level of possibility. When a possibility becomes compelling, then we become engaged. Programs and specific goals are generally too predetermined to be amenable to engagement. What is required is that the intention and the possibility generate the engagement rather than the specific goal or the carefully constructed program.

Engagement is an individual occurrence within a social context.

A corporation cannot be engaged nor can one corporation engage another. Engagement is an interaction that occurs between individuals and it forms the communicative fabric that becomes the background for the other conversations within a corporation. This fabric may cross organizational boundaries, even distinct corporations, but the phenomenon of engagement remains individual. Even though we are interested in engagement for organizational purposes, it exists only in the relationship between individuals and their communication.

It is natural for engagement to occur when people are living together, working together, learning together, or interacting in a community in some way. Our conversations will be natural expressions of engaged speaking and listening to the extent that there is a sense of freedom in our interactions, corporations and communities. To the extent that there is force, coercion, or manipulation in the corporation, engagement will be reduced or largely driven out. Corporations and communities provide the environment or context within which individuals express themselves.

ENGAGEMENT AND TRANSFORMATION

A transformation of perception is required in order to have an accurate and therefore profoundly useful perspective on what is actually taking place. The shift is from a perception that all of management is "getting others to do something." The shift that must take place is that we begin to see a corporation as a complex intelligent system playing itself out and expressing itself; and we must begin to see the individuals in that system as complex intelligent systems who are self-generating, self-renewing, self-intending and self-responsible people working out their own expression within that larger system.

Human beings cannot really be told what to do unless they have chosen the willingness to be told. People do not live their lives waiting to be told what to do, so it is really not surprising when people haven't the slightest interest in what "management" wants them to do. Yes, they do have an interest in being rewarded for actions. And yes, our corporations are loaded with systems through which people are "interested" in appearing to do what executives and managers are asking of them. Human beings aren't waiting to do what others want them to. They are fully engaged in their own affairs, and that is quite sufficient for any individual.

The job of an executive is to create an environment in which engagement is possible, and to communicate in ways that provide a certain focus, call attention to certain things and engage the hearts and minds of people in the possibility of the corporation. None of these specify the nature of that engagement or its results. When we value and respect the hearts and minds of people—that is, the whole human being—we are also able to value and appreciate engagement, which is very distinct from the directed activity of our normal way of working. When we can see human *beings* (instead of human "doings") populating our corporations, the way in which we interact and work with people transforms from manipulation and control to engagement. When we look around ourselves and see full human beings and their possibility, we can easily engage their hearts and minds.

Although we can arrive at this way of perceiving people and corporations through other interests or disciplines, the results tend to be more operational in Western terms if we undertake the journey using the new sciences of complexity theory, information theory and communication theory.

If a system is based on coercion, engagement is not possible within it.

The organizational design principles that we have inherited from the Machine Age do not support engagement; rather, they foster control and limit opportunities for thinking, action and communication between human beings within the production system. In corporations that operate from mechanistic approaches, intelligence is not wanted from individuals unless it is specific and very limited. In these corporations, communication is structured in both its direction and content. The reductionist thinking on which these approaches are based (which leads to more of the same) leaves the individuals within such systems with the sense of being controlled and manipulated; therefore any attempts at engagement made by management end up as just more manipulation. Within a system based on coercion, engagement is not possible. It is not necessary that the coercion be intentional or malevolent—its mere existence affects how interactions and conversations are shaped. It can and often does exist in a purely impersonal manner with nothing but good intentions behind it. Coercion can often be mixed in with some very good intentions, or it can exist as an underlying position of force that can be used as a fallback in cases of disagreement, emergency, and the like. If this is the case, engagement won't occur.

COERCION AND OUR HISTORICAL ORGANIZATIONAL DESIGN

The way human thought has evolved throughout our history has shaped our current structures, so there is nothing for us to be ashamed of as we acknowledge their current ineffectiveness. We are doing the best we can with the knowledge and education we have. It is important to remember that there is no point in attaching shame to our current structures. At about this point in the process of workshops and organizational education sessions, participants from the management level insist they are not using manipulation or coercion and that people are free to speak their minds. They are certain manipulation or coercion do not apply to them, or the corporation as a whole. Yet I have never found a case where this is so. When other levels of the corporation are absent, management will acknowledge the condition of coercion and manipulation on the spot, and say clearly that they have no choice. When I do interviews or other workshops at lower levels in the corporation, there is always agreement that coercion and manipulation *are* part of the working environment. Usually it is also revealed in personal interviews at the highest levels in a corporation that these are the normal working conditions for executives as well, even though that is not acknowledged in public.

Coercion is an operating tool that we aren't ready to give up, given our current designs and ways of thinking.

What's interesting is that when these same executives and managers are confronted about this matter by people in lower positions in the corporation, or suggestions are made regarding organizational designs and practices that would undermine coercion and manipulation, the executives and managers say that the condition must be maintained, if the business is to work. They consider the availability of coercion and force a necessary part of the game.

The practical and the human seem to collide at this point, and the collision produces a great deal of heat and energy. If we can remove the moral tone and simply tell the truth, what will be revealed is that the only designs we are comfortable and competent with are our inherited designs that include elements of coercion and control. Further looking reveals that those who are subjected to the coercion and complain about it are also only competent and comfortable with this way of operating. Even more difficult to confront is that we complain if the method is taken away and we are expected to be fully responsible for our own actions. It is not uncommon for senior executives in large corporations to get very upset when "the boss" won't tell them in great detail what they are accountable for.

We enter the world of engagement by telling the truth about the existing conditions and from there begin to develop structures and practices that

The tendency for even senior executives to wait for a detailed disclosure of their accountabilities most often occurs in larger corporations.

In smaller corporations an executive is closer to the action, less insulated from communication, and more able to observe direct feedback on relevant issues such as performance.

As the size of a corporation increases, an individual can become an executive by responding only to internal realities and internal signals.

The design of larger corporations has often become complicated and therefore distorts the signals coming from and going to the higher levels.

In situations like this, the principles of complexity can be useful. They suggest ways to think about organizational design that open boundaries, include information to and from external marketplaces and establish contact and effective feedback.

are consistent with intelligent *self-responsible* human beings. The main structures will be ones that create simplicity within complex intelligent systems. The main practices will involve communication. Given that the current design of our corporations is based solely on production, there is no room for engagement with anything other than the productive activities at hand. There is no room for possibility. There is no allowance for conversations, meetings, dialogue, testing or experimenting in thought and action in which engagement might occur, let alone flourish. Systems that demand individuals to be accountable for things they have not voluntarily agreed to (i.e. budgets) do not allow for engagement.

ENGAGEMENT, COMMUNICATION AND DESIGN

The phrase "upward feedback" reveals a great deal about the current structures in our corporations that are inimical to engagement; this is also true of other related terms that imply a concern for a specific direction of communication. Communication between human beings does not go in one direction only—and the same applies to communication within corporations. Communication is contained in every action or opportunity for action and it has a set of principles for generating information or extracting it from such opportunities. If it is being used in narrowly defined ways, suitable for inanimate objects and systems, it is certainly not suitable for human beings.

Communication is not unidirectional.

When "direction" is used in referring to communication, it is an indication that what is being considered as communication is actually a narrow mechanistic view of sending and receiving messages. If people are included in this consideration, they are being reduced to less than machines. If you don't think so, take a look at computers. When one computer sends a message to another, it is not a one-way transaction but a multidirectional event. The machines communicate codes that establish identity, they repeat messages so that each is aware of the success of the communication, and they each communicate completion. At no time, except for the initiation itself, is the communication "one-way."

The hierarchical design in our corporations has established information flow so that one kind of communication goes downward (direction, instruction, etc.) and another kind of communication goes upward (market information, results, etc.). The two channels of communication are designed to be totally independent of one another. Such a design or structure has no place for engagement. To increase engagement, the minimal requirement is to increase dialogue at each point of communication, so that intelligence is increased. To maximize conditions supportive of engagement, full recognition of the intelligence of all human beings involved is required, and designs that encourage engagement at all levels must be created. This provides the opportunity for engagement for everyone, and creates information flows that are more accessible and less directional.

When the conversations in our corporations begin to support establishing and encouraging dialogue throughout the corporation and providing access to information, we can begin to tap into the rich possibility that communication can be between human beings and a vast possibility of varied communications can exist within an organizational structure.

TRANSFORMING FROM COERCION TO ENGAGEMENT

The task of transforming our way of communicating is far-reaching. Not only do our inherited organizational designs thwart the natural possibility of engagement, but our social structures do the same. We have grown up in societies that do not promote being engaged or engaging others. Enthusiasm and full expressiveness are not included in the social norms, especially in business. There are individuals who are naturally engaging and naturally expressive. There are individuals who are easily engaged by others. And there are occasional situations that call for engagement. But there is no general openness or appreciation of communication, especially any that is expressive and revealing. Every one of us has experienced countless instances of embarrassment, failure, ridicule, or being taken advantage of; all of these combined have educated us into patterns of suppression in expressing ourselves and not listening to others.

We all have the capacity for engagement and we all have personal experiences of engagement to refer to as we learn.

As our culture concludes an era of control, power and simple linear systems based on mechanistic concepts, we bring with us a long history of domination, be it beneficial or evil. We dot that history with only brief encounters of profound freedom and respect for the individual. Our experience of a world in which information, its generation and its accessibility are the key to individual and group success is extremely limited. In the political, organizational and public arenas, the history of freedom is so short that many of us have never had direct experience of it. Fortunately, the tradition of freedom is not as short as it might seem. If we look into the history of personal freedom, most of us have some experiences with family members, friends, teams, educators, or a mentor, in which there was open communication, and intentions, feelings and information were freely shared. It is this way of communicating that forms the personal basis for a corporation in the current Age of Information.

At a time when cooperation, coordinated action and the interplay of information and ideas are the source of individual and social progress, the old habits of suspicion, power and control no longer have a place. Previously, power was gained from having information and controlling it, but now power will come from generating information and sharing it. Those who provide or offer access to information and participate in information sharing will gain access to the broadest social network—and the most information. Those who hoard their information will be isolated from opportunities for sharing and creating information. We are heading toward a more open society, whether we like it or not. We are being called on to engage and participate, and at the same time abandon our tendencies to direct and control. Contribution has always been the key for entry into a system, and the most valuable key now is the contribution of information or the facility to generate information. If you are not offering that, you will soon be excluded.

The personal and the organizational converge in communication.

By including intentions, meaning and feelings in our communications, transformation occurs at a personal as well as an organizational level. Personal expression is becoming more acceptable and respected as an important part of communication, regardless of the purpose. Business and science are no exception. Even the analytic activities of engineering and planning are considered to be just as much a personal expression as they are impersonal "fact," or "logic."

Given our lack of practice of engagement at a social level, it is not surprising that executives and managers fumble with it. While many are competent at a personal level, very few are competent at an organizational level. Frequently individuals in influential positions acquired their standing through use of power, force of personality, or manipulation of systems and structures. Given that engagement played no part in their success, not only have they not developed the capacity, but they now see no need for it. The current psychology, operating in almost all our corporations, ensures that the little natural engagement that does emerge gets suppressed.

CREATING COMPETENCE IN ENGAGEMENT

Dialogue is the first practice to be developed in order to become competent at engagement. This includes speaking in a way that invites something new, and also listening to what is unsaid as well as what is said. Most executives and managers seem to require substantial work on developing their listening, so begin there. Engagement is not a matter of convincing—most managers are masters at that. Engagement begins with the expression of personal wants, intentions, feelings and possibility. Most people are not comfortable with any of these expressions and the skill of engagement is not something one acquires merely by reading a book—it takes introspection, being present to oneself—and actually trying it out. None of these are common historical requirements for management advancement.

Listening as a capacity for awareness is the single greatest development required for management.

Listening as an open, generous and inclusive phenomenon is not an outstanding skill of those in management. Many people have developed the ability to listen for particular things or to listen in particular ways. Few have developed the ability to listen for a whole communication, let alone to a whole human being. Few have developed the ability to be present to ambiguity, uncertainty or the development of an idea. The ability to listen, in its broadest sense, is at the heart of engagement *with* others as well as engagement *of* others.

Engagement is expressing oneself—and listening to the expression of others.

At this point it should be very clear that engagement is not only a matter of speaking and expression but equally a matter of context, environment and listening. Engagement is not so much about being factual; it is about personal expressions of interest, meaning and intention. It is a way of pointing or indicating so that the communication is compelling to another. It is not a matter of telling what or how to think, but a matter of indicating what might be of interest to consider. Another aspect of this kind of speaking is possibility. Again, it is not a matter of fact or probability but instead the *space of possibility*. It is a conversation in which to speculate and explore, in order to see what shows up. It is a domain of promise, future possibility and potentiality.

Engagement is thinking, inquiring and exploring possibility.

Another aspect of engagement is thinking or conversations that demand thinking. Engagement does not take place when something is already complete, nor does it occur when there is no possibility of creativity or new thinking. Engagement is the ability to sense the presence of something before it is well formulated or completely thought out. This capacity is notably absent in executives, especially in their communications with the people of their corporation. Executives, still living in the mire of linear thinking, be-

Mechanistic theories teach manipulation of circumstances, communications and activities, and thereby reduce engagement to humanistic manipulation at best, or to cynical selling and outright application of fear at worst.

I recall that during my time at IBM, both the sales and nonsales staff were put through a training program that pronounced fear as the basis of *all* action.

In the same vein, my son-in-law attended an MBA course in 1993 in which the role of fear in management was given positive attention. His course went on to include some very creative "how-to" applications of fear!

lieve that they are supposed to know everything and have all the answers thought through—and that they only need to communicate in order to inform others. Executives and managers usually show little respect for another's ability to think or another's interest in thinking.

An organizational design that encourages engagement will include systems that are open to input and provide access to information. These systems will operate via the results of interplay, complex systems integration and dialogue. These systems will require engagement for their creation and call for the same in their application.

Key places to explore to see if a corporation's systems will support engagement are its relationship to responsibility and accountability. There must be choice and freedom in these areas. Also look to see if people are accountable by specific agreement made freely to others; it is not relevant whether the accountability is to a "higher" or "lower" person in the organization. (This hints at the radical nature of what is being proposed and the wealth of human capacities that might be tapped into.) The transformation of executives and management will include the development of their ability to speak, listen and engage in dialogue consistent with the principles of engagement. These are critical if the transition to an organizational design appropriate to an Era of Information is to occur.

QUESTIONS FOR THIS CHAPTER:

- To what extent is engagement the source of action in your corporation? Where is it practiced? Where is it suppressed?
- To what extent does your corporation depend on force, manipulation, authority or coercion? Where and when is it used? Where is it maintained as a fallback?
- When you look at your best performing managers, do they use engagement and have great teams, or do they use domination and speak with an attitude of "just get it done"?
- Which receives the greatest reward in your corporation, engagement or domination? If one predominates, what does it tell you about your organizational principles?
- What initiatives have failed to take off as intended? In regard to each initiative, what attempts were made in the area of engagement and why did they fail?
- Who are the people who aren't listened to in your corporation?
- Is it because of position (level) or personality (style)?
- Listen to them.

IV From Theory to Practice

This section explores the challenges of putting a new theory to work. The first chapter in this section begins by distinguishing the phases of an organizational transformation process. The next chapter considers the nature of the breakdowns created during a transformation and the critical role they play in the success of an initiative. From there come the personal challenges that will confront the thinking, speaking and action of the leaders of any transformation. The last chapter of this section is directed at the importance and power of declaring a period of transition in order to provide a context for change.

In this book
read
Chapter
14

then Chapter
13
Then 7, 12
then book

14 The Process of Transformation

"The most exciting breakthroughs of the 21st century will occur not because of technology, but because of an expanding concept of what it means to be human."
J. NAISBITT & P. ABERDENE
MEGATRENDS 2000

Prelude

The accelerating rate of change in the world and the escalating competitive pressures call for the use of new strategies and new descriptives. Now, one of the most common words connected with any corporate initiative—whether it is re-engineering, TQM, time-based, or teams—is *transformation*. Executives know their organizations need to transform, but what do they mean when they say that?

All organizations are in a process of becoming. The process of transformation is also a process of becoming. *Transformation* means to become something that has a new form, but at the same time is still recognizable as a realization of the original. The term *transformation* implies a major change and at the same time it implies continuation. When viewed from the outside, a transformation is the kind of change that appears to alter dramatically the structure and even the nature of an entity, yet the results of this change can be seen as a continuation of the original entity.

What seem to be missing in almost all initiatives of transformation are sensible well-grounded details for accomplishing the process of transformation. The processes for chemical or biological transformation are well formulated, but this is not so for transformations that involve complex intelligent systems. What is unique about the transformation of complex systems is that the intelligence of the complex system must be involved in its own transformation. To do this effectively, an interactive process based on information and communication must be an instrumental part of the process.

WHAT IS A TRANSFORMATION?

The phrase "organizational transformation" is being heard in conversations everywhere. An increasing number of executives concede that what is needed in their companies is a transformation—and nothing less will do. These executives are not calling for a revolution, although that is how some people are interpreting it. And yet, it is very clear to everyone involved that a slow and evolutionary change is not going to be satisfactory. So what will fill the bill? Is there a unique kind of shift that needs to occur? Is it the kind of shift that is described by the word *transformation*?

Transformation refers to a change beyond predictive ability.

Many of the executives grappling with the idea of transformation know that they are looking for a large change that happens fast. They're not exactly clear how large, but they know that it is larger than can be easily planned and executed. These executives know the change must be larger than can be seen clearly from where they currently stand and that the change must be more substantial than merely extending the past. Those executives working with the idea of transformation are also not certain how fast the process needs to be in order to make it effective. Most of them know that there will have to be an acceleration, so that change will take place faster than is currently happening—and certainly faster than is comfortable for those involved. Although these questions point our attention in the right direction, transformation will have to be more clearly distinguished if we are going to have the power to engage others in the transformation and execute it successfully.

A Texas-based contract-building company recognized that times were changing and that a transformation was needed—and in a few short months the company accomplished that feat.

The company stopped competitive bidding and only accepted exclusive relationship-based contracts. All existing positions were eliminated from the company and teams were created that changed with each job. In addition, all pay became performance based and all job security was removed.

Yet it was easy to see that the company's starting place of commitment to quality, reputation and good relationships (internal and external), which were the foundation of the corporation before the transformation, continued to be the company's core qualities throughout the entire process of transformation.

As is the case with personal transformation, an organizational transformation can only produce what was already inherent in the original entity, even though it was hidden initially.

Transformation builds on what already exists in unpredictable ways.

If the process of organizational transformation is not a revolution or mere evolution, then it must be something that is already in existence in the corporation, but is untapped—and would remain untapped if it were not for certain conditions. Transformation is becoming what is possible; it can be developed from what exists, but is uncertain in process and final form. The pathway is one of development and growth, rather than intervention. What will result from any transformation cannot be known in advance—at least in process and final form. The result will be a realization of what was always possible, but not previously expressed. A transformed corporation will be recognizable and at the same time clearly be something else. For a transformation to take place, an acceleration in the process of becoming and an increase in the space of possibility are necessary.

Very few corporations have attempted an authentic transformation and even fewer have been successful. Many corporations have attempted major changes and called their attempts transformation; and even more have talked about it, but made no real effort. The mythology of transformation continues to flourish everywhere—library shelves are filled with books on the subject and no current business magazine would dare publish without an article on the subject. Yet transformation remains one of those things that is very popular to talk about, but not so popular to do.

A corporation can be designed for a particular purpose or particular time span, become successful, end its existence and be considered a complete success. But very few corporations are designed that way.

We generally speak and act as though our organizations are supposed to last forever. If they are to last for even an extended period of time, then we must act in ways consistent with that. To do this we must make sure that we design into our corporations the capacity to evolve in ways that meet the current demands, and we must support and nurture that capacity. *Becoming* must be seen as a way of life for our corporations.

For those intent on long-term survival and viability for their corporations, I suggest that you ask yourself the following questions on an ongoing basis:

- What is it about your corporation that justifies its long-term existence?
- What is the unique contribution of your corporation that insures its survivability over a long period of time?
- What valued service or product does your corporation provide to the social ecology such that there will always be a place for you?

These questions offer a valuable starting place for considering the objectives and challenges of transformation.

Warning: personal transformation will be a part of any organizational transformation.

Most executives and consultants who talk about transformation have not undergone a personal transformation themselves; most have never actually engaged in an organizational transformation, even though they talk about it while attempting to make changes. But those few executives and consultants who have personally been through a process of transformation and have made serious attempts at an organizational level, stand apart from all others; they are recognizable in their manner of speaking, their way of relating to issues, their deep respect for the difficulty involved in the process and their unwavering consistency of intent. Anyone who has been through such a process is not very interested in engaging in anything else.

Transformation is the process of continuous intelligent living.

A process of transformation cannot be characterized by the idea of a caterpillar changing into a butterfly and then living an exquisite life as a butterfly. In the world of organization, transformation is a process of a rapidly changing life of survival in a rapidly changing world. Typically, the perception of people in a corporation who are anticipating a transformation is that the corporation will get somewhere and then "return to normal." Engaging in a process of transformation wakes people up to two things: one is that *be-*

The North Sea oil industries provide a special opportunity to look at and understand the co-evolutionary nature of transformation in action.

Those on watch at BP Exploration (BPX) realized there would be no more major oil discoveries in the North Sea, and the present-day fields would soon run dry. The company would clearly have to transform itself in a major way.

To survive, BPX would have to become a corporation that could include frequent oil searches as well as be able to extract oil at greatly reduced costs. It became very clear to those at the helm that the way in which work was currently organized would not support the necessary cost reduction. It also became obvious that to accomplish the required cost reduction, the entire industry that supplied BPX with services and equipment would also have to transform how it was organized. To accomplish such a transformation, BPX would have to alter its relationship

to the whole industry, at the same time that the industry was altering all its relationships and ways of doing business.

BPX brilliantly continued to offer the supply industry information on the processes that it was using. In return, BPX was given the knowledge that the supply industry was gaining from its individual transformation processes. As a result of this exchange process, an industry-wide commission was created to enable rapid transformation of companies in that industry. The commission provides learning programs that will facilitate the process.

As a member of the educational force within that industry, I am in the unique position of educating many companies that are in direct competition with one another. As a result of the educational programs, the industry now realizes that competition and cooperation must go hand-in-hand.

coming has been and always will be the condition of any corporation as well as any human being; and the other is that the pursuit of the fulfillment of possibility is what organizational life is all about. Waking up to the ever-present process of becoming and the fulfillment of possibility reveals a profound similarity between individuals and corporations. After living with the satisfaction and freedom that accompanies a life completely aligned with the design of human beings and corporations (a life of continual growth and development), no one would dream of returning to earlier ways of living off past accomplishment, using ineffective formulae, or thinking in a merely linear way.

TQM is renowned for insisting that quality is a way of life and there is no end to the process. The name of the game may change from quality to something else, but the way of life being referred to—one of learning and development—will never end. The notion that there is an end to the process is a product of the way we are conditioned to think and this way of thinking must be addressed in the process. It is not in accord with who we are as human beings for there to be an end; wanting there to be an end is merely in keeping with the social norm of the world.

We grow up in a world in which the lifelong pursuit of mastery, learning and development is not the norm. Yet it is this very possibility that is distinctive to human beings and their institutions. Human beings are designed to continue evolving and the basis of that kind of development occurs in our language. Language provides the capability of continued development throughout our own life and that of our corporations.

HOW THE PROCESS OF TRANSFORMATION UNFOLDS

The actual process of transformation is directly related to the nature of the entity that will transform. Let's consider the issue of transformation in a very general way. The idea of transformation is that of *becoming*. An entity can become something that is related to its design principles, its historical development and its environmental circumstances. In previous chapters, we gave considerable attention to design and historical development, so now let's look at environmental circumstances.

Our operational definition of transformation is *"a process by which an entity creates a new relationship between itself and its environment/ecology by reorganizing its knowledge and operations; the process is coemergent and alters both the entity and the ecology."* The complex system that the entity *is to become* must remain coupled with its environment throughout the process of change and the environment (a larger complex system) must remain coupled with the entity through alterations in the environment. It is this complex emergent process we are indicating when we use the term transformation.

For the purpose of illustration, let's imagine introducing a new species into an existing rainforest. The forest is a complex and thriving ecology that is balanced in a dynamic way. When the new species is entered into the complex system, there is not an empty space waiting for it—the space is already filled with something. Once introduced, the new species is likely to starve, be eaten, or be excluded to the point of death. Resources and energy must be added to create a space for the species' survival until it can begin (if it ever does) to engage with the surrounding ecology in such a way that it can sustain itself and return something to the ecology that will allow the cycle to continue.

When we introduce new ideas, processes, or intentions into the existing system that a corporation *is,* and/or into the existing system that the social ecology (economy, politics, or customs) *is,* we can expect the same kind of results as we would get when introducing a new species into a rainforest. The transformed entity (now a new species) will have to find new ways to integrate with the ecology, while at the same time changing the ecology. If this coevolutionary process does not happen, resources will be required continually to nurture the new entity. To survive, the new entity must be self-replicating, self-generating and self-sustaining within an environment. Any entity that does not have those qualities, or cannot gain them, will not survive—and the *becoming* of the environment (ecology) will continue on its path without pause.

Let's consider a corporation as a linguistic phenomenon. For operational and transformational purposes it may be useful to consider a cor-

From time to time *is* will be put in italics. This is because the English language does not have a recognized way of communicating that something may exist that does not merely *have* specific characteristics, but can be usefully thought of as *being* those characteristics.

For instance, an organization can be thought to *have* systems. An organization can be analyzed or interacted with in ways appropriate to that way of thinking. An organization can also be thought to *be* those systems. This way of thinking provides a new perspective that will initiate different ways of analyzing, or interacting with an organization.

This way of distinguishing *is* is not attempting to say "it is true" that a corporation *is* its systems, but only that it is useful and valid to think about a corporation in this way for particular purposes.

poration as a network of conversations. Our operational definition of a corporation is *"an emergent phenomenon that has arisen from a network of conversations and is now primarily composed of conversations."* These conversations hold together all the elements of the corporation and constitute its culture and its way of being. The continued evolution of the corporation emerges from the interplay of these conversations.

If we consider a corporation a network of conversations, we can see that for transformation to occur we must introduce new conversations into the existing ecology of conversations. Internally, a corporation is a structure of interrelated conversations, so any changes in the way we conduct our conversations will interrupt the existing system. Externally, the marketplace is a network of conversations, and changes in conversation within the corporation will disrupt each of the entities in the marketplace that relate to the overall corporation, and even those entities that aren't directly connected. These changes will ripple through the whole ecology and affect the originator in unpredictable ways.

PHASES OF A TRANSFORMATION PROCESS

We can now distinguish the process of transformation in a way that is consistent with the nature of corporations and the marketplace. The process of transformation can be outlined in such a way that we can see that it is consistent with the principles of complex adaptive systems. Transformation will provide sufficient design to produce conditions favorable to the generation of creativity and innovation. By distinguishing transformation in this way, we can see transformation as an evolutionary process in the world of conversational ecology—such as a corporation. The phases of the process of transformation are:

Phase 1: *Awakening:* The awareness that something is needed, wanted and possible beyond what can be seen as an extension of past circumstances and current thinking. The intention to pursue what's possible is awakened.

Phase 2: *Formulation:* There is a development of possibility for your particular corporation through an iterative process of dialogue. The dialogue moves from tentative propositions to rich and compelling possibilities.

Phase 3: *Experimentation:* Pilot projects and isolated experiments are created that demonstrate the approaches in action and test new theories of organizing work against the realities of circumstances and environment.

Phase 4: *Integration:* Projects that have been isolated from the full challenges of existing production processes are transferred into those processes. This integration alters the organizational structures of support.

Phase 5: *Development:* Continuous improvements are made in the processes that are implemented. Structures for challenging the new, as well as the old, are built into the main organizational structures.

Phase 6: *Mastery:* Understanding and excellence are pursued by a corporation that is teaching and learning continuously, so that knowledge is always being questioned and expanded upon. Becoming is more important than arriving.

It is useful to distinguish these phases for purposes of understanding the process, but the phases are not clear-cut steps. The phases never proceed in a neat order, and they are likely to overlap and repeat at different times. The unfolding of a complex intelligent system, within a larger complex adaptive system, cannot be predicted or planned using today's standard logic; nor can these systems be managed using the logic that currently exists in corporations and management.

Awakening is exploration from the point of view that something is possible.

Awakening begins with exploring the existing ecology, introducing new ways of speaking and thinking and dramatically altering listening. During this period, the changes that will be involved in the transformation are largely unknown, and certainly cannot be known in any detail. Even though there may be a general sense of direction, it is wise to start in an "as if" mode—to be speculative and tentative. The initial direction may turn out to be off course, and surprising developments may occur, but the direction will never begin to approach a well-formed definition without a great deal of input from the complex system and the existing intelligence. The beginning of the process should be exploratory and inclusive, in ways that foreshadow something coming, without being explicit about what it may be.

During the early phases of transformation more people are *dwelling in the language,* until it is a comfortable and familiar way of thinking, speaking and listening.

Until this happens, the new language, and the ideas that it represents are simply jargon. What transforms jargon into useful information-rich language is its integration with existing language and practice. This alters the way things occur and provides new openings for action.

During formulation, education, thinking and dialogue mark a particular pathway out of all that is possible.

Moving into the next phase will be appropriate only when the first phase has created enough dialogue and information which was not previously in existence for a new understanding to emerge about the business of the organization as well as organization itself. The new understanding that has emerged will develop into a greater degree of detail and a more refined level of abstraction. When this more refined understanding can be *formulated* in a way that is tentative, yet generates understanding and agreement when introduced into dialogue, then the next phase begins (the first phase still continues, but mainly at a different organizational level). The formulating phase includes development in the areas of education, abstract thinking and design for exploratory and information purposes, as well as for actual use. *Integration* on any broad scale is premature at this point. To acquire an understanding that is substantial enough to create "permanent" structures, more dialogue and learning are required.

Experimentation occurs when an idea is attractive enough to call forth action. Its purpose is to provide practices and language that encourage further development.

When there is sufficient abstract understanding for practitioners (people at work) to begin to invent projects and trials that put ideas into practice, the phase of *experimentation* and testing begins. Projects and trials will appear throughout the organization and be the occasion for more learning, development and exploration in the direction that is being taken. The new projects and trials will produce rapid returns. In fact, returns may come in even before the experiments start. But don't be fooled by these results. They are merely "loose change" that has been on the table waiting for a little intelligence to pick it up. The results are merely a reflection of the gap between what is possible and the current state of affairs and given the size of the gap

I began initiating our way of working in a construction company. Those in the company who participated in our education program did so on a volunteer basis. When left on their own, the people who had participated in the program launched into a project without sufficient investment in the first two phases of a transformation, and did so without a commitment to the process as a whole.

The self-selected team that had formed for purposes of experimentation came up with a process of reorganizing the flow of work and immediately reduced costs by 25% on existing projects.

Even though the experiment led to permanent changes and continued savings, the transformation effort faltered. This happened for two reasons. First, management focused solely on the savings. Also, management attempted to continue to accomplish cost savings without continuing to develop the initial phases of the transformation or altering the organizational structures so that they were aligned with the ways of working that had produced the savings in the first place.

in most corporations, almost anything will produce immediate gains. The release of inhibitors and the resulting release of human energy, intelligence, and coordinated action will produce immediate returns. But these releases are not a signal that organizational transformation has begun. The pilot projects and experiments will produce results of their own and these too are merely incidental (even though they are capable of paying for the whole process). If we lose sight of the intention of the pilot projects and results, which are only a part of the learning and developmental process, then the value will be lost, the transformation effort will fail and the corporation will revert to business as usual. Remember: your corporation does not yet understand itself as a complex intelligent system.

The phase of *integration* is critical if the initiative is to be transformational. The learning, theory and development of the earlier phases is now ready to be *implemented and integrated* into the "mainstream" way of doing business. Until this stage of the process, the executives have provided the shelter and resources for the initiative to survive. It is now time to take what has been learned in the process of development and integrate it at other levels of the corporation. Remember: this is still a development process and learning is as important as results.

It is crucial that the process of integration has complete integrity; it must be totally consistent with both the way in which the current progress was created and the way that the systems are intended to function. (After all, you cannot establish a democratic process by decree—nor can you institute a dictatorship using open and participative processes.) The understanding of design and structure is instrumental if the processes leading to this point are

In the earlier phases of a major initiative, disagreement is always part of the dialogue. During one of our consulting engagements, the CEO of the company made the request that each executive generate her or his own series of plans that would cut costs by 30%. Some of the executives responded as requested, while others returned with well-researched proof showing that cutting costs so dramatically couldn't be done.

At this stage of the initiative, there was no retribution for not generating plans. When selected plans were implemented, a few of the executives continued to object and failed to lead. Failure to align themselves eventually led to the departure of these executives from the company.

It didn't matter how adequate the efforts of leadership were to educate and develop the opposing executives in the new ways of thinking and working—the time for sorting out how to react was over. Implementation demanded appropriate self-initiated, aligned action from all senior management.

to be integrated. The integration needs to be guided by a corporation's new theories and design principles, or integration won't occur. Integrating the design of communication and information structures will allow each person and department to relate to what is wanted and allow them the freedom to express that in their own way.

It is the process of integration that requires alteration of a corporation's structures so that they are consistent with the new theories.

During the process of integration, all existing structures such as reporting, reward systems, hierarchies and authorities are challenged. Information that has been withheld must be shared and be made accessible. Relationships that undermine the old ways must be formed everywhere and fears of competition must be handled in new ways. There must be strong and clear acts of change designed to work effectively in the new systems, and they must also communicate to all parts of the system an unequivocal message. The message is: the system is transforming and anyone or anything that obstructs it will be chewed up; this is different from the trend thus far, where most of what is new has been chewed up by the old system.

The later phases, or *contextual phases,* must be strategically planned and intended for a transformation process to succeed, because these phases create the depth of the process of transformation. If it is thought that the transformation process is over when the structure and its integration are complete, then the process is not likely to get very far and will almost certainly fail. This is because there is a way of thinking that must be built into the transformation at the start—that is, that you are starting a process that will never end. More accurately, you are in a natural process of *becoming* that is part of the survival of human organizations, and the process flows far

---

Motorola, Disney and Toyota are examples of companies that have reached a level of mastery and have become teachers to the world.

What was the source of their success? Why don't they keep their theories, strategies and practices to themselves? The reason is: the people in these companies are clear that as the level of mastery is approached, learning accelerates by teaching others. They also recognize that information and knowledge increase by sharing, rather than by sheltering or protecting them. By sharing their knowledge, these companies gain access to knowledge that would otherwise be unavailable to them.

Paradoxically, these companies retain their marketplace advantage by giving information away. The executives of these companies are "taking a page" from the scientific world in which papers are published, conferences are held, and information is shared in a combined cooperative/competitive environment for the purpose of accelerated growth of knowledge.

beyond the limits of current corporate intentions. The later stages that continue to provide context are:

- *continual improvement* of the newly invented processes until they begin to reinvent themselves as increasingly complex systems
- *mastery* of the newly invented theoretical structures and designs that eventually lead to recognized world leadership and education of others

The speed of a transformation process can be very rapid, but it need not be. However, the process cannot be too slow because when the speed is slowed down, factors come into play that have a tendency to kill a transformation. Caution or delayed speed often reflect a desire for a level of control that is incompatible with the processes of a complex system; these factors also tend to encourage the use of inappropriate behaviors or structures. At a slow, deliberate speed, linear thinking seems to retain its grip. If the rate of action is insufficient, resistance can be met as a result of the rate of change of competitors or others impacted by the system and this can cause unforeseen problems that could stop the process. Often the best way to generate favorable new information is to speed things up and explore what is revealed in the breakdowns that occur. And finally, some of the most insidious obstacles of all are the already existing, robust systems that have been designed to include whatever disturbances appear within the system or its surroundings. This mechanism of inclusion has the power to chew up or kill what initially look like promising initiatives.

QUESTIONS FOR THIS CHAPTER:

- What expectations do you, or others, have regarding how much effect a transformation process will have on the existing system?
- If your corporation has started a transformation process, what failures or oversights in the first two phases are waiting to undermine your later phases?
- What initiative was started in your corporation more than a year ago? What degree of vitality is still in it, when you compare its current state to its state in the first few months?
- If the initiative is losing its vigor, where do you see deficiencies in the earlier stages and how can they be fulfilled? If your effort seems to be failing, what sources do you see in the areas of individuals, commitment, resources, or the process itself?

15 Breakdowns

"When you fail to bring forth what is inside you, it will destroy you. When you bring forth what is inside you, it will save you."
THE GNOSTIC GOSPELS

"My experience is that when things are non-controversial, beautifully coordinated and all the rest, it must be that there is not much going on."
JOHN F. KENNEDY

Prelude

Our competence is measured by how quickly and effortlessly we can produce results. It is especially measured by how effectively we overcome interruptions, breakdowns and problems in performance of our promises. People who are considered to be the most competent are those who can still make things happen, even when confronted with extremely difficult circumstances. The ultimate measure of competence is that we can accomplish automatically, unconsciously and with a sense of grace whatever the circumstances demand of us.

And then there is learning, growth and life itself.

When we challenge our competence, either intentionally or as a result of circumstances, and go beyond what we are already competent at, it threatens our self-image. If we intend to grow and develop at more than an ordinary pace, we must look more carefully into the nature of self-esteem and begin to redefine what it means for us. Our new definition will have to include the idea that the source of self-esteem lies in the ability to grow, develop and handle circumstances beyond our existing competence.

This same challenge awaits us at an organizational level. We must be able to redefine the nature of organizational competence and create an environment that builds and recognizes that.

TRANSFORMING OUR RELATIONSHIP TO BREAKDOWNS

In the ordinary course of events, we want to avoid breakdowns. We have designed our work and production processes to ensure against breakdowns. Such designs are not compatible with the pursuit of transformation. As we distinguished earlier, the very nature of transformation means that there will be continuous breakdowns and that the successful resolution of these breakdowns will be the source of transformation. The process of transformation is unknowable beforehand and therefore demands continuous learning at all levels and all points along the way. Each breakdown is an opportunity to learn, a demand to rethink, and a challenge to our old way of thinking—all sufficiently beneficial for us to welcome breakdowns.

When we have transformed our relationship to breakdowns, we will have succeeded in transforming our corporation, making it more able to engage continuously in new challenges. The ability to welcome breakdowns as opportunities for learning—and to create them, if none exist—is a fundamental capacity of any corporation that is learning continuously.

A smooth and uninterrupted flow of production does not support growth and development.

An organizational transformation effort reveals the paradox of organizing ourselves to prevent, avoid, or rapidly handle all breakdowns—and of learning or growing at the same time. We have been making predictability and reliability the watchword for our corporations; we have been designing controls that ensure that breakdowns be as minor, as short-lived and as few in number and kind as possible. Organizational transformation demands that we begin to look for breakdowns, welcome breakdowns and even design or create breakdowns. To better suit the realities of transformation, we should change the saying, "If it ain't broke, don't fix it" to "Replace it before it has time to break."

Production is about designing for no breakdowns and being able to apply minimum energy to produce maximum output. We have geared ourselves to systematize things until everything happens reliably and automatically. We take whatever information we have and try to transform it into some kind of concrete results. This is now the only job of production: to organize the flow of things so that there is minimum information and maximum repetition.

The needs of learning and growth are different from the needs of production—and often apparently contradictory. For learning and growth we want unpredictability, breakdowns and interruptions in the flow of things. Ultimately, we want frequent and different breakdowns that interrupt what is automatic and create paradox and uncertainty. When learning

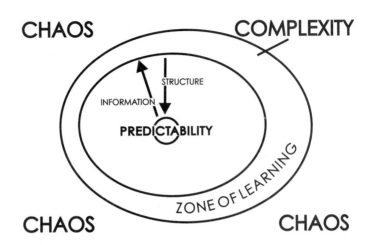

WHEN INFORMATION EXCEEDS STRUCTURAL CAPACITY,
BREAKDOWN OCCURS

CHAOS

COMPLEXITY

STRUCTURE

INFORMATION

PREDICTABILITY

ZONE OF LEARNING

CHAOS

CHAOS

The area of complexity can be considered the zone of learning when information exceeds the capacity of a part of the structure and demands new structure, or reintegration of the particular structure into the whole organization.

and growing, we want to gain the most information possible; we welcome breakdowns and will even cause them, if necessary.

If there are no surprises, there is no information available—and consequently, no development. If there are too many surprises, there is insufficient production and no development—but for very different reasons. What we are seeking is a design that gains maximum information from maximum production. Of course, there is no way of knowing what maximum is, so the measurement itself is a directional statement or, if you prefer, an expression of balance.

Creating conditions for learning is about intention and balance, rather than absolutes.

BREAKDOWN AS INTERRUPTION TO THE FLOW

The language we use for breakdowns tells the whole story—we don't want them.

Our first challenge is to revise our perception of and reaction to breakdowns. Most people relate to breakdowns on a continuum where those that we are able to handle easily, without too much interruption in our flow, are a source of enjoyable challenge, pleasure and pride. At the other end of the continuum are those that totally interrupt the flow of our work and take us into a domain where we lose our sense of competence. These breakdowns are a source of upset and extreme discomfort; they often leave us with a sense of failure and threaten our self-esteem. We seldom bother to call those in the first category breakdowns, but tend to reserve the word for those situations that we are doing all we can to avoid. Our ordinary way of speaking about breakdowns imposes strong, subtle pressures to see and interact with breakdowns in a particular and ineffective way. What we need is a language that will give us power in the arenas of information and maximum intelligence.

Corporations designed for information and maximum intelligence will need an operational definition for breakdowns that will give us the power and freedom to design and generate breakdowns, as well as manage those that occur in the ordinary course of events within a complex coevolving system. Our operational definition of breakdown is *"an interruption to the flow of a system that cannot be handled within the automatic processes of that system."* A breakdown is an interruption that demands thinking, new information, or innovation in order to return to a productive state of flow. That state of flow is likely to be a different productive process, or an alteration of the original larger complex system.

The concept *breakdown* implies that there is an existing design or operational flow that is unfolding according to certain design principles; there must be something regular or predictable in order for it to be interrupted. It is the interruption to such a flow that we consider a breakdown. When merely looking at the operational flow, such an interruption is by definition a disturbance; if the system has feelings and is not the source of the interruption, an upset or annoyance will follow. But when looking at the larger system, in which the operational flow functions, we don't know whether to consider such a breakdown positive or not. How the breakdown is *interpreted* depends on the design principles of the system. If the design principles require the repetition of an uninterrupted process for some end, then the

It is Toyota's practice to allow any worker on its production line to press a button that stops the whole line. This practice is a result of a commitment to continuous learning on those lines. The learning did not start with the button.

The button causes an intentional and focused breakdown. There is a refined quality of understanding, which comes from earlier learning, that allows this process of ongoing learning to work effectively.

When our response to breakdowns produces low levels of predictability, we need to alter our relationship to the breakdowns that happen to us. When we operate at a higher level of predictability in regard to breakdowns, we can declare them into existence for specific purposes. When we reach this level we have gained mastery of our production processes.

breakdown will be considered negative. If the design principles advocate gaining information, then the breakdown is likely to be considered positive. If the design principles include the intention to constantly improve the production flow, then the nature of the breakdown becomes critical for balancing information and production.

When designing to include breakdowns, the size and kind of a breakdown must be appropriate to the larger design of a corporation. Factors that will come into play will be competitive forces, the existing pace of learning and the existing competence in production. When there is low productive competence, the system will tend to learn most from the breakdowns that are occurring in the ordinary course of events, if they are kept to a workable number and kind. When productive competence is high (measured by reliability and predictability), then the number and kind of breakdowns may be intentionally increased to maximize learning. The higher the level of competence, the more learning is likely to occur from the successful resolution of breakdowns. If competitive pressures are high, then the intelligence of the system will need to be greatest. The designed breakdowns need to have a particular nature. They must keep reliable production going and, at the same time, increase the learning from each and every action, during each moment of operation. The design will frequently include experiments that are outside the normal production flow in time, but use the ordinary production equipment and processes.

BREAKDOWNS AND CAPITAL VALUE

Competition engenders the destruction of physical capital value.

To determine the size of breakdowns that need to be designed, look at the relative rate of change in your own corporation and compare it to the corporations with which you are competing. If the competition produces a great deal of change, therefore creating a high demand for change, then the size of the breakdowns to be designed into the process and the resources brought to bear on them should increase. In a relatively stable environment, the size of a generated breakdown can be kept low, so that the risk element is also kept to a minimum. There is no situation that justifies a long-term design to avoid breakdowns within a context of learning or transformation. Wherever there is competition—that is, everywhere—then the new will replace the old. Frequently, there are temporary conditions in which production without information is needed. Even more frequently, it appears that there is a long-term condition (although not permanent) bearing down on us that doesn't allow for immediate experimentation—better known as competition and the continual seeking of the highest result for the lowest cost.

This is actually an occasion for information, intelligence and therefore, breakdowns, not a reason for "heads down" production, as it is usually interpreted.

The value of capital decreases as the value of knowledge increases.

The computer industry provides the starkest example of the new replacing the old. Here the rate of change and the rate of technological development has been faster than in any other major industry in history; it has continued to be so for a longer period of time than in any other industry. Companies that were once leaders have literally gone out of existence. Venture capital poured into new companies. They skyrocketed, made fortunes and went bust. Well-known stars left companies to side with the competition or set up their own competition; they succeeded for a time and then disappeared. Only a few companies have managed to remain leaders for a long period (at least by industry standards). These few have continued to invest in new technology, the latest equipment, the development of science and leading-edge approaches; with each investment they rendered their previous investment obsolete. *The new will always destroy the capital investment of the old.* Until we make the shift and realize that the capital of the new age is knowledge (its development and application), then we will try to protect the existing capital base and the existing structures. Consequently, others will take our place as we fail to adapt and learn fast enough. This lesson comes to us courtesy of the industries that created the Information Age and were first to feel the pressures of a change they created. The changes that have swept through their industry will sweep through every other industry with the same velocity. The speed of change in technology is an indicator of the speed of change we can anticipate in a world organized for information, as opposed to material production.

The message is that intelligence, learning, information and knowledge are the source of competitive advantage. Anyone who ignores this message will be cannibalizing their future. There is no long-term strategy for success that does not include learning in its broadest and most creative sense. Any strategy that is to succeed long-term must focus on increasing knowledge (our real capital) and continually increase the rate at which physical capital is devalued. *Not* to do this is a breakdown indeed.

BREAKDOWNS CALL FORTH INFORMATION

If we alter our organizational principles so that they are consistent with increasing information and intelligence, then we will alter our personal and systemic relationship to breakdowns. They will be welcomed, they will be intentionally caused and they will be designed and used. When there are no occasions for new information, they must be created. What is needed are design principles that balance production and learning.

JIT and other approaches become occasions for learning rather than methods of production.

Most of the management "fads" and initiatives have some gold in them if we transform them into opportunities for information and learning. Whether the creators of JIT (just-in-time) meant it this way or not, we could consider that their processes were developed to learn about a system or gather information about a system and that they were not intended as "the right way" to run a corporation or organize a production process. In other words, the approaches were designed for learning while producing, rather than for production itself. A time-based initiative will produce dramatic results when used to cause interruptions in order to learn more about how a system operates. The benefit to be gained is understanding, not speed itself. However, that understanding may end up producing even more speed, or it may increase quality and flexibility without increasing speed. (One could argue that part of quality is speed and that flexibility is speed of change, rather than speed of production.)

Breakthrough targets offer more in the area of learning than achievement.

Despite popular opinion, the sustaining value of breakthrough targets or objectives is not motivation. If motivation is the intended result for breakthrough targets, they will end up being self-defeating. Even though various conditions can generate extra effort, that effort cannot be generated internally or maintain effectiveness. (We should take the lessons of "the boy who cried wolf" to heart.) Worse, if targets are generated for the purpose of motivation, the focus on immediate results will pollute the information environment. The sustaining value of breakthrough targets is that they can be used to cause breakdowns *for the purposes of learning and gaining understanding of a system.* The targets can be strategically designed to produce the particular breakdowns that are desired. Setting a target that is a breakthrough is an immediate breakdown: it is a breakthrough target *because* a pathway to its achievement isn't currently known, nor does it currently exist in the system, so setting a breakthrough target will immediately interrupt the normal flow of things.

The real value of using breakthrough targets will be realized only if they are used with awareness and open communication. When they are used for their most common purpose—manipulation—they damage the integrity of the system. As a basis for exhortation, they become the object of resistance and trust is lost. But, when breakthrough targets are openly used for the creation of breakdowns and the generation of information, they can be a valuable tool. The greatest benefit will be derived from setting a goal that is beyond the range of commonly understood possibility—not merely beyond the range of usual uncertainty.

A target that lies within known range will produce efforts that demand no creativity and generate little new information. A target beyond a known range will demand new approaches and generate a great deal of information, irrespective of whether or not the target is achieved. In fact, our reward systems need to be aimed at new information, new processes and new approaches, as well as achievement of the target. If they aren't, the system will destroy itself by being in service of something other than its intended purpose.

A recurring breakdown must be transformed into an occasion for learning.

Breakdowns are interruptions to the flow of existing systems that can be used to call forth new information. There are undesigned breakdowns in which the appropriate response is simply to repair the interruption as soon as possible. These types of breakdowns can often be transformed into opportunities for learning through an intentional declaration. If a breakdown is recurring, it is a signal that it needs to become an occasion for learning, rather than an occasion for fixing. Until a corporation is transformed into one that is designed to use every breakdown for learning, creating information and increasing its intelligence, the distinctions will have to be made between breakdowns for information and learning and breakdowns that are to be fixed with as little interruption as possible.

A way to create a useful interruption is to create projects that require learning, thinking, or creative approaches that are outside normal accountabilities. This has the effect of interrupting the normal flow and creating a structure for communication and information that is manageable. To take advantage of and further develop the full intelligence possibility of the corporation, every employee should be involved in such projects. Perhaps the most powerful application of this involves each employee having at least one such project for which she or he is accountable, as well as participating in the projects of others. The nature of these projects can range from "fixes" and improvements to innovations and endeavors that are purely for research, creation and invention.

BREAKDOWNS AS LANGUAGE ACTS

As we explore breakdowns, we discover that they are not as fixed as we might have thought. A breakdown is more an interpretation than an event. A whole range of breakdowns becomes available as we begin to distinguish the area: a challenge, an opportunity, a possibility, a problem, or an unwanted interruption. We can begin to see a rich and varied possibility emerge, as we consider breakdowns in depth. There are breakdowns we want to avoid, those we might welcome and others we might generate.

Breakdown is an interpretation. What is a breakdown for one person may not be a breakdown for another. What is considered a breakdown in one situation may not be a breakdown in another. The gamut of breakdowns ranges from a bare flicker on the screen to an upset that stops all production (or all thinking). The reaction to a breakdown can be anything from mild annoyance, fear, or anger to excitement or anticipation.

A breakdown is also a declaration—a speech act. Something exists as a breakdown when we declare that it is. When we notice an interruption and call it something, then it becomes that. By identifying it as a declaration, we create an enormous amount of freedom in the area and open up the possibility of mastering the situation. Our expanded operational definition of breakdown is *a declaration of interruption to the flow of a system to focus attention on a need for learning from demands beyond the current ability of the system to handle.*

When the idea of creating breakthrough projects is presented, most executives will respond with their version of, "We tried this project approach when we initiated TQM (time-based analysis, re-engineering, etc.) and it didn't work. First, it disrupted things too much. Then, it got chaotic and was unmanageable. And finally, the whole thing died out."

When I suggested this type of project to one of our clients, an integrated engineering and construction company, one of its division leaders said, "That will produce chaos and anarchy; so we can only create project teams in which management approves and directs."

He missed the point—and the design—of the breakthrough project approach. The intention of this approach is to get everyone involved in learning and allow that to happen in ways that are considered most appropriate by those who are learning and their immediate management.

Such a process will indeed cause breakdowns for managers. But isn't that the point?

The idea of breakdowns and learning does not only apply to the work force, it also applies to management and *its function as management.*

The resolution for this company was to replace the doubting people in management, and initiate a continuing education and development program for the management community. As part of the program, managers had to learn to manage the learning loop, as well as the production loop. To do that, they had to become adept at creating and handling breakdowns for themselves and others.

Statements such as "we've tried it" or "that's too chaotic" are red flags indicating that management doesn't understand the nature of the challenge confronting it. In bold terms, they are the kind of statements made by managers who are avoiding breakdowns.

When we recognize breakdowns as declarations, then we can both design the breakdowns and transform our relationship to them. After all, it is a breakdown only because somebody says so. And it is a *particular* breakdown only because somebody says so. That doesn't mean we don't need to take it seriously. It simply means that we have moved the phenomenon into the domain of conversation and made it accessible and amenable to dialogue. It becomes not something that happens to us of which we become victims but something that we create and cause. It becomes not a personal threat to our competence but a designed challenge for our learning. Language transforms. The realization that a breakdown is a speech act transforms the event.

THE PERSONAL CHALLENGE OF BREAKDOWNS

The place that seems to need the most work in the area of breakdowns is the personal development of executives and management. To put into practice effectively the very important, useful and pragmatic things that we have learned about communication, design, language and theory of organization, we must be able to create breakdowns for ourselves and be able to think and act powerfully in the face of those breakdowns. The challenge is to be able to operate with grace under pressure and not merely deflect that pressure onto subordinates.

Executives and managers need to develop the ability to confront situations that are personally challenging and to be able to handle the challenge instead of transferring it onto someone else—to be responsible. It is an unpleasant sight to see a manager avoid the personal upset of a breakdown by blaming others, or transferring the breakdown to his or her subordinates. Even worse is to witness a community of managers colluding in that act of self-protection.

The current rate of failure of major corporate initiatives (about 80%) can be placed squarely at the feet of management. The blame is usually placed on many factors, but the actual source can be found in the failure of executives and managers to handle the breakdowns presented to them by such initiatives. The employees of a company will handle breakdowns with ease when management is able to do the same. Management provides the environment and the security for dealing with breakdowns; therefore any management that is unable to deal with its own breakdowns certainly cannot create the environment for others to do so. The lack of such an environment is evidence that management is failing in the matter.

The breakdown that most management should declare for itself is that it does not have the environment, culture, or attitudes that it needs to manage its accountabilities and that it does not know how to create them. We must begin to develop our ability to see a corporation as a phenomenon in its own right and our ability to relate to people as co-creators of that corporation. We must begin to question our competence in dealing with people as a community, and our competence in the areas of personal communication and relationship. Few managers are willing to say outright that they do not know how to accomplish what they want to. Few will admit that the mood, spirit and culture of their corporation is their responsibility; and that they are unhappy with it and are unable to change it.

Executives and managers complain that TQM is not working in their corporation, but they fail to notice that they have done nothing effective to "drive out fear." They have not taken to heart W. Edwards Deming's claim that more than 80% of all problems are management caused. They have failed to take on any of the challenges that Deming said created the basic conditions for quality. These managers are avoiding the confrontation of the

Skilled trades are considered to be one of the hardest professions in which to initiate change. New methods and projects to develop new ways of working are usually greeted with great resistance.

The welders of a client construction company had a longstanding practice of not accepting new tools or new standards.

Management of the company attempted to force a change in the "ways of the welders" because the latest research showed that enormous productivity gains were possible through new developments in the industry.

Management failed to take into account the needs of the welders within their own culture: a culture in which dealing effectively with a certain set of breakdowns was the basis of their social value and self-esteem.

Doing things according to the dictates of "management engineers" was a direct threat to their culture.

It was not until management stopped making decrees, but instead created a breakdown by having the welders observe the performance of colleagues in other companies, and challenged them to meet those standards, that the welders began to see their job as one of continuous learning. The welding division soon adopted new methods and began to seek out better methods on its own.

As is frequently the case, those who were leaders in the resistance to change became leaders for change when conditions were created that made sense to them.

breakdown on their own doorstep, in hopes that the breakdown will occur with someone else—anyone else.

This is not an indictment of executives and managers. This is simply the way in which the system has evolved until now. If we combine our inherited mechanistic, materialistic and reductionist view of corporations, work, and people with our successful history of production (in which matter takes precedence over information), we cannot expect anyone to welcome breakdowns. With our education (formal and informal) aimed at status, rather than self-responsibility, we cannot expect people to be different than we find them. Nor can we expect to go beyond that way of operating without the aid of personal growth and development supported by something other than the norms of the system. We are going to have to accept the challenges of personal development before we can demand the same of others.

We not only have to give up our investment in physical capital, but also the much more personal investment that we have in our own knowledge, skill and competence. Putting aside our tools may not be so tough; putting aside "what we know," and what we have invested our learning, effort and social standing in, is much more difficult. As we begin to understand self-esteem, we see that one of its pillars is the ability to learn new things, which includes the ability to unlearn what we already know. As we become more competent at that, our attachment to what we already know decreases dramatically.

When we can create a context for living that includes learning, growth and development, we can undertake the process of engaging in breakdowns with a calm spirit and a generous heart. There is nothing inherently painful about creating and working with breakdowns.

Our organizational relationship with breakdowns, problems and interruptions in the flow is currently being determined by our obsession with production and an extreme ignorance of the possibilities of information. Our mechanistic and engineering approach to production and organization do not allow for the pursuit of what cannot be mechanistically measured. The value of learning, information and intelligence is not something that can be measured, as yet, on a direct cause-effect basis. These are the issues that we need to address. They can be accomplished without great difficulty when the possibility and value of creating information is recognized.

QUESTIONS FOR THIS CHAPTER:

- What kind of breakdowns do you welcome or respond to effectively? What kind do you avoid or respond to poorly?
- What protective acts of blame, or transference of responsibility, are being accepted or put up with in your corporation?
- What successes in your corporation's history are the result of the successful resolution of challenges and breakdowns? Which challenges and breakdowns were self-chosen and which were "inflicted"?
- What challenges are currently being avoided by your corporation?
- Where can you declare breakdowns for yourself, your peers and your team that would powerfully generate velocity of learning in important areas?
- What breakdowns could be declared today in your corporation that would create learning challenges substantial enough to resolve outstanding problems or lead to industry domination?

16 New Attributes of Behavior

"The most notable characteristic of the managers I interviewed is their mannerly lack of intensity."
DIANE MARGOLIS

"He exhibits a perfect harmony between his language and his life."
ON THE LIFE OF MOSES

"I have a vision of people in organizations, that involves longer, more thoughtful conversations, more risk-taking, much more tolerance of mistakes, asking questions like, How do we make sense of this organization?"
MEG WHEATLEY
LEADERSHIP AND THE NEW SCIENCE

Prelude

Does organizational transformation occur as a result of personal transformation taking place in all the people who are a part of that entity? Or must all the structures of a corporation go through a process of transformation, thus transforming the people in it? The debate rages on and fails to reveal any useful information because it uses a linear approach, suggesting that it is a matter of one *or* the other. Transformation is not a linear one-comes-first phenomenon.

In any transformational effort, we can count on the fact that many different things are going to change. The challenge for each of us personally will be to let go of the behaviors that we have found comfortable and relied on in the past. Most of us see our past behavior as the source of our success to date. Given we have that relationship to our behaviors, we aren't going to give any of them up in a hurry—particularly when we are under pressure.

What behaviors will be best suited for a corporation whose design principles are aimed at the emergence of intelligence? Where will we begin in our approach to shape these new behaviors? If we have not explicitly undertaken an initiative of transformation, what new behaviors will be demanded of us merely because of the dramatic changes that are occurring globally? If we declare our intentions for intelligent organization or any kind of transformation, that declaration will generate valid expectations from others that our behavior will change in some way.

THE NATURE OF BEHAVIOR

The behaviors, capacities and practices suitable for successful action in a corporation that values intelligence are different from those required and rewarded in a corporation that values only production. When there is a change in circumstances, a change in systems, or a change in intended results, new, more suitable behaviors must emerge that are a better fit with the new environment being created.

At an organizational level, changes in the structure and changes in behavior influence one another.

Executives and managers must learn new ways of acting and communicating, and new ways of being, if they are going to work effectively in a corporation committed to intelligence and learning. However, it may be a mistake to think that new behaviors can be practiced independently, or ahead of the demands of a system. Generally, it is more effective to begin by initiating design changes in a system and then supporting the behavioral changes that are appropriate to that. Why? Because behavior occurs in response to an environment (the complex systems with which we interact). Developing new ways of communicating and interacting will not be as hard as you might imagine. After all, we shaped our current behaviors by selecting them from a rich, dynamic set of possibilities, because they were the ones that were the most appropriate to the situation and the most rewarded at that time. So as new intentions, new objectives, and new systems of reward emerge within our organizational structures, an environment will be generated in which learning compatible behaviors will be quite easy. We will simply select and develop a different constellation from the array of human possibilities.

The most difficult introduction to make in any organizational transformation is that of a new language that is to be used as the structure of interpretation. Many of the currently acceptable ways of speaking, listening (or not), relating, reacting, or approaching problems will not be consistent with the new structure of interpretation being introduced. The behaviors that we are competent in (those appropriate for a system organized around a mechanistic world) are not the same as those appropriate to a complex system within a world in which information takes precedence. The pursuit of organizational intelligence, organizational learning and success in a new era demands that each one of us makes changes; and if we are going to be a part of an organizational transformation then we must make the appropriate changes.

Behavior is an emergent phenomenon in complex intelligent systems.

In our attempts to understand behavior and the dynamics of transforming it, we are challenged immediately by the way in which we perceive human beings. If we consider them to be mechanistic cause/effect systems, then behavioral changes should be quick and easy once we understand the mechanism and can "program in" changes. But when we see ourselves as complex intelligent systems, then the alteration of behavior takes on a new dimension. The process of change in behavior occurs as a result of an interplay between interpretation and structure. During this interplay, the transformation of behavior is not expected to be immediate. Instead it emerges and evolves in a dance with the circumstances.

When management declares that transformation is underway, it is not uncommon to hear rumblings throughout a corporation such as, "Management says things are going to be different but *they* haven't changed." What kind of change is everyone looking for? They're looking to see if there are changes in the way people are communicating—and they're looking at every action or nonaction as a form of communication. Communication is embodied not only in language but in the moods, habits, reactions, time allocations, and multitude of day-to-day actions that create the interactions within a complex system. The expressions and practices of people are a reflection of the linguistic world in which they live, and are interpreted through the linguistic world of the corporation and every person in it. The term linguistic world means that we create and attach meaning to everything that occurs. This meaning is expressed in our words and ideas. It is this meaning that is the world that we respond to.

BEHAVIOR CHANGE WITHIN A CORPORATION

Executives and managers who are initiating an organizational transformation face a particularly rugged challenge in the area of making behavioral changes, due to the public nature of their position. Every action and response made by the executives and management is being watched and interpreted by others in the corporation. This precarious position of high visibility can either provide the incentive needed to maintain a sense of discipline when facing the challenges of personal change or it can ignite seemingly unbearable discomfort resulting from an attempt to meet everyone's expectations.

If the process of organizational transformation is not possible unless and until the executive and management levels are totally consistent with the new ways of speaking and acting, then any such initiative will undoubtedly be doomed. It is only possible to become totally consistent with a new language and a new approach through the unfolding integrative process of living it. Awareness in each moment will lead us to integrity of intention and to closer approximations of these intentions in our actions.

Unless those promoting the initiative exhibit *some* level of consistent integration of the new thinking and speaking, it is understandable that others will question the validity, integrity and meaning of the initiative. Any skepticism encountered during the initiative is part of an attempt to conserve power or security in the old system by complaining about those who are attempting the new. The needs of those yet to "jump on board" the initiative will vary dramatically: some will demand that those promoting the initiative have complete integrity with the new approaches down to the last detail, and others will be satisfied with only a small sign of authenticity. But whatever the needs, their origins can be traced back to the old structure exerting its tendency to protect its identity and its mode of functioning.

THE DANCE BETWEEN INITIATING CHANGE AND BEING CHANGED

Anyone's attempt to formulate and articulate the new behaviors required for an organizational transformation will be influenced by that particular person's understanding of what is "good" based on her or his own values. The behavioral changes suggested very often exceed what is implied by the theory also being proposed. Often these behavioral suggestions are a result of someone's personal or spiritual beliefs about how people should relate to one another. Even though these suggestions may offer some insight for a personal transformation, they are not necessarily valuable or essential for an organizational transformation. Perhaps a better approach would be to observe what behaviors are being suggested by the circumstances themselves rather than trying to shape them using someone's personal idealistic philosophy.

Behavior reorganizes itself when the world occurs for us in ways that call for that behavior.

As stated earlier, developing new attributes of behavior is not the place to begin an organizational transformation; instead it is more effective to begin with designing new theories, ideas and possibilities for the corporation that are best expressed through changes in structure. These structural changes will then begin to call forth new dimensions in behavior. As structure continues to unfold in alignment with our theories and practices are implemented, behavioral changes will continue to be suggested and demanded by the structures. These behaviors will in turn be a natural expression of both the new theories and the new structures. Behavior is shaped by how the *world is occurring* and the world occurs consistent with our linguistic interpretation. When our interpretation changes, then our behavior changes quite naturally. Both the way in which the world occurs and our behavior are shaped through our response to the social environment. Like every other complex phenomenon, it is not necessary to force something to happen. In fact, it cannot be forced. We merely need to begin the process and let the unfolding indicate to us the possibilities that are now available.

When the tales of major initiatives disclose pain and struggle amid the executives, this is usually an indication that there has been a premature emphasis on behavioral change. Often executives are too demanding of themselves and others "up front," well before the new thinking and language has been adequately integrated into the system. Action communicates. If that's so, what results can be anticipated by taking actions that are consistent with an idea that is not well enough formulated to know what those actions should be? Answer: something between minimal benefit and significant detriment. One of the developmental aspects of the approach being suggested is that initial results of behavioral change will provide introspective value while beginning desired action.

THE CURRENT CONDITIONS

The water we are swimming in isn't clear—it is polluted by our history.

It is useful to remember that the structures of interpretation that currently exist in our corporations are not particularly friendly or forgiving. The relationships within corporations designed using a mechanistic model (certainly any that consider themselves in need of transformation) are fundamentally adversarial, no matter how personally pleasant they may be. These structures and relationships have been primed to be antagonistic toward individual initiative and creative expression. The hierarchical nature of organization became a part of society long before your corporation came into existence, so this style of organizing has a long career of interfering with the profound possibility of generous and cooperative relationships. Many of us understand these systems and can operate within them without taking personal offense, but the costs are enormous in our communications and relationships as human beings.

Any effort at transformation is attempted within an environment that is more separated, more adversarial and more exclusive than the intended one; therefore, the environment is somewhat inimical to the requirements of the transformation effort. Our current way of relating to one another renders us nearly incapable of undertaking a transformation effort together, or for that matter, to do anything together that is risky or new. We remain at a standstill until we establish relationships that make it safe and appropriate to undertake such a venture together. Yet we cannot begin to establish the necessary mosaic of relationships until some transformation has taken place. A classic double bind. Escape from a double bind is always the same. Move to a new level of abstraction and create a context that alters the situation. We create a context by declaring intention and possibility. Next, we must demonstrate and call for the kind of relationships suitable to meet the challenges of the future. We begin this process by communicating our own responsibility for the past and our responsibility for its continuation or not.

An executive for a construction company woke up to the need for change and began a program of personal development for himself and his executive team. The program focused on behavioral aspects of communication, relationship and participation.

The team being educated began to move out into the corporation and exercise what was being developed in its program. Their actions included asking others for their opinions, encouraging disputes to come to resolution through mediation, and treating people as intelligent, responsible, sensitive human beings.

Given the fact that this executive's company as well as the entire industry was predisposed to an autocratic and authoritarian way of management, the changes were not welcomed by the lower levels of management. Those lacking in a similar education could only interpret the new behaviors as "losing it."

To further complicate the situation, the executive team could not maintain consistency in their expression of the behavioral changes in their day-to-day practices.

Following a period of lack of success, the old behaviors soon reappeared and the new completely disappeared. Those who witnessed the cycle interpreted the executives' new behaviors and attempts at developing relationships as manipulative gestures.

The situation was resolved by providing development opportunities at all levels throughout the company and by taking the pressure off the executive team by shifting the context. This was done by managing the project as though it was an organizational process, rather than an effort directed at behavioral change.

THE PERSONAL CHALLENGE

Attachment to identity increases the challenge of a behavioral change.

Even when the need for behavioral change is blatantly obvious, we tend to keep our feet in the mud because of our strong attachment to our existing behaviors. Our behavior and our identity are closely intertwined, and let's face it—we are very attached to who we are. This tendency of attachment to oneself is further magnified by our society, which encourages individuality and therefore discourages the detachment from our identity which is essential for introspection and growth. In our efforts to protect our identity, we end up cutting off our access to flexibility, intelligence and adaptation. Much of the personal pain and struggle experienced by executives in a transformation effort are caused by the fact that they are being forced to look very closely at themselves and see that what they are doing is not working. Our efforts should not be focused on behavioral change, but instead on introspection and a willingness to look at oneself. What is needed is awareness.

As human beings we are designed to be infinitely adaptable, but we have brilliantly mastered restricting that.

Environment and circumstances play significant roles in shaping our identity. Our continuing adaptation to our environment and circumstances allows us to function and be accepted. So it makes perfect sense that we have become attached to our identity, given its survival value and social significance. What we fail to notice is that our identity is extremely malleable to circumstances. We are different things for different people. We become a different person in different circumstances and we differ over time. To the extent that this is not true, we are attached to some particular behavior or way of being for survival or social reasons. Attachment to identity is the source of our inability to adapt to different circumstances.

If organizational transformation is managed as though it is merely a matter of personal transformation, then unnecessary problems arise during the process. The problems result from the misconception that a corporation is merely a collection of individuals, and if they all transform, then the corporation will transform. An even more popular delusion is that a corporation is a creation of its executives, and if they transform, then the rest of the corporation will follow. Neither approach works because both fail to see a corporation as it really is—a complex system in its own right.

Even though an organizational transformation will probably transform the individuals in it, their personal transformation will be a *result* of the organizational transformation and not the other way around. If too much attention is placed on behavioral change, the organizational nature of the process will be overlooked and important elements will be neglected. The approaches used to launch the initiative will create a process that will unfold in unpredictable ways, because a complex intelligent system is involved. The process will also transform individuals in unknown ways. We can, however, anticipate the direction of some of the new ways of being that will result, especially if the shift is from a mechanical model to an information model. While appropriate ways of being will naturally emerge throughout the process itself, those ways of being for initiating a process may not be identical to those of later regular functioning. There are, however, ways of listening and dialogue behaviors that will go a long way in both circumstances.

The struggle to become something one is not, or something that the circumstances are not calling for is arduous and generally leads to failure. Many executives, upon being requested to change their style, lose their strengths and fail to compensate with other gains. For example, executives assessed as being "too autocratic" become weak as they attempt to become "more democratic." Their error lies in not interpreting others' requests as useful information to be ongoingly accessed for incremental development; instead they try to become something that they are not. These executives are being requested to exhibit behaviors that they have not yet developed and to limit the actions they currently use to produce results effectively. And they are being asked to do that even though the system and the circumstances are not calling for those changes. This recipe is certain to produce pain and failure.

The senior executive of a very large multinational engineering contractor invited me to work with one of his managers to prepare him for a position as vice-president.

The guy was unbeatable when it came to producing sales and successful deliveries, and a promotion was in order. However, the other executives felt his behavior was too autocratic and that he was incapable of developing and working with teams—so my task was to reshape that.

What I found interesting was that although the executives were a little uncomfortable with his style, it wasn't too different from the rest of the successful people in the company. Plus, the system produced rewards and no penalties for his behavior.

The promotion candidate was mildly interested in our work together and exhibited enough of a shift in his behavior to get the promotion. The change lasted only as long as it took to get the promotion. After that he reverted back to his old style with a vengeance.

Was he a phony? Absolutely not. He did what the system asked of him from start to finish. And until the corporate system changes, there will be no lasting behavioral change in the company's new vice-president or any others like him.

A threat to one's sense of competence is considered a threat to one's identity.

We usually consider it a personal threat when our competence is called into question, especially when it is caused by the circumstances within our immediate vicinity. We are very attached to our competence and our sense of our ability to survive. When that is threatened, especially in areas where it was previously considered to be sufficient, we find ourselves in the midst of one of the worst possible scenarios. When undertaking an organizational transformation or any other major initiative, it is the element of competence being challenged that calls for a level of relationship beyond what already exists. Undertaking anything that lies within the boundaries of our existing sense of competence does not require a relatedness stronger than we now have or are capable of building. However, in order to create a future for ourselves and our corporations that is not merely a continuation of our past, new dimensions in the area of relationship are required, because transformation always demands the kind of change that will threaten our sense of competence.

It is not that we are inadequate to meet the challenges that emerge in the process of transformation; it is that we are not already *unconsciously competent* for such a process. Transformation constantly challenges us to look at ourselves and create ourselves to *become* more than we are right now. We are accustomed to a certain level of mastery and it is not challenged in the normal course of operation. Although we have become competent at managing interruptions to the normal flow of things, this way of managing takes place at an unconsciously competent level. When things go wrong outside our realm of competence, we are not only challenged but frequently threatened. Most human beings have attempted to design their lives to avoid such circumstances and have succeeded all too well.

NEW DIMENSIONS IN BEHAVIOR

Develop capacities—don't limit options or possibilities.

As the environment of a corporation begins to transform, behavioral changes that will be called forth will not be a specific set of ideals, nor should they be considered better than the old ideals. A wider range of behaviors should be developed, to be called on as needed, rather than a new and exclusive set of behaviors. Developing these behaviors will be intentional and directional rather than working toward a specified end.

The direction of behavioral changes will be toward increasing intelligence, improving our ability to generate information, and compounding the computational capacity of our corporation. This direction will create coordination within the complex system of the corporation as well as maximize the expression of our personal intelligence within that system. We might indicate the intended direction as being toward the right from the left in the following columns. The behaviors are best interpreted as a whole rather than as pairs:

closed	open
secretive	accessible (regarding information)
exclusion	inclusion
impersonal	expressive
authority-based	self-responsible
bureaucratic	accountable
direct control	trust in processes
hierarchical	interconnected
rule-bound	value-based
tightly controlled	loosely coupled
produced	learned
directive	listen
argument	dialogue

Movement toward the right column is not movement away from the left. These columns are not opposites but, instead, a complex system out of which a wider variety of responses may emerge. These distinctions do not represent values but, instead, diverse ways of being. Our flexibility with them is instrumental in adapting, learning and increasing intelligence.

"Whatever is flexible and flowing will continue to grow. Whatever is rigid and blocked will wither and die."
I CHING

THE IMPORTANCE OF DIALOGUE

The one behavioral change that will produce the largest shift in our corporations as we transform our relationship to information, learning and intelligence is dialogue. Although we all have the capability of dialogue, there has been little room for its practice in our organizational life. Few managers have developed the necessary skills or are effective with the art of dialogue. Few have been called upon to generate, lead, or even engage in dialogue throughout their entire career.

Our operational definition of dialogue is *"a conversation in which the intention is to generate something in the conversation itself that did not exist in any one of the participants before the conversation began."* Dialogue is a

215

distinctly different kind of conversation from those in which we are attempting to pass information between people, convince others of the rightness of our ideas, or persuade others to do what we want. Dialogue has a creative and generative intention supporting it.

There are numerous skills we can develop that will enhance our effectiveness in dialogue. However, the best place to start is with the realization that dialogue is essential for increasing information, intelligence and learning. Until we realize its value and are committed to the results that it can produce, we will not commit ourselves to developing the necessary skills, nor will we apply them. Our development of the skills of dialogue will emerge through our intention to engage in dialogue and our ongoing awareness and application during the process of our conversations.

As we begin to move in the direction of developing new capacities and ways of being, we meet with no real mysteries. There are programs that make the assimilation of new behaviors easier, support their development and provide practice. But the greatest opportunities will be found right on the job, in real situations. The integration of theory and our behavioral practices will occur as they continue to inform one another. Velocity in the development of these practices can be increased dramatically by coaching from a credible source, one whom you trust. The coaching must be developmental rather than interventionist. There is not a right way and no required timeline. New behaviors will emerge in the process of implementation itself. Mismatches in speed of development will cause various breakdowns, which can be used as a source of information to guide the developmental process. The personal challenge will be to orchestrate the dance between the pace of development of the corporation and the pace of your own development. If the "dance" does not sound attractive and inviting, then organizational

The biggest obstacle that we must overcome in engaging in dialogue is its threat to our identity. Although there is no *real* threat, it is strongly perceived as a threat.

One of the positions dialogue threatens is any authority with which we have identified. Even more threatening for some people is that it opens our thoughts, values and beliefs to question and challenge.

Through the course of dialogue the very structure of our identity is exposed and can no longer be protected, not even from internal influences.

If you're now thinking that you do not fall within the category of those who feel threatened by dialogue, invite a group of subordinates to open dialogue and get feedback on your behavior or strategies.

transformation is not a good thing to initiate. If it has already been initiated, then there is nothing to do except learn to dance or get out of the way.

QUESTIONS FOR THIS CHAPTER:

- In past efforts to change, has the focus been on personal behavior or on the corporation?
- Have past change efforts been based on intervention or development?
- If you have suffered during a change effort in the past, locate the source of that in inconsistencies between personal demands and system demands.
- If there has been resistance in past change efforts, locate the source of that in attachments to identity.
- What organizational structures inhibit dialogue and will block change efforts in the future?
- Are any behavioral attributes needed that you don't have?
- Are you sure?

The Transition Period

"The important thing is this: to be able at any moment to sacrifice what we are, for what we might become."
CHARLES DUBOIS

"The teacher (or leader) must present a structure of knowledge that he does not fully understand to a student who also cannot hope fully to understand it."
WILLIAM BARTLEY III
UNFATHOMED KNOWLEDGE, UNMEASURED WEALTH

Prelude

No matter where we look in our lives, whether it is a day, a period that spans a year or two, our career, or our own body—we are always in transition. Anything that is alive is in a state of *becoming* and therefore constantly in transition. Transition is so much a part of everything that it remains transparent, unless there is a jarring major shift, such as leaving a comfortable situation and not yet settling into something new.

We have grown up in a culture where we are always supposed to know where we are and where we're going. Yet life is a process of constant changing, shifting and becoming. The more awake we are in our lives, the less fixed we are about exactly where we are and exactly where we're going and the more open we are to what's possible. How many times have you heard someone ask, "How are we supposed to know what to do if we aren't clear about the goal?" A powerful answer to that might be, "We'll discover where we're going as we go. Simply take the action that most fully engages with the world."

If you are about to enter a process of transformation, then you know that most people will be disrupted in their comfort and familiarity with existing operations. This is the kind of period when a declaration of a "state of transition" might be useful. Such a declaration will remind not only others, but also those who made the declaration, that normal expectations, actions and ways of being will not be sufficient to the times.

DISTINGUISHING A TRANSITION PERIOD

An emergency is an event in time. It has a beginning and an end. When a state of emergency is a permanent state, it is not an emergency; it is just a peculiar way to live. If an emergency goes on for a long period and continues to be considered an emergency, we begin to see it as incompetence. The point that will mark the end of an emergency can be stated beforehand by declaring the conditions that will be considered its end, such as the recovery of a stable level of health. In other situations, we can decide beforehand how long we will consider a certain condition an emergency before we declare it a matter of incompetence, or a new state of normalcy.

A transition period has a declared beginning and a specified end.

A transition period is similar to an emergency in that it has a declared starting time and an ending that can be declared as a specific time or specific conditions. Declaring a beginning and an end is a way to provide a context for a transformation or a major change effort. It is important to declare an end because the transition we are talking about (from a linear mechanistic state to a robust information state) will not have a clear end. The transition itself will begin to look like the desired result. Another example of this phenomenon is quality: quality is a way of life and the transition, from what was to what shall be, has no ending point. But the transition period should have a beginning and an end.

The declaration of a transition period informs everyone in the corporation that the effort is developmental and that there will be room for the failures and inconsistencies that are part of any transition period, that is, a grace period. This declaration also warns people that things will be happening that are beyond what is normal or familiar and that actions will be monitored and measured. Declaring a transition period also encourages people to sort out how they will relate to the initiative and prompts them to begin to explore their own expression as they participate in the initiative. It also announces clearly to everyone what the conditions of satisfaction are for the transition period.

A transition period is not something to be identified; instead, it is something that is declared. Our operational definition of a transition period is *"a declared condition or state of being that has a beginning in time and an ending that is specified in time or by a condition."* The purpose of a transition period is to announce a period of change, learning, and relative uncertainty. The announcement of a transition period has a dual purpose: it alerts people

219

to the conditions of the near future and it places a demand on those declaring it to think and act in a way consistent with a specified intention.

PRESENT ACTION AND FUTURE UNCERTAINTY

The typically concealed, but always pressing question of what the future will hold rushes to the foreground whenever we consider major changes that might impact our future in unusual ways. Every action that takes place now is related to the future. Each action in the present leads toward something that has not yet happened. Every action we take today will have consequences in our lives, predictable or not.

You are being paid for creating the future of your corporation.

For everyone at every level of a corporation, the future is relevant. We are not being paid for the past, nor are we being paid for mere repetition or action that has only immediate results. We are being paid to create a future for our corporation that is healthy and has the potential for generating long-term survival.

The question "What will the future be?" is not a question designed to be answered. It is a question to be lived with, to be used to inform our current thinking and actions, and to remind us that the uncertainty of our future de-

---

After having discovered some radical new ways of organizing, based on approaches derived from biology, information and intelligence, the chairman of a construction company asked his executive group to consider these approaches and to present its ideas at the next management meeting.

After the presentation was made, those in management concluded that they would design radical changes for their own organization based on the ideas that had been generated.

They declared and announced a period of transition during which every structure and practice of the company would be turned on its head. It was requested that, during that time, everyone was to carry on according to their operational accountabilities to the best of their ability.

Needless to say, everyone's working life was greatly disrupted due to the amount of attention focused on redesigning everything.

The amount of time allowed for major changes to take place was declared at the onset and was set at three months. The organization was redesigned within that period.

A second period of transition was declared for individuals who were either not accepting the change or were not able to succeed with all of the necessary changes within the first period. During the secondary phase, anyone not up to speed could continue with their development, or decide on other career paths.

The entire process of redesign was accomplished within six months and the year's sales and profit results were positive at a time considered by the industry to pose difficult trading conditions.

mands that we remain awake, vigilant and continually challenging ourselves. Any corporation that has ceased to question itself has become complacent, has forgotten that there are no guarantees in our future, and has chosen a path that is seductively leading to its own extinction.

Human beings and corporations have inherited a culture that includes a way of thinking and speaking that is proficient at recalling and even creating a past, but is impoverished when it comes to thinking about or creating a future. In the midst of this culture, the most that we can accomplish is to take our past and extend it into the future, and then attempt to be usefully informed by that. Such a culture leaves us desperately trying to preserve the past, instead of inspiring us to think and be innovative about our future. After all, the past worked—we're still alive! When people operating from this culture are confronted with the issue of not placing enough attention on their future, their response will inevitably be one of the following: "We think about the future. We invest in planning for the future." Or, "We're clear that our survival isn't guaranteed." Maybe so. But I'm suggesting that what most people are doing, regarding their future, does not affect the day-to-day actions of their corporation because it is done in isolation from the daily functioning of the corporation. The current design of almost all corpo-

When our consulting firm takes on a new account, one of the first things that I do is meet with an executive group. When I ask the members of that group about their strategies, they're insistent that the future gets plenty of attention.

But after establishing relationship and being pressed a bit, the members of the executive group reveal that their idea of thinking about the future entails operational questions of how to impact the next quarter, what the next move is on current contracts, how to secure subsequent contracts, and so on.

Next I ask them the somewhat embarrassing question, "How much useful time do you spend in dialogue together developing the future of your corporation five to ten years from now?"

Their answer always reveals that it is extremely little time and definitely not enough.

The reason behind this always turns out to be that people don't know how to explore the possibilities of their future, rather than pressures such as time and required results. I notice there's also a sense of futility in people's speaking about the future because they don't know how to go about making a different future happen.

This is where a transition period becomes essential. Any executives that are taking on an initiative need the awareness and humility to declare that they too are in a learning or transition period—at least to themselves. Carrying on as though *others* need to change but *we* are fine will not produce dramatic results.

rations encourages concern for the immediate and little, if any, concern for the future.

It is not that we aren't doing anything in our corporations to influence our future. We are. We do what everybody does. We know that our actions have implications for the future and we act accordingly. But what we fail to do is fold our future back into our present with any real creativity or power in the course of our day-to-day activities—and day-to-day activities are where the future occurs. Our future emerges from the interplay of today's actions. Enough of the "right" actions and we will survive and prosper. Too many of the "wrong" ones and we will disappear. Enough of a fuzzy mixture and we will take a little longer to disappear, with a few of us waking up to discover what path we are on and working out a recovery.

An extension of the past is a good predictor of the future—until something changes. Then it is the most dangerous predictor of all.

Our ineffectual approach to thinking and speaking about the future is one that we have inherited and for the most part, we have left it unexamined. We think and speak about the future using language based on a muddled view that the future is an extension of the past and therefore knowable. So we approach our work involving the future with a concern for knowing the future. But the future is not knowable. It is knowable only when looking back. Most of the future that occurs is merely an extension of the known past and therefore contains no surprises. Looking back into the past for a view of what the future will be is pretty safe, provided there is no change in conditions. Driving your car by looking in the rearview mirror only works as long as the road continues in a perfectly straight line.

At times the future is a complete surprise. However, later when we look back on it we generally can see how it was predictable. Very few people predicted the collapse of the Soviet Union or the Berlin Wall, but today very few people recall those events as the complete surprise that they were when they happened. IBM was considered by "everybody" as one of the best managed companies in the world but, of course, now "everyone" knows exactly what was wrong with the company and speaks about it as though it was always obvious. "Everyone" knew that EuroDisney was not going to work *after* it ran into problems.

THE NEED FOR A DECLARED TRANSITION PERIOD

For almost everyone, the question "What will the future be like?" takes a backseat to the more burning question "Will the future work out for me?" Prediction, if it could be counted on to be accurate, would undoubtedly be useful. So any prediction efforts that are working should be continued. Keep in mind that the longer they work the more suspect they become, unless they are also changing or developing in some way. (Don't forget the inherent double bind: if the prediction theory or model is changing, how do you know that it is working?) All of this uncertainty points one in the direction of developing a new way of thinking.

New thinking, new questions and new ways of being need a grace period for development.

This new way of thinking leaves prediction to those who practice magic and unremittingly looks for what will provide the best means of survival ongoingly into the future. A new way of thinking will initiate a different approach altogether, one which leads to discovering the actions, capacities, skills, information and flexibility needed to provide the best possible chance of survival for the corporation—no matter what the future. This way of approaching the future promotes engagement with people and the environment, rather than isolation and protection from them, and also introduces a different set of questions with which to live, inform our thinking and actions, and remind us what our intentions are on a daily basis.

The future of a transformation is certain to be uncertain.

As a transformation begins to unfold, the problems and pitfalls that will arise will not be familiar ones and the responses that we must bring to these will not be our old ones. Our once-valued predictions won't offer us much aid, because the future of a transformation is certain to be uncertain. We must create new tools and approaches that will assist us in meeting the challenges of transformation and support our success. And equally important, we need the time and support to develop them.

It seems almost contradictory to establish a "transition period" when what we are working toward is a way of life or a way of organizing that we expect to continue. But using the terminology of a transition period, especially in the *initial phases* of an organizational transformation, provides the context for the events that are likely to unfold or the reactions that are sure to surface from the corporation and its environment. This context will offer us some sense of preparedness so that we can set out on the path with enthusiasm.

THE PROBLEMS OF A TRANSITION

The specifics as to the methodology of implementation can vary enormously from corporation to corporation, even though the design principles are the same. In much the same way, the specifics of reaction and breakdown will vary in relation to circumstances, yet they will be similar in kind. One of the principles of action is, "you don't know what you do," that is, you cannot know the full implications of an action before the event. No matter what your intentions are and how much planning and analyzing you do, the results of action will not be as expected. Recognizing this creates a sense of humility that will be very useful for staying open to the uncertainty that is part of any major initiative.

I have yet to work on a transformational activity during which the client hasn't said, "Why didn't you tell me that the results were this powerful and that there would be such a dramatic impact?" My response always resonates with, "I told you as best I could and I told you that you'd ask that question. Two factors make it this way: one is that I don't know exactly how it is going to work out. The other is that you don't have the ears to hear until you've experienced it yourself."

As a leader in a transformation, one must gracefully straddle what appears to be a wide gap. On one side, you don't know how the initiative is going to unfold, and on the other, you are working within an environment of people who expect you to know just that. In the past, if you didn't know, you acted as if you did. But that won't work in this situation. A transformation will also not take place as a result of the ideas you have about how it is going to turn out, or as a result of you directing the process. Instead, it will emerge from the interaction, the dialogue and the *working out in action* that occurs between hundreds or thousands of people in the course of millions of interactions. Plus, if you try to figure out the whole thing beforehand, it won't be right and people will know it. They will consider it more bureaucratic nonsense. If a small group tries to figure it out, the same holds true,

The founder and CEO of a German design company discussed our consulting processes with us in great detail before deciding that we would work together.

In the agreements we made with one another, the CEO committed his company to a major education and development program that would include 60 of the top people in his management group.

But as we started to get the ball rolling, he balked and ended up committing himself to only about half of the program we had previously decided to undertake.

When asked why, he said he doubted that the paybacks could be accomplished as promised. He also said he was doubtful that anything could make the difference that we had described to him.

We had no sooner started moving forward when very clear changes began to occur, followed by unprecedented results.

About four months into the process, he complained to us that we had done a poor job in explaining to him how powerful the results of our approach were. He immediately increased the scope of work to what we had originally suggested.

Later, he made the same complaint, although this time, in a lighter spirit. We increased the extent of work even further based on the paybacks.

but with others feeling excluded. If you announce the initiative before you have it all worked out and communicate to people that it will be worked out in action by everyone, they will declare your incompetence and start asking for real leadership in the company. Within the current model of organization and leadership, there is no way to win this one.

In any major initiative, you start at the wrong place and at the wrong time.

There will be an infinite variety of opinions about who should have done what during the initiative. In retrospect, you will think others should have been included from the start. You might think that some of those included shouldn't have been. Others will think that the wrong group was chosen initially, or that specific people should or should not have been included. But when the initiative is finally successful, no one will care that it was the wrong group. Opinion will finally give way to reality.

Starting in the wrong place with the wrong people provides the information out of which the transformation will emerge.

So what do you do in a situation where it looks like the wrong time and the wrong people? Some would throw up their hands and say that it is a "no win" situation. I would say that it is just a normal situation, that "winning" is not the issue, and that anything worth doing includes this kind of challenge. There's nothing wrong with the situation; it's just the nature of the challenge. The best approach is to act in ways that are consistent with your intentions, to have speaking and action exhibit integrity, and to do the best you can to include people in information and in action. No matter how you approach the initiative, there will be gaps in information and understanding. Rather than being a problem or "something wrong," these gaps act as fuel to ignite communication, information, and dialogue—all of which are the basis for developing new ways of thinking and formulating a corresponding organizational design. Gaps that occur between information and understanding are always uncomfortable because we cannot deal with them competently using approaches that we typically use. Even so, gaps are occasions for high levels of communication and creativity.

The problem is not the situation. The problem is our tendency to react and communicate in old ways. Gaps in information and understanding are not only new opportunities to learn but also opportunities to demonstrate integrity. Of course, our tendency will be to want to look good, and to do that we'll have to appear to be in control and say what was typically expected of leaders in the old organizational models. Because we have not yet developed our ability to count on others, allow others to be self-responsible, and trust the system to be self-organizing, we will tend to revert to previously accepted modes of hierarchy, linear thinking and low-information/high-control. In fact, everyone around us will suggest that we revert to old approaches, and if we do, those same people will condemn us for hypocrisy.

What is occurring isn't personal; it is the unfolding of a process.

When we are being criticized for our new approach, it is important to remember that what is happening is not personal; it is merely the organization and the people in it attempting to get old patterns, styles, behaviors, and so on back in place. The complex system that is already in existence is attempting to survive. The comments that are made, the upsets that emerge, the questions that are raised and the threats that are made are merely the old system attempting to destroy the new. The information contained in people's comments is invaluable, because it points out the existence and the particulars of the old system in ways that have been concealed until now. The comments, questions, and so on are revealing not the personalities of the people but the operation and design of the existing system that has emerged into a phenomenon that has avoided the particular stresses of change up to this point.

Some of your best supporters can end up being your worst enemies.

Another inevitable occurrence in a transformation will be the emergence of "true believers": people with very strong convictions who actually become impediments to the process because of their approach. The basis of transformation is understanding at a very fundamental level the nature of corporations, markets and human beings. Transformation is not about believing something; nor is it something that can be formulated and then sold. It is a process of *becoming* which is not available to individual perception. Apart from a mood of enthusiasm (if that is one's bent) there is only the process of unfolding, dialogue and being awake. Those that do not allow others to engage in the process in their own way defeat the purpose and the intent of a transformation.

Those who are not able to see the process of transformation as an organizational unfolding, but see it only as a matter of individual conversation or personal transformation, will find it difficult to stay in sync with what's actually occurring. This is inevitable, and the inability to understand the process merely reveals the current social condition of human beings. This condition will continually provide opportunities for the process of transformation to demonstrate its integrity. The design flaws that currently exist in the corporation allow situations to get out of hand and interrupt the productive and learning purposes of the corporation. If the purpose of our corporations is coordinated information and action, then there must be structures that allow some of the "human nature" that is so much a part of our culture to be expressed and, at the same time, limit its potentially damaging impact on the corporation.

TRANSITION AND STRUCTURE

To the extent that our organizational design has as its intention the creation of a complex intelligent system, each instance of communicative incompetence or blockage is an opportunity for discovering some of the corporation's design or developmental needs. The essence of such a design is its ability to access, generate and discover the meanings of information. Every breakdown is an opportunity to discover the nature of the old structures that are currently in place and an occasion for creative application of the newly developed design principles. Each instance of communicative breakdown is also an opportunity to return to the basic design principles of the evolving complex system, observe them in action and reinforce or change them as the foundation from which a rich variety of productive action may emerge.

The already existing structure is designed to continue the past as a means of survival. This will always work against change needed for the future.

There will be conflicts between the rigid hierarchical structures already in existence and the new self-organizing principles being developed. These conflicts will appear contradictory to the transformation in the rational linear mind of the corporation. They are not contradictions, no matter how many difficulties the conflicts create. The existing structures are currently a perfect match for the existing corporation. A corporation and its structures are like the front and back of the same hand; they are related in an essential way, but are not the same thing. Conflicts between the old and the new are occasions for discovery, information and possibility; they must occur. These conflicts will occur until the new design principles are fully formulated and integrated in such a way that they are the system. The process of formulation and integration cannot happen without passing through the phase of the old "battling it out" with the new, and this will include the practical resolution of countless issues and infinite instances of application. This will be important to remember, especially during conflicts and getting lost in the heat of the moment.

At some point during the transition period, all the structures must go through the process of being redesigned. Some may be changed at the onset of the transformation for communication purposes or for immediate operational purposes. Other structures may be changed early in the process to support the flourishing of learning and information. Others may not go through their process of formulation and integration for some time. It is even conceivable that many of the old structures will remain in place; however, their importance will decline. For instance, the old cost accounting methods are not suitable for most complex activities, even though they are ideally suited for specific local purposes and should be retained for those. This may be viewed as a reduction in importance, but it is also an increase in power and usefulness, because now these systems are being utilized in the areas for which they are best suited. They can now renew themselves, regain integrity and become welcome tools instead of bureaucratic burdens.

The tendency will arise in many people to keep the old structures (pay, reporting, advancement, authority, lines of communication) long beyond the time they are useful. Anyone wanting to do so will justify it by saying that these structures are vital for survival and must not be tampered with. Pilot projects will often be explained away, even if successful, and will not be transferred to the larger system. One of the ways to prevent this type of undermining is to run a parallel system, as was done during the transformation from manual to computer accounting. At some point the cost of parallel systems will run too high and the decision must be made to switch over. The indicators for when to switch are related to the principles of the approach; that is, notice where information and creativity are being suppressed by a system and let go of those systems, even though it may feel like losing control. This is like mountain climbing. Novice climbers will cling to the hillside which moves the center of gravity away from their feet and increase their chance of slipping. Although leaning away is much safer and effective, the

In every corporation in which a major initiative is undertaken, there are departments or individuals that can be clearly seen to be working against the process. These are excellent places to make structural changes because they will have the dual purpose of communicating to the whole corporation what is intended in the initiative as well as facilitating the process of redesign.

In a manufacturing company undertaking a major initiative, it was a pretty common opinion that the Industrial Relations Department managed its accountabilities in a controlling and manipulating fashion. This was a natural development that resulted from earlier days of union battles. Even so, this demeanor was not compatible with the intended new ways of relating to the workforce.

Dramatic action was taken by disbanding all the structures that encouraged manipulation and control. This facilitated the process of change at the same time as it made a bold declaration to the corporation.

In another part of the corporation, a seasoned director of manufacturing dominated and controlled all his responsibilities by inciting fear. To facilitate the initiative he was moved to a new position in which he could offer advice for manufacturing, but no longer exercise any control. His talent for understanding all the nuances of the manufacturing process was put to good use by making him responsible for investigating opportunities for buy-outs and joint ventures.

instinct is to cling because leaning away *feels* like losing control. This is similar to leaning away from the mountain to execute a turn when skiing, or steering into a spin when a car goes out of control.

The transition period is not complete until the new system has emerged sufficiently for its continued emergence to be assured. However, the transition can be considered complete when the old system cannot remain intact, cannot reassert itself, or cannot return to its former state. While there is still uncertainty as to the specific direction that the new system will take, there is certainty that there has been enough education, development and information inserted into the old system for a new organization to emerge that has a stronger grip than the old.

The test for completion of the transition period is the new structures' level of robust viability in the face of the old structures trying to reassert themselves.

A corporation cannot be said to have emerged into a transformed organization if the new organization that results is what was intended, in detail. An emergent system may have predictable qualities, it may have specifics that were intended, and it may be generally consistent with the originating ideas, but it will not look exactly like a previously planned system. An emergent system can have design principles guiding the way in which it unfolds, but it cannot be specifically engineered. The richness, variety and creativity (which is the very purpose of such a system) can only emerge from a complex intelligent system.

The final trap to watch for is control.

The final trap will be that executives and management will want to apply rigid control to make sure that the new system is working. They will want to be certain that the new system can survive in the future and that the transformation does not go off track. This kind of control can kill the process before it even starts if it is attempted very early on in the process. If brought in later, this kind of control can turn the transformation (however great its initial success) into another bureaucratic monster that will require a further transformation in the not-too-distant future. Controls themselves are not the danger, but rather the fact that they are designed from, and can only be satisfied with actions that are inconsistent with the intentions of the transformation. The kinds of controls we tend to bring are those of the mechanistic path that lead the corporation back to a rigid form with minimum information.

A similar danger is present when we apply tests too early. These will often be the wrong ones. Worse, if they're applied too early, the effect is like checking to see how the new shoots in your garden are growing by pulling them up by the roots. Realistic thinking is required to develop tests that are appropriate to the new systems and their current state of development.

Without a clear *declaration* of a transition period, the purpose of such a phase begins to lose its meaning. The organization is developing into the kind that intends transition—yet the word transition implies that there is a beginning state and an end state. *Becoming* is a process of unfolding with no end state; it consists of merely an historical record and a current state which is itself becoming and will be part of the future historical record. When the point is reached in which becoming is considered to be the ongoing state of the corporation, both in people's experience and in theory, then the idea of a transition period will lose its usefulness.

Declare the completion of a transition period.

An important feature of declared states (transition, emergency, etc.) is that the completion of such a state is also declared. In many cases, the completion of a transition should be marked by a celebration that announces both its success and its completion. In other cases, it should be marked by an analysis verifying its lack of success. But in all cases, a state that is originated by declaration must also be completed by declaration or acknowledgment. Failure to declare something complete that was initiated through a declaration will ensure that the process of making declarations will cease to have meaning in the listening of others.

Declaring completion provides a clean environment for the next effort.

At the beginning of any transition phase, we are usually concerned with getting the initiative off the ground, and the concern for how it will end is remote. If the initiative is successful, we assume that everyone knows it. We are anxious to move on to whatever is next and often neglect declaring the completion. If the initiative is unsuccessful—or worse, somewhere in between—our tendency is not to acknowledge the failure but instead to move on as though nothing ever took place. When failure is ignored, we begin to think and act without conscious attention. By completing a failure through declaration, we create a clean space in which to make new declarations and create new beginnings that are not contaminated by failures from the past.

It is time to declare the transition phase complete when there is sufficient realization that the corporation will always be in a state of transition. This realization is a difficult one for executives to live with because their sense of confidence, security, risk, control, satisfaction, and ultimate well-being are the result of the match between their thinking and their experience. During any transformation, the thinking is always ahead of what is actually occurring; this causes unsettled feelings that will probably result in ineffective action. It is here that a mentor, coach, or someone experienced in supporting such efforts will be invaluable. It is also helpful to remember that a corporation won't have these unsettled feelings and will probably be operating effectively long before your feelings match the actual state of affairs.

Perhaps the most useful thought that I can leave you with is to trust the self-organizing ability of both your corporation and the individuals in it. These are the complex intelligent systems that you can count on to produce the intelligence, information and necessary interactions with the world that are needed for a successful transformation.

QUESTIONS FOR THIS CHAPTER:

- Was the beginning of your most recent initiative declared publicly? Was a transition period also declared? Were the conditions for its completion known?
- If you have an earlier initiative that is complete, no longer in operation, or barely alive, how would it impact the corporation to declare it complete and have an event that marks the occasion? Consider doing that. When it is complete, notice what becomes available as the next phase of growth and development in your corporation.
- If you are currently in an initiative and dealing with uncertainty, expressions of confusion, or unsettled conditions, what conditions could you declare as the completion of a transition period? What kind of declarations could you make that would make a transition period clear for others? Do it.
- If you are about to embark on a new initiative, how much time will you allow yourself to become operational, and what are the conditions that will mark the completion of that phase?
- Spend the time required to make sure that the transition period is understood by everyone and, as you begin the phase, declare the phase that you are starting.
- If you are engaged in an initiative, use the process of interview as well as checking your own experience to continually monitor the process of the initiative. Check to see if the methods of implementation used in the initiative are consistent with the outcomes being sought in process.

Reference Reading

The ideas in this book are the result of the reading I've done, the conversations I've had and the application of the resulting thinking with clients. The interactions have been part of the learning process and have altered the meaning of the written works for me. While I found each of the mentioned books interesting on their own, it is as a body of knowledge that have become extraordinarily powerful. It is the interplay of the various ideas from the various fields that has created the richness of the model that I am presenting.

There are many books, articles, workshops, individuals and experiences which are not mentioned. The books that I refer to here provide a network of thinking that intertwines, while never completely overlapping, and is, I think, enough to make a complete web of reality.

I have created a course for managers from a more extensive set of readings which guides the student through the highlights of the authors' ideas for the purposes of developing principles of organizational design and management practices. This is accompanied by exercises, projects and practices to explore in action what is being developed in the reading. A management group could easily construct their own development program from the readings below. I would be delighted to hear about other sources of material that would increase and enrich the body of knowledge which is being developed here. Happy reading!

THE SOCIAL CONSTRUCTION OF REALITY
Berger & Luckman (Penguin), 1966, ISBN 0 1401 3548 0, has a simple and clear approach to the way that culture is formed and transformed. It reveals the linguistic and social nature of our structures of interpretation and provides insight into how we can access and impact the reality we live in.

GRAMMATICAL MAN
J. Campbell, (Simon & Schuster) 1982, ISBN 0 6714 4062 4, reveals the linguistic nature of human beings and their institutions. The nature of infor-

mation and its creative possibilities are explored. Startlingly simple presentations of theories, communication and information which have been at the center of communication and information technology—the information age—are made available for insight into organizational design.

THE TREE OF KNOWLEDGE
Maturana & Varela, (New Science Library), 1988, ISBN 0 8777 3403 8, shows how language and knowledge develop in an interactive manner with the environment and survival requirements. Provides an understanding of intelligence, learning and knowledge which reveals them as phenomena larger than something individual.

COMPLEXITY: LIFE AT THE EDGE OF CHAOS
R. Lewin, (Macmillan Publishing), 1993, ISBN 0 4608 6092 5, makes the concept of complexity simple. Lewin shows that systems can self-organize and how they can innovate and adapt as they coevolve. He shows how central the operation of central values or "attractors" is to the continuing viable production of results that fall within a range of values rather than being individually specified. He reveals the operational principles for an organization of free and independent agents—human beings.

COMPLEXITY
M. Waldrop, (Simon & Schuster), 1992, ISBN 0 6708 5045 4, presents simple definitions of complexity and talks about what the research being done reveals for organization, strategy, learning, evolution, adaptation and various other issues. He shows how thinking from biology, evolution and the sciences can—at least metaphorically—inform the thinking of corporations.

THE MATHEMATICAL THEORY OF COMMUNICATION
Shannon & Weaver, (U of Illinois Press), 1963, ISBN 0 2527 2548 4, contains the fundamental theory of communication—accompanied by mathematical proofs of the nature of information in a communication flow. These ideas suggest how to relate to communications of all kinds and the principles by which communication challenges can be successfully approached.

AUTOPOIESIS AND COGNITION
Maturana & Varela, (D Reidel Publishing Co.), 1980, ISBN 9 0277 1016 3, a difficult but profound analysis that reveals the way intelligence

and the environment arise together or coevolve. This work shakes the foundations of our accepted view of intelligence, learning, knowledge and the relationships between individuals and their organizations and environment.

UNFATHOMED KNOWLEDGE, UNMEASURED WEALTH
W. W. Bartley III, (Opened Court Publishing), 1990, ISBN 0 8126 9106 7, presents an approach of inquiry and a relationship to knowledge that reveals the always unfinished nature of our state of knowledge. This book reveals the possibility of continual learning and the cost of inhibiting learning and points the way to practices, structures and ways of thinking that will allow us to tap the greatest source of wealth.

INVENTING REALITY: PHYSICS AS LANGUAGE
B. Gregory, (John Wiley & Sons), 1988, ISBN 0 4716 1388 6, shows the inherently metaphorical nature of physics and reveals that the sciences are creating ways of speaking which give us more effective action in the world and are, ultimately, unconcerned with "the way it really is." This book removes any suggestion that the idea that we are "making it up in language" leads to capricious or subjective approaches to reality.

THE SIX PILLAR OF SELF-ESTEEM,
N. Brandon, (Bantam Books), 1994, ISBN 0 5530 9529 3, presents the fundamentals of self-esteem by the leading researcher of the field with practical methodologies and questions at the end designed specifically for executives and managers. (Breakdowns, Learning Loop)

FLOW: THE PSYCHOLOGY OF HAPPINESS
M. Csikszentmihalyi, (Harper & Row), 1992, ISBN 0 7126 5447 1, presents a view of learning and growth that not only shows this to be the natural human condition but indicates the boundaries which will combine the maximum learning with the maximum in personal satisfaction and self-esteem. (Breakdowns, Learning Loop)

MICROCOSM
G. Gilder, Touchstone (Simon & Schuster) 1989, ISBN 0 6717 0592 X, presents, in a few short pages of the preface, the best statement about the occurring era of change. A presentation of the theory that is continually driving the computer and information industries and of the importance of theory itself. Tells the story of winners and losers based on theory. (Broad Outline of Thinking, Theory)

BEING-IN-THE-WORLD

H. L. Dreyfus, (MIT Press), 1991, ISBN 0 2625 4056 8, a most profound yet easy to read book on the nature of human beings and how they relate to each other and the world. Explores the inherent challenge in a world where it is up to us to choose and to create the reality that we live in and up to us to give our lives—and organizations—meaning. His presentation of how we relate to everything as "tools" in service of our ends and what that means for humanity provides insight into much of what is not working in our corporations today.

A PATTERN LANGUAGE

Alexander, Shikawa & Silverstein, (Oxford University Press), 1977, a book which reveals the nature of design and the way it unfolds from fundamental principles rather than being something that is invented whole and independently. In revealing the design principles of architecture and community development, he shows us the power of language in the unfolding of a design in practice.

Index